WAR-PATH AND BIVOUAC
OR THE CONQUEST OF THE SIOUX

A Narrative of Stirring Personal Experiences and Adven-tures in the Big Horn and Yellowstone Expedition Of 1876, and in the Campaign on the British Border, in 1879.

JOHN F. FINERTY
War correspondent for the Chicago Times

CONTENTS

Preface And Dedication..v

THE BIG HORN AND YELLOWSTONE EXPEDITION

Chapter 1:   Bound For The Plains..2
Chapter 2:   The Black Hills Fever..10
Chapter 3:   The March Of The Platte..15
Chapter 4:   On To Fort Fetterman..21
Chapter 5:   Marching On Powder River..26
Chapter 6:   Glimpses Of The Big Horn Range...............................38
Chapter 7:   The First Fusillade...46
Chapter 8:   Indians In War Paint...52
Chapter 9:   Scout And Buffalo Hunt...59
Chapter 10: Battle Of The Rosebud..66
Chapter 11: In The Shadow Of The Mountains...............................80
Chapter 12: Across The Snowy Range..86
Chapter 13: The Sibley Scout. A Close Call...................................92
Chapter 14: The Custer Massacre..106
Chapter 15: Merritt's Fight On The War Bonnet............................117
Chapter 16: Marching In Darkness...127
Chapter 17: Crook And Terry Meet...132
Chapter 18: Under A Deluge...140
Chapter 19: Half-Rations And Horse Meat...................................145
Chapter 20: Fighting At Slim Buttes. Awful Scenes.......................151
Chapter 21: Marching In The Mud..163
Chapter 22: Invading The Black Hills..168
Chapter 23: Closing The Campaign...174

Chapter 24: Defeat Of Dull Knife. Surrender Of Crazy Horse 179

THE CAMPAIGN ON THE BRITISH LINE

Chapter 25: Beginning Of The '79 Expedition 184
Chapter 26: Miles' Battle With Chief Joseph 188
Chapter 27: Encamped On The Big Muddy 194
Chapter 28: Miles Arrives At Fort Peck 199
Chapter 29: Sitting Bull's Last Fight 208
Chapter 30: On John Bull's Frontier 214
Chapter 31: Face To Face With Sitting Bull 222
Chapter 32: Hobnobbing With The Hostiles 234
Chapter 33: The French Half-Breeds.balaklava's Charge 240
Chapter 34: In The Last Ditch 248
Chapter 35: "Desserters And Dog Robbers" 251
Chapter 36: "Sandy" Forsyth's Famous Fight 257
Chapter 37: General Crook's Career 264
Chapter 38: Gen. George A. Custer 270

Appendix: Echoes From The Little Big Horn 279

PREFACE AND DEDICATION

It had long been my intention to publish the volume which I now submit to the public. The book is, as far as human fallibility will permit, a faithful narrative of stirring events the like of which can never again occur upon our continent.

Stories of Indian warfare, even when not founded entirely upon fact, have ever been popular with people of all nations, and more particularly with the American people, to whom such warfare is rendered familiar both by tradition and experience.

These memoirs aim at laying before the public the adventures, privations, heroism, and horrors of our last great Indian wars, exactly as they presented themselves to the writer in battle, on the march or in bivouac.

The valor of the American army has never been impugned, but millions of our own citizens do not know, even yet, what privations our brave soldiers endured, and what noble sacrifices they made, in advancing our banner in the wilderness of the West and in subduing: the savage and sanguinary tribes that so long barred the path of progress in our Territories.

The soldier who falls wounded while battling against a civilized foe feels certain of receiving humane consideration if he should fall into hostile hands, but our soldiers who were disabled in the Indian campaigns had ever before them the terrors of fiendish torture and mutilation in case of capture by the savages.

Buried for months at a time in the very heart of the wilderness, excluded from every solace of civilization, exposed to the stealthy strategy of the most cunning and merciless of all existing human races, unsheltered, for the most part, from the fury of the elements, deprived of the ordinary food of mankind, and compelled to live at times on that against which the civilized stomach revolts, the soldiers of the regular army seldom or never complained and always went cheerfully into "the gap of danger."

In former years the Congress of our country, through a strange system of reasoning, rewarded the bravery and devotion of our regular troops by assuming that their deeds of arms against savages in revolt should not be ranked among acts of warfare deserving of national recognition! It is some satisfaction, even at this late day, to know that the national legislature no longer looks upon services rendered by the troops against hostile savages with contemptuous eyes and that the bill granting brevet rank to the more distinguished among the Indian fighters of the regular army, has now become a law.

If these frankly-written pages serve to place before the Congress and the people of the United States the deeds and the sufferings of the national army while struggling in several most important campaigns for the extension of our peaceful borders, the safety of our hardy pioneers and the honor of our martial name, I will feel greatly recompensed for the labor of their production.

The gallant service in which Harney, Fremont, Sully, Stanley, Connors, Crook, Miles, Merritt, Terry, McKenzie, Gibbon, Carr, and other heroic chiefs distinguished themselves against the intrepid hostile Indians, and in which Custer, Canby, Fetterman, Kidder, Elliot, Brown, Grummond, Yates, McIntosh, Calhoun, Keogh, McKinney, and many more as brave as they were, died fighting against overwhelming numbers, deserves honor at the hands of the nation, whose glory it has maintained and whose progress it has insured.

Whether as regulars or volunteers, our soldiers, at all times and under all circumstances, have deserved well of their country. From the day of Concord bridge, when the citizen-soldiery of Massachusetts "fired the shot heard 'round the world," to that of the Little Big Horn, when Custer, at the head of his three hundred, died like Leonidas at Thermopylae, the American army, whether in victory or disaster, has ever been worthy of the flag which it carries, and of the nation which it defends. In this spirit, I respectfully dedicate this book to the American army and the American nation.

JOHN F. FINERTY.
CHICAGO, April 1890.

PART I

THE BIG HORN AND YELLOWSTONE EXPEDITION

CHAPTER I

BOUND FOR THE PLAINS

In the beginning of May 1876, I was attached to the city department of the Chicago Times. One day Mr. Clinton Snowden, the city editor, said to me, "Mr. Storey wants a man to go out with the Big Horn and Yellowstone expedition, which is organizing under Generals Crook and Terry, in the departments of the Platte and Dakota. There is apt to be warm work out there with the Indians, so if you don't care to go, you needn't see Mr. Storey."

"I care to go, and I'll see Mr. Storey," was my answer.

The famous editor of the Chicago Times did not, at that period, show any significant indication of that "withering at the top" which subsequently obscured his wonderful faculties. He was a tall, well-built, white-haired, white-bearded, gray-eyed, exceedingly handsome man of sixty, or thereabout, with a courteous, but somewhat cynical, manner.

"You are the young man Mr. Snowden mentioned for the Plains?" he asked, as soon as I had made my presence known by the usual half shy demonstrations, because everybody who did not know him well, and who had heard his reputation on the outside, approached the formidable Vermonter in somewhat gingerly fashion.'

I replied in the affirmative. "Well, how soon can you be ready?" he inquired.

"At any time it may please you to name," was my prompt reply.

"You should have your outfit first. Better get some of it here—perhaps all. You are going with Crook's column," said Mr. Storey, with his customary decisiveness and rapidity.

"I understood I was to go with Custer," I rejoined. "I know General Custer, but am not acquainted with General Crook."

"That will make no difference, whatever," said he. "Terry commands over Custer, and Crook, who knows more about the Indians, is likely to do the hard work. Custer is a brave soldier—none braver—but he has been out there some years already, and has not succeeded in bringing the Sioux to a decisive engagement. Crook did well in Arizona. However, it is settled that you go with Crook. Go to Mr. Patterson (the manager) and get what funds you may need for your outfit and other expenses. Report to me when you are ready."

It did not take me long to get ready. I called first upon General Sheridan and asked him for a letter of introduction to General Crook, and also for a general letter to such officers as I might meet on the frontier.

The gallant General very promptly, and in a spirit of the most generous cordiality, acceded to my request. He gave me some advice, which I afterward found valuable, and wished me every success in my undertaking.

"I'll try and do your kindness no discredit, General," I ventured to remark, as I took my leave.

"I am fully confident of that, but let me warn you that you will find General Crook a hard campaigner," said he, laughingly.

My next care was to purchase arms and a riding outfit, and, having said farewell to friends and received the final instructions of Mr. Storey, who enjoined me to "spare no expense and use the wires freely, whenever practicable," I left Chicago to join General Crook's command on Saturday morning, May 6, 1876.

The rain fell in torrents, and the wind shrieked fiercely, as the train on the Northwestern road, well freighted with passengers, steamed out of the depot, bound for Omaha. I reached the latter city on Sunday morning, and found General Crook at his headquarters, busily engaged in reading reports from officers stationed on the Indian frontier. He was then a spare but athletic man of about forty, with fair hair, clipped close, and a blonde beard which seemed to part naturally at the point of the chin. His nose was long and aquiline, and his blue-gray eyes were bright and piercing. He looked, in fact, every inch a soldier, except that he wore no uniform.

The General saluted me curtly, and I handed him the letter of introduction which I had procured in Chicago from General Sheridan, who then commanded the Military Division of the Missouri. Having read it, Crook smiled and said, "You had better go to Fort Sidney or Fort Russell, where the expedition is now being formed. You will need an animal, and can purchase one, perhaps, at Cheyenne. Can you ride and shoot well?"

"I can ride fairly, General. As for shooting, I don't know. I'd engage, however, to hit a hay-stack at two hundred yards."

He laughed and said, "Very well. We'll have some tough times, I think. I am going with my aide, Mr. Bourke, to the agencies to get some friendly Indians to go with us. I fear we'll have to rely upon the Crows and Snakes, because the Sioux, Cheyennes and Arapahoes are disaffected, and all may join the hostiles. However, I'll be at Fort Fetterman about the middle of the month. You can make messing arrangements with some officer going out from Fort Russell. You had better be with the cavalry."

I thanked the General, and proceeded to my hotel. Next morning found me *en route*, over the Union Pacific road, to Cheyenne. The weather had greatly improved, but, after passing the line of what may be called Eastern Nebraska, nothing could beautify the landscape. Monotonous flats, and equally monotonous swells, almost devoid of trees, and covered only partially by short, sickly-looking grass, made up the main body of the "scenery." In those days the herds of antelope still roamed at will over the plains of Nebraska and Wyoming, and even the buffalo had not been driven entirely from the valley of the Platte; but there was about the country, even under the bright May sunshine, a look of savage desolation. It has improved somewhat since 1876, but not enough to make any person mistake the region between North Platte and Cheyenne for the Garden of Eden. The prairie dogs abounded by the million, and the mean-looking coyote made the dismal waste resonant, particularly at night, with his lugubrious howls.

That night I stood for a long time on the rear platform of the Pullman car, and watched the moonbeams play upon the rippled surface of the shallow and eccentric Platte. I thought of all the labor, and all the blood, it had cost to build the railroad, and to settle the country even as sparsely as it was then settled; for along that river, but a few years previously, the buffalo grazed by myriads, and the wild Indians chased them on their fleet ponies, occasionally varying their amusement by raiding an immigrant train, or attacking a small party of railroad builders. The very ground over which the train traveled slowly, on an upgrade toward the Rocky Mountains, had been soaked with the best blood of the innocent and the brave, the air around had rung with the shrieks of dishonored maids and matrons, and with the death groans of victims tortured at the stake. Nathless the moonlight, the region appeared to me as a "dark and bloody ground," once peopled by human demons, and then by pioneers, whose lives must have been as bleak and lonesome as the country which they inhabited. Filled with such thoughts, I retired to rest.

"We're nearing Sidney, sah," said the colored porter, as he pulled aside the curtain of my berth. I sprang up immediately, and had barely dressed myself, when the train came to a halt at the station. The platform was crowded with citizens and soldiers, the barracks of the latter being quite close to the town. Nearly all the military wore the yellow facings of the cavalry. I was particularly struck by the appearance of one officer—a first lieutenant and evidently a foreigner. He wore his kepi low on his forehead, and, beneath it, his hooked nose overhung a blonde moustache of generous proportions. His eyes were light blue; his cheeks yellow and rather sunken. He was about the middle stature and wore huge dragoon boots. Thick smoke from an enormous pipe rose upon the morning air, and he paced up and down like a caged tiger. I breakfasted at the railroad restaurant, and, as the train was in no hurry to get away, I had a chance to say a few words to the warrior already described.

"Has your regiment got the route for the front yet, lieutenant?" I inquired.

"Some of it," he replied in a thick German accent, without removing his pipe. "Our battalion should have it already, but 'tis always the vay, Got tamn the luck! 'tis alvays the vay!"

"I guess 'twill be all right in a day or two, lieutenant!" I remarked.

"Vell, may be so, but they're always slighting the 3d Cavalry, at headquarters. Ve ought to have moved a Veek ago. "

"I saw General Crook at Omaha, and he said he would be at Fetterman by the 15th."

"You don't zay so? Then ve get off. Veil, dat is good. Are you in the army?"

"No; I am going out as correspondent for the Chicago *Times*."

"Veil, I am so glad to meet von. My name is Von Leutwitz. The train is going. Good-bye. We shall meet again."

We did meet again, and, to anticipate somewhat, under circumstances the reverse of pleasant for the gallant, but unfortunate, lieutenant, who, after having campaigned over Europe and America, and having fought in, perhaps, a hundred pitched battles, lost his leg at Slim Buttes fight on the following 9th of September.

The train proceeded slowly, toiling laboriously up the ever-increasing grade toward Cheyenne, through a still bare and dismal landscape. Early in the afternoon we passed the long snow sheds, and, emerging from them, beheld toward the southwest, the distant summits of Long's and Gray's peaks of the Rocky mountains. Less than an hour brought us to Cheyenne, which is only three miles from Fort D. A. Russell, my immediate objective point. As at Sidney, the railroad platform was crowded with soldiers and citizens, many of the latter prospectors driven from the southern passes of the Black Hills of Dakota, by the hostile Indians. I "put up" at an inviting hotel, and was greatly interested in the conversation around me. All spoke of "the Hills," of the Indian hostilities, and of the probable result of the contemplated military expedition.

As I was well acquainted in Cheyenne, I had little difficulty in making myself at home., Nobody seemed to know when the expedition would start, but all felt confident that there would be "music in the air" before the June roses came into bloom. At a book store, with the proprietor of which I was on friendly terms, I was introduced to Col. Guy V. Henry, of the 3d Cavalry. He was, then, a very fine-looking, although slight and somewhat pale, officer, and, what was still better, he was well up in all things concerning the projected Indian campaign.

"We will march from this railroad in two columns," said he. "One will form at Medicine Bow, ninety miles or so westward, and will cross the North Platte Paver at Fort Fetterman. The other will march from Fort Russell to Fort Laramie, cross the North Platte there, and march by the left bank, so as to join the other column in front of Fetterman. This I have heard not officially, but on sufficiently good authority. From Fetterman we will march north until we strike the Indians. That is about the programme."

I asked the colonel's advice in regard to procuring a horse, and was soon in possession of a very fine animal, which subsequently met with a tragical fate in the wild recesses of the Big Horn mountains. Colonel Henry's "mess" being full, a circumstance that he and I mutually regretted, I made arrangements with a captain of the 3d Cavalry to join his, and, having thus provided for the campaign, I set about enjoying, myself as best I could until the hour for marching would strike. Cheyenne, in 1876, still preserved most of the characteristics of a crude frontier town. Gambling was openly practiced, by day as well as by night, and the social evil, of the very lowest type, was offensively visible wherever the eye might turn. No respectable maid or matron ventured out unattended after nightfall, while occasional murders and suicides "streaked the pale air with blood."

Notwithstanding these almost inevitable drawbacks, there were then, as there are now, level heads, and loyal hearts, in Cheyenne, and I can never forget the many pleasant evenings I spent there in company with some officers of the Fort Russell garrison, and such distinguished citizens as Editors Swan and Glascke, Col. Luke Murrin, Dr. Whitehead, Sheriff O'Brien, Messrs. French, Harrington, Dyer, MacNamara, Miller, Haas and many other "right good fellows," who will ever live in my grateful remembrance. I believe that all of the gentlemen mentioned, with the exception of Mr. MacNamara, still survive. If I have omitted the names of any of the friends of that period, the omission, I can assure my readers, is entirely unintentional, for a manlier, more generous or hospitable group of men it has rarely been my good fortune to encounter.

On the 12th or 13th of May, it was known that General Crook and his staff had arrived during the night, but were off on the wings of the wind, overland, to Fort Laramie in the morning. Captain Sutorius, with whom I had arranged to mess, sent me word, on the 14th, that the command was under orders, and that I had better take up my residence at Fort Russell during the night. Messrs. Dyer and MacNamara insisted on taking my "traps" to the Fort in a spring wagon, drawn by a spirited horse. I rode on horseback beside them. Just as we neared the entrance of the parade ground, their beast took fright and ran away with great skill and energy. I attempted in vain to keep up with the procession. In front of the quarters of Captain Peele, of the 2d Cavalry, an officer who has since suffered many misfortunes, the wagon was upset. MacNamara, a pretty heavy man, described the arc of a circle in the air, and fell upon the crown of his head. His high hat was crushed down upon his face, and he presented a ludicrous spectacle enough, but, most fortunately, he escaped serious injury, and relieved his feelings by thundering anathemas against the runaway animal, and all concerned in the catastrophe. Dyer was thrown out also, and suffered a gash over the eye-brow, the scar of which still remains. My effects were strewn all over Fort Russell, and half a dozen orderlies were, by the courtesy of Captain Peele and other officers, engaged for some time in picking them up. I have since learned the wisdom and the beauty of moving in light marching order. Both Captains Peele and Sutorius treated us most kindly, and, in view of their subsequent misfortunes, I feel bound to bear witness that on that occasion, as on many others, they showed that their hearts were in the right place, although their heads might be sometimes weak.

Next day I called upon the commandant of the fort, Gen. J. J. Reynolds, colonel of the 3d Cavalry, who received me with that courteous bearing so characteristic of the American regular officer. He spoke pleasantly of the approaching campaign, but regretted that he personally could have no part in it. He did not say why, but I understood perfectly that he and the department commander, General Crook, were not on good terms, owing to a disagreement relative to Reynolds' action during the short Crazy Horse village campaign of the preceding March. Reynolds stormed the village, but was unable to retain it, and, in his retreat, the Indians attacked his rear guard and stampeded the pony herd of 800 horses he had captured. General Crook held that General Reynolds ought to have shot the ponies rather than allow them to fall again into the hands of their savage owners. A court martial grew out of the controversy, but nothing serious came of it, as far as I can remember, and General Reynolds was soon afterward, at his own request, placed upon the retired list of the army.

As I was taking my leave, General Reynolds said: "As you have not been out after Indians previously, allow an old soldier to give you this piece of advice—Never stray far from the main column, and never trust a horse or an Indian."

I promised to follow the General's advice as closely as possible, and made my adieux. Orders had readied the Fort that the troops were to move to Fort Laramie on the morning of the 17th, and all felt grateful that the period of inaction was almost at an end.

Before giving my account of the famous campaign, I must briefly relate the causes that led to the great Indian War of 1876.

CHAPTER II

THE BLACK HILLS FEVER

There had raged for many years a war between the Sioux Nation, composed of about a dozen different tribes of the same race under various designations, and nearly all the other Indian tribes of the Northwest. The Northern Cheyennes were generally confederated with the Sioux in the field, and the common enemy would seem to have been the Crow, or Absarake, Nation. The Sioux and Cheyennes together were more than a match for all the other tribes combined, and even at this day the former peoples hold their numerical superiority unimpaired. There must be nearly 70,000 Sioux and their kindred tribes in existence, and they still possess, at least, 5,000 able-bodied warriors, more or less well armed. But times have greatly changed since the spring "of 1876. Then nearly all of Dakota, Northern Nebraska, Northern Wyoming, Northern and Eastern Montana lay at the mercy of the savages, who, since the completion of the treaty of 1868, which filled them with ungovernable pride, had been mainly successful in excluding all white men from the immense region, which may be roughly described as bounded on the east by the 104th meridian; on the west by the Big Horn mountains; on the south by the North Platte, and on the north by the Yellowstone river. In fact, the northern boundary, in Montana, extended practically to the frontier of the British possessions. About 240,000 square miles were comprised in the lands ceded, or virtually surrendered, by the Government to the Indians — one-half for occupation and the establishment of agencies, farms, schools and other mediums of civilization; while the other half was devoted to hunting grounds, which no white man could enter without the special permission of the Indians themselves. All this magnificent territory was turned over and guaranteed to the savages by solemn treaty with the United States Government. The latter made the treaty with what may be termed undignified haste. The country, at the time, was sick of war. Colonel Fetterman, with his command of nearly one hundred men and three officers, had been overwhelmed and massacred by the Sioux, near Fort Phil Kearney, in December. 1866. Other small detachments of the army had been slaughtered here and there throughout the savage region. The old Montana emigrant road had been paved with the bodies and reddened with the blood of countless victims of Indian hatred, and, indeed, twenty years ago, strange as it may now appear to American readers, nobody, least of all the authorities at Washington, thought that what was then a howling, if handsome, wilderness, would be settled within so short a period by white people. Worse than all else, the Government weakly agreed to dismantle the military forts established along the Montana emigrant trail, running within a few miles of the base of the Big Horn range, namely, Fort Reno, situated on Middle Fork of the Powder river; Fort Phil Kearney, situated on Clear Fork of the same stream, and Fort C. F.

Smith, situated on the Big Horn river, all these being on the east side of the celebrated mountain chain. The Sioux had no legitimate claim to the Big Horn region. A part of it belonged originally to the Crows, whom the stronger tribe constantly persecuted, and who, by the treaty of '68, were placed at the mercy of their ruthless enemies. Other friendly tribes, such as the Snakes, or Shoshones, and the Bannocks, bordered on the ancient Crow territory, and were treated as foemen by the greedy Sioux and the haughty Cheyennes. The abolition of the three forts named fairly inflated the Sioux. The finest hunting grounds in the world had fallen into their possession, and the American Government, instead of standing by and strengthening the Crows, their ancient friends and allies, unwisely abandoned the very positions that would have held the more ferocious tribes in check. The Crows had a most unhappy time of it after the treaty was ratified. Their lands were constantly raided by the Sioux.

Several desperate battles were fought, and, finally, the weaker tribe was compelled to seek safety beyond the Big Horn river.

Had the Sioux and Crows been left to settle the difficulty between themselves, few of the latter tribe would be left on the face of the earth to-day. The white man's government might make what treaties it pleased with the Indians, but it was quite a different matter to get the white man himself to respect the official parchment. Three-fourths of the Black Hills region, and all of the Big Horn, were barred by the Great Father and Sitting Bull against the enterprise of the daring, restless and acquisitive Caucasian race. The military expeditions, under Generals Sully, Connors, Stanley and Custer —all of which were partially unsuccessful—had attracted the attention of the country to the great region already specified. The beauty and variety of the landscape, the immense quantities of the noblest species of American game; the serrated mountains, and forest-covered hills; the fine grazing lands and rushing streams, born of the snows of the majestic Big Horn peaks; and, above all else, the rumor of great gold deposits, the dream of wealth which hurled Cortez on Mexico and Pizarro on Peru, fired the Caucasian heart with the spirit of adventure and exploration, to which the attendant and well-recognized danger lent an additional zest. The expedition of General Custer, which entered the Black Hills proper—those of Dakota—in 1874, confirmed the reports of "gold finds," and, thereafter, a wall of fire, not to mention a wall of Indians, could not stop the encroachments of that terrible white race before which all other races of mankind, from Thibet to Hindostan, and from Algiers to Zululand, have gone down. At the news of gold, the grizzled '49or shook the dust of California from his feet, and started overland, accompanied by daring comrades, for the far-distant "Hills;" the Australian miner left his pick half buried in the antipodean sands, and started, by ship and saddle, for the same goal; the diamond hunter of Brazil and of "the Cape;" the veteran "prospectors" of Colorado and Western Montana; the "tar heels" of the Carolinian hills; the "reduced gentlemen" of Europe; the worried and worn city clerks of London, Liverpool, New York or Chicago; the stout English yeoman, tired of high rents and poor returns; the sturdy Scotchman, tempted from stubborn plodding after wealth to seek fortune under more rapid conditions; the light-hearted Irishman, who drinks in the spirit of adventure with his mother's milk; the daring mine delvers of Wales and of Cornwall; the precarious gambler of Monte Carlo—in short, every man who lacked fortune, and who would rather be scalped than remain poor, saw in the vision of the Black Hills, El Dorado; and to those picturesquely sombre eminences the adventurers of the earth—some honest and some the opposite—came trooping in masses, "like clouds at eventide."

In vain did the Government issue its proclamations; in vain were our veteran regiments of cavalry and infantry, commanded by warriors true and tried, drawn up across the path of the daring invaders; in vain were arrests made, baggage seized, horses confiscated and wagons burned; no earthly power could hinder that bewildering swarm of human ants. They laughed at the proclamations, evaded the soldiers, broke jail, did without wagons or outfit of any kind, and, undaunted by the fierce war whoops of the exasperated Sioux, rushed on to the fight for gold with burning hearts and naked hands! Our soldiers, whom no foe, white, red or black, could make recreant to their flag upon the field of honor, overcome by the moral epidemic, deserted by the squad to join the grand army of indomitable adventurers. And soon, from Buffalo Gap to Inyan Kara, and from Bear Butte to Great Canon, the sound of the pick and spade made all the land resonant with the music of Midas. Thickly as the mushrooms grow in the summer nights on the herbage robbed sheep range, rose "cities" innumerable, along the Spearfish and the Deadwood and Rapid creeks. Placer and quartz mines developed with marvelous rapidity, and, following the first, and boldest, adventurers, the eager, but timid and ease-loving, capitalists, who saw Indians in every sage brush, came in swarms. Rough board shanties, and hospital tents, were the chief "architectural "features of the new "cities," which swarmed with gamblers, harlots and thieves, as well as with honest miners. By the fall of 1875, the northern segment of the irregular, warty geological formation, known as the Black Hills, was prospected, "staked" and, in fairly good proportion, "settled," after the rough, frontier fashion. Pierre and Bismarck, on the Missouri river, and Sidney and Cheyenne, on the Union Pacific railroad, became the supply depots of the new mining regions, and, at that period, enjoyed a prosperity which they have not equaled since. All the passes leading into "the Hills," from the points mentioned, swarmed with hostile Indians, most of whom were well fed at the agencies and all of whom boasted of being better armed, and better supplied with fixed ammunition, than the soldiers of our regular army. The rocks of Buffalo Gap and Red Canyon, particularly, rang with the rifle shots of the savages, and the return fire of the hardy immigrants, many of whom paid with their lives the penalty of their ambition. The stages that ran to "the Hills" from the towns on the Missouri and the Union Pacific rarely ever escaped attack—sometimes by robbers, but oftenest by Indians. All passengers, even the women, who were, at that time, chiefly composed of the rough, if not absolutely immoral, class, traveled with arms in their hands ready for immediate action. Border ruffians infested all the cities, and, very soon, became almost as great a menace to life and property as the savages themselves. Murders and suicides occurred in abundance, as the gambling dens increased and the low class saloons multiplied. Notwithstanding these discouragements, the period of 1874, '75 and '76 was the Augustan era, if the term be not too transcendental, of the Black Hills. The placer mines were soon exhausted, and, as it required capital to work the quartz ledges, the poor miners, or the impatient ones, who hoped to get rich in a day, quickly "stampeded "for more promising regions, and left the mushroom "cities" to the capitalists, the wage workers, the gamblers, the women in scarlet, and to these, in later days, may be added the rancheros, or cattle men. Morality has greatly improved in "the Hills" since 1876, and business has settled down to a steady, oldfashioned gait, but the first settlers still remember, with vague regret, the stirring times of old, when gold dust passed as currency; when whisky was bad and fighting general; when claims were held dear and life cheap; when the bronzed hunter, or long-haired "scout," strutted around in half savage pride, and when the renowned "Wild Bill," who subsequently met a fate so sudden and so awful, was at once the glory and the terror of that active, but primitive, community. But enough of historical retrospection. I will now resume my narrative of the long and weary march, which began at Fort Russell in "the ides of May," and terminated at Fort Laramie in the last days of September, 1876.

CHAPTER III

THE MARCH OF THE PLATTE

The final order to move out on the expedition readied Fort Russell, as I think I have already stated, on May 16th. On the morning of the 17th, several troops of the 3d Cavalry, and, I think, one or two of the 2d Cavalry, under the orders of Col. 'W'. B. Royall, marched northward toward the Platte. It was my desire to accompany this column, but Captain Sutorius, Company E, of the 3d Cavalry, had to wait, under orders, until the morning of the 19th. Captain Wells, Troop E, of the 2d Cavalry, had orders to march with Sutorius. As I messed with the latter, I was compelled to wait also, and I occupied myself during the brief interval in visiting Cheyenne, and taking final leave of my kind friends in that city. I met there Mr. T. C. McMillan, now a State senator, who was going out as correspondent for another Chicago newspaper. Mr. McMillan was in feeble health at the time, but he was determined not to be left behind. He was fortunate in making messing arrangements with Captain Sutorius, who was the soul of hospitality. As McMillan had to purchase a horse and some outfit, we determined to follow, rather than accompany, the two troops mentioned, who marched for Lodge Pole creek, eighteen miles distant from Fort Russell, at daybreak. When McMillan had made his purchases, we set out on horseback, accompanied for a few miles by the late George O'Brien, to overtake the command. Neither of us had been used to riding for some time, and, as the day was fairly warm, we did not over-exert ourselves in catching up with the column. There was a well-marked road to Lodge Pole creek, through a country greatly devoid of beauty, so that we had no difficulty in keeping the trail. Mr. O'Brien bade us adieu on a little rising ground, about five miles from the Fort, and then Mac and I urged our animals to a trot, as the afternoon was well advanced. A little before sundown we came in sight of the shallow valley of Lodge Pole creek, and saw tents pitched along the banks of that stream, while, hobbled or lariated, horses were grazing around. Several canvas-covered army wagons, and a number of soldiers engaged in attending to their horses, completed the picture. Captain Sutorius welcomed us warmly, and explained that he had no lieutenants — one being on sick leave and the other detailed for other duty. He introduced us to the two officers of the 2d Cavalry, Captain Wells and Lieutenant Sibley. The former was a veteran of the Civil War, covered with honorable scars, bluff, stern and heroic. Lieutenant Sibley, with whose career I was destined to be linked under circumstances which subsequently attracted the attention of the continent, and which will live long in the tales and traditions of our regular army, was a young West Pointer, who had distinguished himself under General Reynolds in the attack upon, and capture of, Crazy Horse's village on March 17th of that eventful year. He was about the middle height, well but slightly built, and with a handsome, expressive face. It does not take very long to become thoroughly at home with soldiers, if they take a liking to you, and we were soon seated in Captain Sutorius' tent, partaking very industriously of plain military fare. The conversation turned chiefly on the campaign upon which we were enter ing. Captain Wells said that the Indians were in stronger force than most people imagined, and that General Crook, accustomed mostly to the southern Indians, hardly estimated at its real strength the powerful array of the savages. He joked, in rough soldier fashion, McMillan and myself on having had our hair cropped, as, he said, it would be a pity to cheat the Sioux out of our scalps. The bugle soon sounded, the horses were placed "on the line "— that is, tied by their halters to a strong rope stretched between wagons — curried and fed. The mules joined in their usual lugubrious evening chorus. 'We had a smoke, followed by a moderately strong "toddy," and, very soon, the sentinels having been posted, Sutorius, Mac and I lay down to rest on blankets and buffalo robes spread in the captain's commodious wall tent. I slept the sleep of the just, although I was occasionally conscious of McMillan's eternal cough and the captain's profound snore, and thus opened, for me, the Big Horn and Yellowstone campaign.

In the midst of a dream, in which Indians, scalping-knives, warwhoops and tomahawks figured prominently, I was aroused by the shrill blast of the cavalry trumpets sounding the reveille. I sprang up instantly, as did my companions, made a very hasty and incomplete toilet, and, having swallowed a cup of coffee, served in an army "tin," was ready for the road. The little "outfit" moved like clockwork, and, by six o'clock, everything had "pulled out" of camp. The previous day's ride had rendered me quite stiff in the knee joints, as I had been riding with short stirrups. I soon learned that if a man wishes to avoid acute fatigue on a long march, it is better to lengthen the stirrup leathers. I accordingly adopted the military plan, and found some relief. Indians, by the way, generally ride with short stirrups on long journeys. I suppose they get used to it, but I never could.

The country through which we were passing was monotonously ugly. In most places the ground was covered with sage-brush and cacti, and the clouds of alkaline dust, raised by the hoofs of the troop horses, were at once blinding and suffocating. I was tormented by thirst, and soon exhausted all the water in my canteen. The captain, who was an old campaigner, advised me to place a small pebble in my mouth. I did so, and saliva was produced, which greatly relieved my suffering. I found afterward, on many a hard, hot, dusty march, when water was scarce, that this simple remedy against thirst is very effective. The less water a soldier drinks on the march, the better it will be for his health.

The command was halted several times in order that the horses might have a chance to graze, and also to enable the inexperienced among the soldiers to get some of the soreness out of their bones. I was devoutly grateful for every halt. The shadows from the west were lengthening as we rode into camp at a place called Bear Springs, where wood and water abounded. The scenes and incidents of the preceding camp were duplicated here, but I learned that, on the morrow, we were to catch up with the column in advance, which was under the orders of Col. William Royall, of the 3d Cavalry, since colonel of the 4th Cavalry, and now retired.

We were in the saddle at daybreak, and marched with greater rapidity than usual. There were no halts of any great duration. About noon we encountered a stout young officer, attended by an orderly, riding at break-neck pace toward us. He halted, saluted the captain, and said, "Colonel Royall's compliments, and he requests that you march without halting until you join him. The other battalion is halted about a dozen miles further on. I am going to the rear with orders, and will rejoin tomorrow or the day after."

The captain introduced me to Lieut. Frederick Schwatka, whom I was to meet often afterward in that campaign, and whose name has since become familiar to all the reading world as the intrepid discoverer of the fate of Sir John Franklin, amid the eternal snows and unspeakable perils of the polar regions. Schwatka briefly but courteously acknowledged the captain's introduction, and, having drained a little "elixir of life" from his superior's canteen, set out like a whirlwind to fulfill his mission.

"Close up there! Trot!" shouted Captain Sutorius, who was in advance. "Trot!" repeated Captain Wells, in stentorian tones; and away we went, up hill and down dale, leaving the wagon tram to the care of its ordinary escort.

After going at a trot for what seemed to me, galled and somewhat jaded as I was, an interminable time, we finally reached an elevation in the road, from which we beheld, although at a considerable distance, what seemed to be a force of cavalry, apparently going into camp. We continued advancing, but at a slower pace, and, within an hour, came upon the rearmost wagons of Royall's train, guarded by a troop of horse. We soon reached the main body, and I had then the pleasure of meeting Colonel Royall, a tall, handsome Virginian, of about fifty, with a full gray mustache, dark eyebrows, overhanging a pair of bright blue eyes, and a high forehead, on the apex of which, through the cropped hair, as he raised his cap in salute, appeared one of several scars inflicted by a rebel sabre in front of Richmond during the Civil War. Among the other officers to whom I was introduced, I remember Col. Anson Mills, then in his prime; Lieutenant Lemley, Captain Andrews, Lieutenant Foster, Lieut. Joseph Lawson and Lieut. Charles Morton, all of the 3d Cavalry; and Captain Rawolle, Lieutenant Huntington and others of the 2d Cavalry. As it was still early in the day, and, as our halting place was not desirable for the horses, Colonel Royall, after our wagon train had closed up, changed his mind about going into camp, and the march was continued to a place called Hunton's Ranch, in the Chugwater valley, where, having ridden over thirty miles since morning, I was rendered exceedingly happy by the order to halt and pitch our tents. These latter did not come up for some time, and, being as hungry as a bear, I was glad to satisfy my craving with raw army bacon, hard tack and a tin full of abominably bad water. Then I lay down on my horse-blanket, under a tree, and fell fast asleep.

Supper was being served in Captain Sutorius' tent before I thought of waking up, and it took a good, honest poke in the ribs from the hardy captain to recall me from the land of dreams. In spite of my long nap, I slept soundly throughout the night, and awoke early in the morning to hear the rain falling in torrents, and pattering on our canvas shelter like a thousand drumsticks. An orderly came with the compliments of the commanding officer, to instruct the captain not to strike tents, as, if the rain did not cease before 8 o'clock, the battalion would remain in camp, as the wagons could not be moved in the dense mud. This was welcome news to Mr. McMillan and myself, as we were both exceedingly fatigued. The rain did not cease to fall for twenty-four hours longer, and it was well on toward noon, on the morning of May 23d, when we dragged ourselves painfully out of the Chugwater mud and took up our march to Fort Laramie. This march was brief and uneventful, and we were in camp on the prairie surrounding the Fort shortly after 1 o'clock. We picked up a few more troops at this point, and, as Colonel Royall was fearful of being late at the rendezvous of still distant Fort Fetterman, no time was lost in getting the command ready for the hard road before it. The entire column crossed the Laramie and North Platte rivers early on the morning of the 24th. The sky was cloudy, and a raw wind blew from the east. All of us hoped that the cool weather would continue, but we were doomed to sore disappointment in that, as in other, respects.

The men of the command were, for the most part, young, but well seasoned, and in their blue shirts, broad felt hats, cavalry boots and blue, or buckskin, pantaloons, for on an Indian campaign little attention is paid to uniform, looked both athletic and warlike. Their arms were bright as hard rubbing could make them, and around the waist of every stalwart trooper was a belt filled with sixty rounds of fixed ammunition for the Springfield carbine. Each man carried also a supply of revolver cartridges. The sabres had been left behind at the different posts as useless encumbrances. I well remember the martial bearing of Guy V. Henry's fine troop of the 3d, as with arms clanking, and harness jingling, it trotted rapidly along our whole flank, in the dawn twilight, to take its place at the head of the column. "There goes Henry !" said our Captain, as the troopers trotted by. They were fine fellows that morning, and proved themselves to be as brave, and enduring, as they were imposing in appearance, throughout the campaign.

CHAPTER IV

ON TO FORT FETTERMAN

Our route was over an unfrequented path, known as the Old Utah route, through the Indian reservation on the left bank of the North Platte. This road was selected in order that the delay and expense of crossing the rapid river at Fetterman might be avoided. The portion of the territory through which we moved had not been described, at least by the newspapers, for the reason that very few people cared to roam at that time through so dangerous and desolate a region in small parties.

Our first day's march from Fort Laramie was begun at 6 o'clock A. M., and by 12:30, including two halts, we went into camp on a bend of the Platte, twenty-four miles from our starting point. The first part of our route lay through an undulating grass country, lying within easy distance of the river. Ten miles through this kind of land brought us to an immense "park," situated in the midst of five dotted bluffs, where we halted for some minutes. This "park" was simply the portal to one of the longest, darkest and most tortuous "passes" that can well be imagined.

It was a perfect labyrinth. Bluffs rose on each side to an immense altitude, and the turns were so abrupt that our advancing column frequently expected to bring up in a culdesac. It was up hill and down dale for eight long miles, and had Colonel Royall been opposed to a capable foe, his part of Crook's expedition would never have reached the rendezvous. A couple of hundred resolute men could there have prevented the march of a vast army. In fact, the larger the latter the less chance would there be for successful battle. But we passed on unharmed through this "Killecrankie" of Wyoming.

The sun shone magnificently, and it was a splendid sight to see our seven companies of cavalry, their arms glittering and their equipments rattling; as they "wound like a monstrous serpent around that gloomy vale." In some places, the ascents and descents were so steep and rugged that the command had to dismount from front to rear, and lead their horses. "Sitting Bull" lost a fine opportunity for clipping Crook's wings, and nearly all the officers recognized the fact. But we neither saw, heard, nor felt any Indians. Our troops moved on unmolested.

Where's the embattled foe they seek?
The camp or watch-fires, where? For save the eagle screaming high
No sign of life is there.

A solitary elk, standing on the edge of a cliff far above our pathway, was the only living thing that, to all appearances, beheld our column.

After more than two hours of unceasing travel through the gorge, we finally unwound ourselves therefrom and struck a red-clay country, where we could not find enough grass to give our weary horses a decent lunch; we did not, therefore, halt, but pushed on to a camp on the river bend, when we thankfully left the saddle and stretched our limbs upon the parched earth. Owing to the roughness of the road, the wagon-train and rear guard were more than five hours behind. Yet, in that lone camping ground, we found the graves of two Mormon emigrants, killed, it was supposed, by Indians. One grave had over it a rude slab, with the name, "Sarah Gibbons, July,1854," cut upon it. The other inscription was absolutely indecipherable. Reveille sounded at dawn on Thursday, May 25th, and the march was resumed one hour later. Prepared as we were to encounter a desert country, the scene that met our view was far beyond all expectation.

Our line of march was through what appeared to be a succession of brick-yards and extinct limekilns. In order to secure a good wagon-road, we were compelled to avoid the Platte, and, with the exception of one stagnant pool, during that weary ride of thirty-five miles we saw no water until we struck the river again. The sun burned us almost to the bone, and every man's complexion was scarlet. Despite all injunctions to the contrary, the tired and thirsty troops made a general raid upon the Platte, when we reached that stream, and drank to satiety. The cheekiest of land speculators, or the most conscienceless of newspaper correspondents, could not say a word in behalf of that infernal region, which it would be the acme of exaggeration to term "land." But some of our old Indian scouts said it was Arabia Felix compared with what lay between us and the Powder river. Why the government of the United States should keep an army for the purpose of robbing the Indians of such a territory, is an unsolvable puzzle. It is a solemn mockery to call the place "a reservation," unless dust, ashes and rocks be accounted of value to mankind. Not even one Indian could manage to exist on the desert tract over which we rode. Trees, there were absolutely none, unless down by the river, where some scrub timber occasionally appeared.

Some of the scenery was striking and savage. In the early morning we had the huge peak of Laramie, snow-covered, on our left. At 10 o'clock it was behind us, and at 2 o'clock, when we went into camp, it was almost in our front. This will give some idea of the zig-zag course we had to follow. Laramie peak is a gigantic landmark, a fit sentinel over that portion of the great American desert.

"Boots and saddles" put us once more on the road, Friday morning. Instead of growing better, the country increased in worthlessness as we proceeded. We struck what are significantly termed "the bad lands"—a succession of sand-pits and hills, with neither cacti nor sage-weed—which are almost universal there—nor blade of grass to relieve the wearied eye. Persons afflicted with weak vision are compelled to wear goggles while riding through those sands which are white as chalk and dazzling as quicksilver. After making over twenty miles, we again went to sleep upon the Platte, and our colonel said we were just twenty miles from Fort Fetterman.

Daybreak, on Saturday, May 27th, found us once more *en route*. The company of the 3d Cavalry with which I messed, having been in advance on the previous day, formed the rear guard, and, consequently, marched at will. It was pretty tedious, as the unfortunate mules of the wagon train were nearly worn out, their backs galled by heavy loads, and their legs swollen by a long march.

We again struck a hilly country, full of red sandstone, and cut up by countless ravines, some of which were of incredible depth. The captain determined to take a short cut from the wagon road, in order to explore the nature of the ground. Mounting a high hill, some ten miles from where we had camped, we beheld a long, low, white building on a bold, bare bluff, to the northwest. This was our first glimpse of Fort Fetterman, called after the gallant and unfortunate Colonel Fetterman, who perished only a few years previously in the Fort Phil Kearney massacre. Taking "the short cut," we found ourselves in a regular trap, and were obliged to ride up and down places that would make some of our city riders feel like making their wills. Our captain had, however, a sure-footed horse, and did not dismount. Neither did any of his men, and I, for the honor of my calling, was compelled to follow their example. Our horses nearly stood upon their heads, but they did not go over. They were all bred in that country, and were sure-footed as mules. Try to hold them up with the rein, and down they go. Give them their own way, and they'll carry you in safety over a glacier.

Having traversed about fifty ravines, we again reached the upper trail, much to my delight, for I had grown tired of steeple-chasing. Our experiment revealed nothing new in the character of the soil—if sand can be designated by that name. If neither flat nor stale, it certainly was unprofitable. By the time we regained the road, the place of rendezvous lay right beneath us, and long lines of tents and clouds of cavalry horses and pack mules grazing in the valley informed us that Colonel Evans' column from Medicine Bow, the shorter route by one-half, had already gone into camp. At the same moment a long cloud of dust, through which carbine-barrels and bridle-bits occasionally flashed, four miles ahead, showed us our main body entering the lines. The march was then down hill. Our teamsters lashed up their beasts until they cantered. The rear guard put spurs to their horses and trotted after. Half an hour later we were on the camping ground, and saw the desolate fort grinning at us from the bleak hill on the other side of the Platte. And thus we completed the ride from Russell to Fetterman.

Some officers informed us that the ferry between the camp and Fort Fetterman had broken down, and that we could not get our mail or send despatches. The river at that point is so rapid and so full of whirlpools that few men care to swim it, and most horses refuse to do so. A wagon driver, together with a sergeant and two private soldiers of the 2d Cavalry, tried the experiment of swimming their horses over a few days before and all were drowned. It was absolutely necessary for me to cross the river, and some other correspondents were in the same position. When we reached the ferry, we found that it had been patched up in a temporary manner, and concluded to go across. When near the Fetterman bank, the rope broke, and we should have been swept down stream, at the imminent risk of drowning, but for the heroism of Lieutenant and Commissary Bubb, who plunged into the stream on horseback, caught a cable which somebody threw toward him, and towed us in safety to shore amid the plaudits of the spectators. We proceeded to the fort immediately, and found General Crook at the commandant's quarters, busily engaged in forwarding the organization of his troops. He appeared to be in high spirits, and laughed grimly at our rough and miserably tanned appearance, stubble beards, dirty clothes and peeled noses.

"Oh," said he, "this is only the prelude. Wait until the play proper begins. After that you can say you were through the mill."

"We came over a pretty rough road, General," said one of our party.

"Yes," he answered, "that is a bad road, but there are worse in Wyoming. We've got to go over many of them."

He kindly invited us to dinner, but we preferred the sutler's establishment, and he directed an orderly to show us there. Fort Fetterman is now abandoned. It was a hateful post—in summer, hell, and in winter, Spitzbergen. The whole army dreaded being quartered there, but all had to take their turn. Its abandonment was a wise proceeding on the part of the government.

CHAPTER V

MARCHING ON POWDER RIVER

General Crook, impatient for action, hardly gave us time to have our soiled clothing properly washed and dried, when, everything being ready, he marched us northward at noon on the 29th of May. Two companies of the 3d Cavalry, commanded by Captain Van Vliet and Lieut. Emmet Crawford, had preceded us on the road to Fort Reno, to look out for the expected contingent of Crow Indians from Montana. The remainder, a formidable cavalcade, cemented, as it were, by a few companies of stalwart infantry, who furnished escort for the long wagon-train, streamed away from the Platte at a brisk pace, and came to a halt at Sage creek, thirteen miles north of Fetterman, in the afternoon. We were then fairly on the road to the Indian country proper—the lands secured to the Sioux, so far as that intangible instrument called a treaty could secure them anything. By the precautions taken in posting pickets and keeping the command well closed up on the march, even the most inexperienced could understand that we were in a region where active hostilities might begin at any moment. At the Sage creek camp, I was introduced by General Crook to Mr. Robert A. Strahorn, a distinguished 'Western newspaper correspondent, who had made a reputation over the *nom de plume* of "Alter Ego," and who, in every situation, proved himself as fearless as he was talented. The General also introduced me to Mr.

Davenport, of the New York *Herald*, and to Mr. Wasson, of the California *Alta*, who had had extensive experience in many Indian campaigns. Mr. Davenport was entirely unused to frontier life, and some of the young officers and his brother correspondents used to banter him a good deal with regard to the horrors of Indian warfare. He took it all in good part, at the time, but he found means, before the campaign closed, to get more than even with some of the jokers. As a rule, all the correspondents got along well together, but one or two of them did not succeed in making themselves liked by several of the officers. Of all earthly experiences, none so tests the strength and weakness of human nature as an Indian campaign, especially when attended by hardship and hunger.

As we advanced, the commanding officers of the "outfit" increased and multiplied exceedingly. First, as a matter of course, came General Crook. Then Colonel Royall, frank and direct of speech, and often very emphatic in his observations to his subordinates. Then came Major Evans, a melancholy, philosophically inclined officer, devoted to literature, suffering from an old wound, and having, to all appearance, registered a vow never to smile, in any sense. Maj. H. E. Noyes, commanding a company, was appointed commander of the five troops of the 2d Cavalry; while the ten troops of the 3d Cavalry were divided into three batallions, under the three senior company commanders, Col. Guy V. Henry, Maj. Anson Mills and Capt. Fred Van Vliet. Maj. Alexander Chambers commanded the five companies of the 4th and 9th Infantry, a very efficient body of men. Maj. John V. Furey looked after the wagon train, as he was quartermaster of the expedition, and Chief Packer, Tom Moore—an old follower of General Crook's— looked after the pack mule train, and all that appertained thereto. Nearly all of the officers mentioned had aides and adjutants, all of whom had orderlies, who blew their bugles with startling frequency, and rode from one end of the line to the other, as if the devil himself was after them. It is astonishing how much our bold dragoons can swear on proper provocation. The sentimental fair ones who so much admire our shoulder-strapped and be-frogged cavalry officers in a brilliant ball room ought to see and hear them when out on a rough campaign. They are then innocent of "boiled shirts;" their beards become a stubble, and only for the inevitable yellow stripe, which the weather turns muddy in color, on their pantaloons, they could hardly be distinguished from the private soldiers of their respective commands. The same is also true of the infantry officers. In contrast, however, with the professional mule packers, and whackers, the officers were models of the early Christian type of mankind.

We had along a trifle over 1,000 mules, all immensely loaded with ammunition and other supplies. They were unamiable and unattractive animals, awkward, yet "handy with their feet," and vilely discordant. The General, however, knew their value on a campaign, and had great respect for their eccentricities of manner and habit. Notwithstanding, I consider that the average mule is obstinate, and even morose, in manner, and filthy, not to say immodest, in habit. But the animal has his fine points also. He is surer, if slower, than the horse, and can live where the latter would surely starve. Ears polite would be immeasurably shocked by the sounds and observations that accompany the starting of a pack train from camp in the early morning. The hybrids are "cinched" or girthed so tight by the packers that they are almost cut in two. Naturally the beasts don't want to move under such circumstances. They therefore stand stock still. This irritates the packers, who swear in a most artistic and perfectly inexhaustible fashion. They welt the animals with their rawhides most unmercifully, and the brutes reply with their heels and the batteries of nature, in a most effective, if somewhat obscene, manner. Suddenly, and generally simultaneously, they dash forward, and matters run more tranquilly during the rest of the day. Such is a part of "the romance of war." The mule-drivers used to have an excellent time of it, and lived far better than the soldiers. The latter were expected to do all the fighting, while the mule-whackers had the better part of the feasting.

Although the country through which Colonel Royall's column moved, along the left bank of the Platte to Fetterman was practically a wilderness, the section between that Fort and Crazy Woman's Fork is not particularly bad; but there are enough "bad lands" here and there to about counterbalance the more fertile portions. The grass ranges along a few small streams in spring time and the early summer are fairly good, but the soil is, as a rule, poor and sandy, and the winter tarries long on the old Bozeman trail, which General Crook's brigade traveled over for several hundred miles. In fact, the whole country had a kind of arid, half-starved look in the beginning of June, 1876, and I fancy it has hardly improved much in appearance since that period. The grass seemed to be exceedingly coarse in most places, and was disfigured, wherever the eye turned, by the omnipresent sage brush and cruel cacti. I wrote at the time, to the paper I represented, that ranchmen who cared little or nothing for the comforts of civilization could raise large herds of cattle in that region, if the Sioux were subdued or friendly, but that for purposes of tillage, the soil was unavailable. My candid judgment was that, during a march of about 300 miles, I had not seen a twenty-acre tract that could approach even the medium agricultural lands of Illinois or Iowa in productive power. I had not seen a single acre that could compare with the prime farming lands of the old States. The wealth of the soil must have been very deep down, for it certainly was not visible on the surface, except in the form of alkaline deposits, which resembled hoar frost. It lacked then, and I suppose it lacks still, several essentials toward making it reasonably habitable: first, water; second, timber; third, climate. In rocks, hills, ants, snakes, weeds and alkali, that portion of Wyoming is rich indeed. If there should happen to be any gold in the heart of the Big Horn mountains, God must have placed it there to make up for the comparative worthlessness of a large portion of the Territory. I observed, also, that it needed neither a professor nor a philosopher to predict that that particular range of country could never become a part of that great agricultural Northwest which is justly called the granary of the world; and that its highest destiny was to become a mammoth cattle range. My humble prediction has been fulfilled. Myriads of domestic cattle have taken the place of the picturesque buffalo, and where the red Indian used to ride on his wild forays, the enterprising cowboy now cracks his horse-whip and "rounds up" his herds.

Colonel Royall, at the outset of our march, used to have us on the road at 5 o'clock in the morning, but General Crook, on assuming command, fixed the hour at 6 o'clock for the infantry and at 7:30 o'clock for the cavalry, in order that the horses might have sufficient rest, as he intended to make night marches in pursuit of the hostiles, accompanied by his pack train only, after the campaign had been fully developed.

He detached from Sage creek two companies of the 3d Cavalry, under Captains Meinhold and Vroom, to patrol the country to the westward, and report the presence of fresh Indian trails, if any such existed. The detachment took along four days' rations, and was ordered to rejoin us at old Fort Reno, on the Powder river. On the 30th of May we marched from Sage creek to what is called the South Fork of the Cheyenne river, a puny, muddy-looking rivulet, the rotten banks of which were fringed with cottonwood trees and tangled, rich undergrowth. The water was shockingly bad, and made many of the men quite sick. It was at this point, during the scout of the preceding March, that the Indians shot and killed the chief herder of the expedition, the very first day out from Fort Fetterman. We all felt that we were on hostile and dangerous ground, but we were allowed to sleep in peace. The pickets, however, were doubled, and every precaution against a surprise was taken.

On the 31st of May the weather, which had been rather mild and pleasant for several days, suddenly changed. The thermometer fell to zero, and the wind rose to the proportions of a hurricane. The sky became deeply overcast with ominous-looking clouds, and whirlwinds raised columns of alkaline dust, which scalded our eyes and gave to every object a hazy and filthy appearance. Many of the tents were blown down, and the men shivered around their watchfires, as if it were midwinter. It was a relief to everybody when morning came and "the general" was sounded. We marched on Wind creek—a very poor apology for a stream— about twenty miles northward. Our course lay over a somewhat bare, but undulating, country. About noon the clouds partially lifted, and the sun of the last day of May shone out fitfully to cheer our weary road. We soon gained the summit of an unusually high swell in the prairie, called in frontier parlance "a divide," and beheld, with some degree of joy, to our left and front, distant perhaps one hundred miles, the chilly, white summits of the mighty Big Horn mountains. From this same "divide" we had an exceptionally fine view of that portion of Wyoming which we had marched over. Looking backward, we could see the faint blue outline of Laramie Peak, almost dipping below the horizon. On our right, and almost due east, tho dark group of the Black Hills of Dakota could be descried through a fieldglass. On our right front, northeastward, the Pumpkin buttes, four long, somewhat irregular, but mountain-like, formations, several hundred feet in height, arose abruptly from the very bosom of "the bad lands." Those buttes run very nearly north and south, the northernmost being nearly abreast of Fort Reno. But soon the lurking storm came back upon us with renewed fury, and there was an end, for that day at least, of our enjoyment of savage scenery.

Wind creek did not belie its name. A more comfortless bivouac rarely fell to a soldier's lot. Every inch of ground was covered with some species of cacti, each seemingly more full of thorns than its neighbor. The water was simply execrable, the wood scarce and the weather bitterly cold. By order of General Crook, who did not desire to be hampered with too many impediments, we had left our tent stoves at Fort Fetterman, and as the thermometer continued to fall, we began to think that we had accidentally marched into Alaska. The storm, as night advanced, increased in fury, and came near playing us the shabby trick which it inflicted on the English army in 1854, when nearly all the tents of the Crimean expeditionary force were swept into the bay of Balaklava. When the grim morning of Thursday, June 1, 1876, broke upon Wind river, snow was falling as thickly as it does in Chicago about New Year's. The shower did not continue very long, and when it ceased, we found the temperature much more comfortable. We marched on that day to a dreary place known as the "dry fork" of the Powder river—something over twenty miles. As every officer and soldier wore a service overcoat, the brigade looked much better, because more uniform, than usual. The first half of our journey lay through and over a mountainous region, but when we reached the highest crest of "the divide," and the valley of Powder river lay stretched out before and beneath us, mile on mile, we concluded that we had, at last, struck a portion of Wyoming which we could praise with a fairly good conscience. Although the soil was marred by the brushwood and weeds which disfigure, more or less, most portions of the Territory, the valley showed evidences of fertility. It is inundated periodically by copious mountain torrents, which follow the "snow melts" and the rain storms. The vegetation is comparatively good, and a belt of cottonwood timber follows the whole course of the river, from its source among the Big Horn mountains to where it falls into the Yellowstone, opposite Sheridan buttes, in Montana. We found many traces of Indian villages near our encampment, which indicated that the valley was a favorite haunt of the savages in the days, not so long removed, when the buffalo covered the range as far as the eye could reach. Antelope were the largest game we found in the locality, because the buffalo had chosen, temporarily, to graze on the then great ranges of the Yellowstone and Tongue rivers.

As we approached the river, a young staff officer raised his field-glass to his eyes, and looked steadily to the westward for some minutes. He soon rode up to General Crook, and informed him that he had observed what he believed to be a cloud of Indians hovering on our left. The distance was too great to allow any of us to make out the precise character of the rapidly moving objects. Colonel Henry's company of the 3d Cavalry was at once ordered to reconnoitre, and set out at a fast trot over the prairie. Our column had begun to straggle somewhat, owing to the uneven character of the road, and an aide-de-camp came riding rapidly from front to rear, shouting, "Close up, close up!" which we did with great alacrity. Judging by the amount of bustle, the uninitiated among us began to believe that Sitting Bull and all his warriors must be close upon our heels. A fight was expected—muskets were examined and carbines unslung. The saddle girths were tightened, and nearly every man in the outfit assumed a proper look of martial ferocity. Very soon we observed Henry's command approaching the rapidly-moving "enemy," who seemed to be coming on with great fearlessness. The troop came to a halt, while the other party continued their movement in advance. Through our field-glasses we could then see that those dreaded "Indians" wore blue uniforms, rode American horses, and had a small pack train with them. They were, in fact, the two troops of cavalry detached under Meinhold and Vroom, at Sage creek, by the General, returning from their scout. "What a fuss about nothing!" observed Crook, as he closed his telescope and resumed his place at the head of the column. We rode almost immediately into camp on the "dry fork "of Powder river, and then we learned that the scouting party had seen no Indians, or traces of Indians, during their long ride. Captain Meinhold, a very fine-looking German officer, with a romantic history, told me smilingly, that the party had found no water since leaving the Platte, but that they had shot some deer, and, in order to quench their thirst, had emptied their brandy flasks with true military promptitude. Captain Vroom was then a magnificent specimen of the human race, tall, well-built and good-looking. He has since grown much stouter, the result, doubtless, of the absence of Indian campaigns, which would now seem to be almost at an end. One of Meinhold's men had wounded himself mortally by the accidental discharge of his pistol, and the poor fellow had suffered intensely on the subsequent march. He was placed in an ambulance, and made as comfortable as possible.

The absence of Indians surprised the men who had been over the road previously. Around the camp-fires, that evening, both officers and rank and file asked, "Where are the Sioux?" This interrogation was addressed by Captain Sutorius to Captain Wells, at a bivouac fire of the 3d Cavalry.

"Don't be alarmed," said Wells, in his grim, abrupt way, "if they want to find us, we will hear from them when we least expect. If they don't want to find us, we won't hear from them at all, but I think they will."

"They have neglected us strangely up to date," remarked Lieutenant Lemley. "Last time they serenaded us with rifle-shots every evening after we crossed the Platte. You have heard, I suppose, the joke on Lieutenant Bourke, of Crook's staff?"

"No, let's hear it," shouted half a dozen future generals.

"Very well. We were camped on Crazy Woman's—ad—d mean place—and no Indians had been disturbing us for some nights. The thing was growing stale, and we were all impatient for some kind of excitement, as it was awfully cold, and we were slowly freezing to death. 'Let us go up to Bourke's tent,' some one suggested that night, and there all of us went. The lieutenant was engaged in scanning a military map by the light of a candle. 'Hello, Bourke,' said one of the party,' ain't you afraid the Indians will ventilate your tent if you keep that light burning?'

"'Oh, no,' said Bourke. 'The Indians that have been firing into us are a small flying party. You may rely on it that you won't hear anything more from them this side of Tongue river. The distance is too great from their villages and the weather is too cold. Mr. Indian doesn't care to be frozen. Now, I'll show you on this map the point where they will, most likely, make their first real at—'

"Whizz! pop! bang! zip! came a regular volley from the bluffs above our camp. A bullet struck the candle and put it out. Another made a large-sized hole in the map. The group scattered quicker than a line of skirmishers, and Bourke was left alone to meditate on the instability of Indian character."

It doesn't take much to make men laugh around a camp fire, and there was general hilarity at the expense of the gallant and genial staff-officer, who was one of the most efficient men connected with the expedition, and who has since been so much distinguished in successive Indian campaigns.

"Now, Lieutenant Schwatka, tell us about that Pawnee Indian picket you had on Powder river, last March," said Captain Sutorius to a young officer, already introduced to my readers.

"You mean about the watch?" inquired Schwatka. "It happened in this way: We were ordered to make a detail for picket duty, and as the Pawnees were doing nothing in particular we thought we would give them a turn. My sergeant took half a dozen of them with the regular guard, and, having placed the picket post, explained to the chief Indian, as well as he could, that he and his men would have two hours on and four hours off duty until the guard was relieved. He said to the Pawnee: 'I will lend you my watch.' He struck a match and pointed to the dial. 'It is now 6 o'clock,' said he. 'When the shorter hand moves two points your first watch will be relieved. Do you understand me?'

"'Hey—hey—good!' said the Indian, and stalked away upon his rounds. The sergeant, who was greatly fatigued, dropped into a fitful sleep by the low watch-fire of the main guard, and was suddenly aroused by a hand laid heavily upon his shoulder. He started up in some affright, and saw the Pawnee standing over him, with the watch he had lent him in his hand. 'Well what the deuce do you want?' asked the startled sergeant. 'Injun heap cold—much heap stiff,' replied the warrior. 'Ugh ! that thing (indicating the watch) much lie. Long finger (the minute hand) him all

right. Short finger (the hour hand) him heap d d tired!'

"The sergeant laughed and tried to enlighten the chief as to his mistake, for he had really been but a short time on guard. 'Ugh!' was all the disgusted brave would say, and, thereafter, he would have nothing more to do with picket duty."

"By the way," said Lieutenant Reynolds, "you all remember how on the night Bourke's tent was fired into at Crazy Woman, a soldier got out of his tent, and in the frosty air of midnight, shouted loudly enough for all the command to hear him, 'I want to go ho-o-o-ome !'"

A roar of laughter rewarded the Lieutenant's anecdote, and we all, soon afterward, "turned in "for the night.

Next morning, June 2d, we marched for old Fort Reno, sixteen miles distant. It was one of the three forts abandoned by the government, under treaty with the Sioux, in 1868-9. We approached the dismantled post through Dry Fork canon, which extended about three-fourths of the way. The bottom lands were covered thickly with cottonwood, and showed very many remains of Indian villages. Emerging, at last, from the canon, we mounted a bluff, and saw, about two miles ahead of us, a small line of what appeared to be shelter tents, with animals grazing in the foreground. We soon discovered that they belonged to the two troops of the 3d Cavalry, sent forward under Captain Van Vliet and Lieut. Emmet Crawford, to meet the expected Crow Indian allies, who were, however, not yet visible. Above their little camp, on the left bank of the Powder river, we observed the ruins of Fort Reno—nothing left but bare walls, scorched timbers and rusty pieces of iron. We forded the stream, which was at low water, and speedily reached the camping ground. We were very kindly received by the officers who had preceded us. Captain Van Vliet, now Major, was tall, thin and good looking. He introduced his second in command of the company, Lieutenant Yon Leutwitz, whom I had already seen at Sidney. Lieutenant, since Captain, Emmet Crawford was over six feet high, with a genuine military face, and a spare but athletic form. He and I formed a friendship then and there which was only terminated by his unfortunate death on Mexican soil, and by Mexican hands, several years later, while he was leading a scouting party in search of the murderous Apaches. The scout was made under what may be called a treaty, and I have always looked upon the shooting of gallant Crawford as a deliberate and cruel murder, which ought to have been promptly avenged on the dastardly perpetrators. Crawford treated several officers and myself to a most welcome stimulant. He was one of the most abstemious of men, but the virtue of hospitality had a large place in his noble nature. Van Vliet also did much for our comfort, and Von Leutwitz made us all laugh heartily at a ballad of lamentation he had written, because of the non-appearance of the Crow Indians, and the refrain of which was, "Crows, dear Crows, vere the d—1 you are?"

Powder river is narrow, but rather rapid. In the rainy season it rises above its banks and inundates the country for miles on both sides of its course. Then it is both difficult and dangerous to attempt a crossing. The clay that composes its banks is generally of a black, brittle, gunpowdery appearance, and hence, it is commonly believed, the peculiar name of the river. The water is, at most seasons, exceedingly muddy, and is thoroughly impregnated with alkali, as many soldiers discovered to their sorrow before and after we left the place. The fort was beautifully situated, commanded a view of the country far and near, and to surprise it would have been impossible, with even ordinary vigilance. The low lands along the river were plentifully wooded, a circumstance that caused the death of many a brave fellow of the former garrisons, as the Indians used to lie in wait for the small wood parties sent out to cut timber, and massacred them in detail. The grazing was about the best we had seen in Wyoming Territory up to that period. The entire mountain barrier of the Big Horn, softened and beautified by distance, is visible to the westward. Fort Reno had been the main defense of the old Montana road, and since its abandonment, up to within about ten years, few white people, even in large parties, were venturous enough to travel that route. The fort had a strong stockade, and must have been quite a fortress. Loads of old metal, wheels, stoves, parts of gun carriages, axles and other iron debris, sufficient to make a Chicago junk dealer rich, were lying there, then, uncared for. I suppose most of the stuff has since passed into nothingness.

Two hundred yards north of the abandoned site is the cemetery, where thirty-five soldiers and one officer, all victims of the Sioux Indians, sleep their last sleep. A small monument of brick and stone had been erected above their resting place, but this the Indians did not respect. The moment the garrison that had erected it crossed the river, it had been set upon and almost razed to the ground. The slab on which were distinguishable the words: "Erected as a memorial of respect to our comrades in arms, killed in defense," was broken. The stones placed to mark the graves were uprooted by the vengeful savages, and many of the mounds were either leveled or scooped out. Even the rough headboards, which proclaimed the names of the gallant dead were shivered into fragments, but the patronymics of Privates Murphy, Holt, Slagle, Riley and Laggin, nearly all of the 18th Infantry, killed May 27, 1867, could be distinguished by putting the pieces together. The most stoical of mortals could hardly fail to look with some degree of emotion at the lonely and dishonored resting places of those hapless young men, so untimely, and even ingloriously, butchered by a lurking foe. They sleep far away from home and civilization, for even yet the place is only visited by the hardy rancheros and cowboys, who are little given to sentiment of any kind. For the poor soldiers lying out there, Decoration Day never dawns, and neither mother, wife, sister nor sweetheart can brighten the sod above their bones with the floral tributes of fond remembrance. "The Indian knows their place of rest," and follows them with his implacable hatred beyond the eternal river.

While the column was *en route* from Dry Fork to Reno, we came upon the trail of a party of Montana miners bound for the Black Hills. We found several rifle pits thrown up in good military fashion, which showed that some among them were old soldiers, and up to every species of Indian deviltry. Captain Van Vliet, while in advance, had picked up the following, written on a piece of board:

Dry Fork Of Powder River, May 27, 1876.

Captain St. John's party of Montana miners, sixty-five strong, leave here this morning for Whitewood. No Indian trouble yet. Don't know exactly how far it is to water. Filled nose-bags and gum boots with the liquid and rode off singing, "There's Room Enough in Paradise I"

The names signed to this peculiar, and rather devil-may care, document were Daniels, Silliman, Clark, Barrett, Morrill, Woods, Merrill, Buchanan, Wyman, Busse, Snyder, A. Daley, E. Jackson, J. Daley and others.

As the Crows, who had promised their alliance, still failed to appear, General Crook resolved to send his three reliable half-breed scouts, Frank Gruard, Louis Richard and Baptiste Pourier, to the Crow agency, some three hundred miles away, in Montana, to bring the friendly Indians into camp. Each man was provided with an extra horse, and all were advised to travel as much as possible by night, so as to avoid any bodies of hostiles that might be "scouring the plains." It was a risky journey, and, as will be seen later on, was successfully performed. The General was particularly anxious to secure the Crows, because of their well known enmity to the Sioux, and also because it was a matter of boast with all the members of the tribe that they had never killed a white man. The latter statement is, however, open to doubt.

CHAPTER VI

GLIMPSES OF THE BIG HORN RANGE

Than the morning of Sunday, June 3, 1876, a lovelier never dawned in any clime. It was 6 o'clock when our entire command — no company or troop being detached — struck their tents and prepared for their day's march. An hour later we had turned our backs on Powder river, with its gloomy associations and its three infernal "forks," facetiously christened by Lieutenant Schwatka, "Charcoal," "Sulphur" and "Spitfire." We had to make nearly thirty miles in order to reach Crazy Woman's Fork, so called on account of some obscure Indian tradition. Very little water lay between the two streams, but the "bunch grass" was plentiful, and we found some fresh "buffalo wallows "—holes made in the ground by the humps of the animals when they refresh themselves by an earth bath — but none of the noble bisons, now, alas, all but extinct, showed themselves that day.

Our column, including cavalry, infantry, wagon train, pack train and ambulances, stretched out a distance of, perhaps, four miles. The infantry generally accompanied the wagon train, and acted as a most efficient escort. On June 3d, the ten companies of the 3d Cavalry, under Major Evans, formed the van of the horse brigade, while five companies of the 2d Cavalry, under Major Noyes, formed the rear. Crook, with his staff, was away in advance of everything, as was his custom. Colonel Royall, commanding the whole of the horse, and mounted on a fast-going charger, regulated the time of the column, and we marched like greased lightning. Were I to live to the age of the biblical patriarchs, I can never forget the beauty of that scene. A friend and myself allowed the soldiers to file somewhat ahead, in order that we might enjoy a complete view. The cavalry rode by twos, the intervals between the companies, except those which formed the rear guard behind the pack mules, being just sufficient to define the respective commands. The wagons, 120 in all, with their white awnings and massive wheels, each drawn by six mules, covered the rising ground in advance of the horsemen, while the dark column of infantry was dimly discernible in the van, because Crook always marched out his foot, for obvious reasons, an hour or two ahead of his horse. 'We used to joke about the infantry, and call them by their Indian nickname of "walk-a-heaps," but, before the campaign was over, we recognized that man is a hardier animal than the horse, and that "shank's mare" is the very best kind of a charger. Our course lay over a gently swelling or billowy plain, nearly bare of trees, but sufficiently carpeted with young grass to render it fresh and vernally verdant. A slight white frost of the previous night, just beginning to evaporate, laid the dust and seemed to cover the prairie with countless diamonds. The sun beamed with a radiance rarely seen in the denser atmosphere of the East. Fifty miles in our front — we were marching almost due westward — rose the mighty wall of the Big Horn mountains, Cloud Peak, the loftiest point of the range, seeming to touch the cerulean-hued canopy of the sky, its white apex standing in bold and broad relief against the firmamental blue. The base of the mountains, timber-covered, as we discovered on nearer approach, had that purple beauty of coloring which we sometimes see in the masterpieces of the great landscape painters. The snow line, under the influence of the solar rays, gleamed like molten silver, and all this, taken in conjunction with the green fore and the dark middle ground, produced an effect of dazzling grandeur. Even the rudest among the hardy soldiery appeared to be impressed by the spectacle. It was like a glimpse of the promised land, albeit not from the mountains of Moab, but from the plains of 'Wyoming. Perhaps never again did the splendid panorama of the sierra of the Big Horn appear so magnificent to the eyes that gazed upon the fullness of its glory on that brilliant morning of leafy June.

We observed on this march, along toward noon, supposed Indian signal fires. Our pickets had been much strengthened already, but now the General sent forward a strong cavalry detachment to feel for the expected enemy, who might attack us at any moment. We then suspected, what we afterwards knew to be correct, that the main body of the Indians was in Montana, keeping watch on the columns under Terry, and particularly the command of General Gibbon, who had under him the infantry of the expedition. It was well known that General Custer, with the 7th Cavalry, had left Fort Abraham Lincoln in the middle of May, and was liable to be heard from before many days. Now, however, that they knew of the presence of Crook's brigade in their country, we all knew that the Indians would not leave us unmolested much longer. Bugle calls were abolished, and all orders were transmitted through the officers of the respective staffs.

Crazy Woman's Fork, like all of its sister streams, is fed from the snows of the Big Horn, and its water is icy cold, even in summer. But it was a treacherous spot in which to camp, and had been the theatre of many a direful tragedy. Scrubwood and gullies abound at the crossing of the Montana trail, and these always induce Indians to form ambuscades. The Montana miners had evidently preceded us, for we saw their well-devised fortifications. The wagons had also moved on two tracks, which showed that, in passing ravines, and other dangerous places, the practiced frontiersmen had marched between their teams, so as to be ready for instant defense. Our pickets were soon posted, supper served and we fell off to sleep as tranquilly as if there were no Indians to disturb our happiness or no gory imaginings to tinge our dreams.

Our next march was a short one, Clear Fork being only a little over twenty miles from Crazy Woman. The water of Clear Fork is absolutely translucent, and in the days of which I am writing there was not in America a more prolific haunt of the exquisite brook trout. This stream is also a tributary of the Powder, but flows independently, thus escaping contamination, through very many miles of as charming a game country as ever the eye of man rested upon.

On that day, for the first time, I saw an Indian "grave." It was situated on a little bluff above the creek. After dismounting I went up to observe it. The Sioux never put their dead underground. This "grave" was a buffalo hide supported by willow slips and leather thongs, strapped upon four cotton-wood poles, about six feet high. The corpse had been removed either by the Indians themselves or by the miners who had passed through a few days before. Around lay two blue blankets, with red trimmings, a piece of a jacket all covered with beads, a moccasin, a fragment of Highland tartan, a brilliant shawl and a quantity of horse hair. Scarcely had I noted these objects when a squad of young fellows from the 9th Infantry walked up the hill after firewood. They, evidently, were lacking in the bump of veneration, as the following remarks will show:

"Hello, Sam, what in h— is that?"

"That—oh, that is the lay-out of some d—d dead Indian. Let's pull it down. Here, boys, each of you grab a pole and we'll tear it up by the roots."

They did tear it up by the roots, and within ten minutes the Indian tomb was helping to boil the dinners of the 9th Infantry.

Thus the relationship of all men to each other in point of savagery was established. The Sioux defaced the white graves at Reno. The whites converted the Sioux funeral pedestal into kindling-wood. It was all the same to the dead on both sides.

In the evening two rough-looking fellows came into camp and reported that they belonged to a party which was coming from the Black Hills to the Big Horn. The main body, they said, was a day's inarch behind us. It was their fires we saw the day before. The men went away like Arabs, and only when they had gone did it strike our officers that they were "squaw men" from the Sioux camp, who visited us in the capacity of spies in behalf of their Indian people in-law. It seemed stupid not to have detained the rascals as prisoners.

June 5th was one of our shortest marches—only sixteen miles. We got into camp at old Fort Phil Kearney about noon, and were located in a most delightful valley, at the foothills of the Big Horn mountains. This is a celebrated spot. Here it was that Colonel Carrington founded the fort made bloodily famous by the slaughter of Fetterman, Brown, Grummond and eighty-three soldiers on December 22, 1866. The world has heard the story how the wood party was attacked down Piney creek, half a mile from the post. How Fetterman and the rest, being signaled, went to their relief. How a party of Indians decoyed them beyond the bluffs and then fell upon them like an avalanche, killing every man and mutilating everybody except that of Metzker, a bugler, who fought with such desperate valor that the Indians covered the remains with a buffalo robe as a token of their savage respect. They attempted to take this brave bugler alive, but be killed so many of the warriors that he had to be finished. This much lied Cloud's people subsequently told our soldiers. From our camp we could plainly see the fatal ravine on the old Fort Smith road, where those brave but hapless soldiers fell. They call the place surrounding it "Massacre Hill." Alas, for glory! I visited the cemetery near the site of the fort that afternoon. The humble railing around it was torn down by the Sioux. The brick monument above the bodies of the officers was half demolished, and a long, low mound, upon which the grass grew damp, rank and dismal, indicated the last resting place of the unfortunate men who met their dreadful fate at the hands of the very Indians who were then being fed on government rations at the Red Cloud agency. Red Cloud, now old and half paralytic, was a prime mover in that butchery. The event closed Colonel Carrington's career, although the court of inquiry acquitted him, chiefly on the ground that he positively ordered Col. Fetterman not to pursue the Indians beyond the bluffs.

We passed, on our road to Phil Kearney, Lake De Smet, called after the famed Jesuit,—a sheet of salt water without visible outlet, about two and one-half miles long by about half a mile average width.

Somebody came into camp in the afternoon and told General Crook that there were buffalo grazing beyond "Massacre Hill." Acting on the information, he, with Captain Dickerson, of his staff, and Major Chambers, of the infantry, mounted his horse and rode out in pursuit. They went far beyond our lines, saw a dozen deer, one grizzly bear, but no buffalo. Crook, however, shot a cow elk.

Whosoever selected the site of Fort Phil Kearney, did not do so with an eve to the safety of its garrison. It was commanded by high wooded bluffs, within easy range, on every side. Indians could have easily approached within a couple of hundred yards of the stockade, without much fear of discovery. A dozen better sites could have been selected in the immediate neighborhood.

It was said that the officer who made the selection—Colonel was influenced thereto by his wife, a lady of some will. He used to delight in sounding the bugle calls himself. One morning, it is related, he was proceeding to sound reveille, when his wife asked him: "Where are you going with that bugle ?" He explained briefly.

"You may march all you please," said she, "but here I will remain. This is as good a place for your fort as any other."

The colonel, who desired domestic happiness, gave in right away, and so Fort Phil Kearney, of bloody memory, came to be built.

Crook wanted to establish his permanent camp at a place called Goose Creek, reported to be only eight miles from Phil Kearney. The whole command—wagons and all— started out to find it early on the morning of June 6th. We crossed the "Great Piney," a rapid mountain torrent, and marched through the fatal ravine in which Fetterman's column got cut to pieces. So perfect a trap was never seen. There was no way out of it. A small party had no more chance of escaping those 1,500 Sioux, in such a position, than an exhausted fly has to break away from the strong spider who has it fast in the web. Fetterman, it is said, was in bad humor with las commanding officer when he left the fort, and hence his rashness and the tragic result thereof. "Not unavenged he died," however, for 180 Indians, by their own acknowledgment, were killed or wounded. Every man of the expedition looked with interest at a spot scarcely second to Fort William Henry as a gloomy memorial of Indian warfare.

Our road lay through one of the richest grass ranges that I have ever seen. It is capable of high cultivation. The air was laden with perfume, the ravines being filled with wild flowers of many species. We marched on for hours, but no Goose creek appeared. Crook had evidently changed his mind, for we diverged to the northeast somewhat abruptly, following the course of a stream called Beaver creek. It ran at the base of a range of red hills, scraggy and wild, and we were not long in leaving the beauteous scenery of the morning far behind us. We found out that we were on the old Bridger trail, and marched five and twenty miles before halting at the desired point. *En route* we struck a buffalo herd and our men killed six of the animals—all in prime condition. We saw a number of deer, and wild fowl sprang up at almost every step. The plain was indented with buffalo tracks, showing that we had struck a belt of the hunting grounds. The veterans said where you find the buffalo there you find the Indians too. But we saw no red hides that day. A heavy thunder-storm, accompanied by fierce rain, made our camp rather dreary. At the camp-fires an adjutant told us that Crook was marching on Tongue river.

The continuous marching over rough roads told severely on our stock. Many of the pack mules were half flayed alive, their loads having galled them dreadfully. Several cavalry horses looked worn out, and not a few of the men were suffering from inflammatory rheumatism — a disease quite prevalent in Wyoming. We had only one cavalry and four infantry ambulances, and three doctors looked after the whole command. "Put the sick in the wagons," was the order, the ambulances being full. A sick man might as well be stretched upon the rack as in an army wagon. But a man has no business to be wounded or taken ill while engaged in that kind of enterprise. In the words of Marshal Massena, before Torres Vedras, the soldier on an Indian campaign must have "the heart of a lion and the stomach of a mouse."

We reached the Prairie Dog branch of Beaver creek early on the morning of the 7th of June, and we followed that creek over hills and rocks for about eighteen miles. It was an execrable road, the stream being of a winding character, and we had to cross and re-cross it several times, drawing our knees up on our saddles, and shouldering our carbines to save them from being wet. The wagons also had a hard time in keeping up, and it was quite late when they and the rear guard finally reached camp at the junction of Prairie Dog creek with Tongue river. It was a point where few white men had been previously, and was situated about half a dozen miles from the Montana line, in the very heart of the hostile country. Tongue river wound around the neck of land on which our tents were pitched, like a horse shoe. Prairie Dog creek bounded us on the south ; a low ridge rose to our left, and in front, beyond Tongue river and commanding it and our camp, there stood a bold, steep bluff. The bottom lands were well covered with timber. Some of the officers found fault with the position, on account of its rather exposed situation, but others treated the matter lightly, and said there was nothing to be apprehended.

At that period General Crook seemed to be a man of iron. He endured heat, cold, marching and every species of discomfort with Indian-like stolidity. If he felt weariness, he never made anybody the wiser. While apparently frank to all who approached him, he was very uncommunicative except to his aides. He was also a born Nimrod', and always rode far in advance of the column, attended by a few officers and an orderly or two, chasing whatever species of game he might happen to find. Looking back at his conduct of that time, I cannot help thinking that luck was greatly on his side, because, as we very soon found out, the General might have run into a strong war party of the Sioux any day, and then nothing could have saved him and his few attendants. He was frequently warned of the risk he ran, but paid no attention to the advice.

At this camp Private Francis Tierney, alias Doyle, born in Albany, N. Y., and a member of Company B of the 3d Cavalry, who had accidentally shot himself in the bivouac on the dry branch of the South Cheyenne river, on the evening of May 30th, died. He was buried during the afternoon with military honors. Every officer and soldier not on duty attended the funeral, and the burial service was impressively read by Col. Guy V. Henry, over the grave, which was dug in a lonely spot among the low hills surrounding the place. The body was wrapped in an overcoat and blanket, and Captain Meinhold shoveled the first spadeful of clay on the cold remains. A rough granite boulder was rolled upon the grave, and the young soldier was shut out forever from the living world. Three volleys—the warrior's requiem—pealed above his tomb, and we left him to his ever-enduring sleep. Except, perhaps, the burial of a human being in mid ocean, the interment of a soldier in the great American wilderness of that epoch was about the gloomiest of funeral experiences. It was, indeed, a sad destiny that led this young man to <lie, accidentally, it is true, by his own hand—the first of Crook's brigade to lay his bones in the terra incognita of Wyoming.

CHAPTER VII

THE FIRST FUSILLADE

At about 11 o'clock, on the night of June 8th, I was aroused from sleep by the loud and persistent howling of what seemed to be a band of coyotes—animals that the Indians often imitate when approaching a camp. Soon afterward a deep voice was heard shouting down by the river, to the men encamped there. Captain Sutorius, who was also aroused, said, "That sounds like the voice of an Indian." The sound appeared to come from the tall bluff above Tongue river. General Crook's attention was called to the matter, and he sent Arnold, a half-breed scout, to interview the mysterious visitor. Arnold recognized the Crow dialect, but, thinking it rather imperfect, had his suspicions aroused. The savage was invisible, being concealed among the rocks and brush on the opposite bank.

"Any half-breeds there—any Crows?" he asked, as Arnold challenged him. The scout made some reply which was not understood by the party of the first part, for the Indian asked in louder tones than previously, "Have the Crows come yet?"

The scout, unfortunately, replied in one of the Sioux idioms, whereupon the savage became silent, and was not heard from again that night. General Crook was very angry, because he believed that the nocturnal visitor was a runner from the expected Crow Indians, whose arrival had been so long delayed. And we were not very long in finding out that the General had made a correct guess.

It is rather singular that in 1876 most of the people skilled in mining seemed certain that gold would be found in the Big Horn mountains, and the streams that had their sources among them. A few stray miners had attached themselves to Crook's column, in the hope of "prospecting" for the precious metal. A man named Wyatt was particularly enthusiastic on the subject. He was a strange genius, and had explored most of the out-of-the-way places on the frontier. Wyatt told me, in Tongue River camp, that the two miners suspected of being "squaw men," who followed us to Clear Creek, said to him that they were from Montana, and four of them had left there for the Black Hills early in the spring. Being a small party, they were afraid to keep the lower road, and therefore footed it through the mountains, living on game. When they reached "Crazy Woman's Fork," they saw a bar in the middle of the river and determined to prospect it. Having no pan, they extemporized one out of a blanket and a willow hoop. In two days, they told Wyatt, $70 in gold was "panned out." Then they left for the Black Hills, where one of the party died. Matters not being prosperous there, they organized a party of sixty men and started for "Crazy Woman," which they reached one day after we left. They had followed Crook's command to buy sugar and coffee, of which they obtained a small quantity. They did not show Wyatt any gold specimens. It was their intention, they said, to keep track of the expedition, and to let General Crook know what success they might meet with. Wyatt gave their story for what it was worth, but was not prepared to vouch for the truth of all they said. In view of the fact that no gold has been discovered in that locality since, the story of the two tramps must have been a fabrication.

On the morning of the 9th some cavalry soldiers, who had been out hunting buffalo, reported having found a fresh Indian trail, and during the night Captain De wees' company of the 2d Cavalry had been disturbed by something, and the firing of their pickets had aroused the whole camp, so that expectation and excitement began to run pretty high. Some of the veterans swore that a recruit had been alarmed by the swaying of a bunch of sage brush in the night breeze, and it remained for Indians in the flesh to appear, before many of them would believe that there were any hostiles in the country.

At about 6:30 o'clock, on the evening of the 9th, just as the soldiers were currying their horses on the picket line, a shot was heard on the right of the camp, and it was quickly followed by a volley which appeared to come from the commanding bluff beyond the river. This opinion was soon confirmed by the whistling and singing of bullets around our ears, and some of us did lively jumping around to get our arms. The Indians had come at last, and were ventilating our tents, by riddling the canvas, in a masterly manner. We were taken by surprise, and the men stood by their horses waiting for orders. Meanwhile Sheol appeared to have broken loose down by the river and all around the north line of our camp. If the casualties had borne any proportion to the sound of the firing, the mortality must have been immense. On our extreme left, the pickets of the 2d Cavalry kept up an incessant fire, which was very spiritedly responded to by the Sioux. The higher bluff, which commanded the entire camp, situated almost directly north, seemed alive with redskins, judging by the number of shots, although only two Indians, mounted on fleet ponies, were visible on the crest. They rode up and down in front of us, repeatedly, and appeared to act in the double capacity of chiefs and lookouts. Although a great number of soldiers fired upon them, they appeared to bear charmed lives. But the savages were rapidly getting the range of our camp, and making things uncomfortably warm. Crook's headquarters and the infantry lines were immediately below them, while our tents, on the southern slope, offered a very attractive target. Their guns carried admirably, and made loungers, who thought themselves comparatively safe, hop around in a very lively, if not over-graceful, manner. The firing had lasted ten minutes, when a brilliant flash of inspiration came upon the officer in command. The men had instinctively fallen in line—the worst thing they could have done under the circumstances. All at once a young staff officer, excited and breathless, rode into the camp of the 1st Battalion of the 3d Cavalry.

"Colonel Mills! Colonel Mills!" he shouted.

"Here, sir," replied the commander of the battalion.

"General Crook desires that you mount your men instantly, Colonel, cross the river and clear those bluffs of the Indians."'

"All right," said Col. Mills, and he gave the order.

All at once the four companies of our battalion—A, Lieutenant

Lawson; E, Captain Sutorius; I, Captain Andrews and Lieutenant Foster, and M, Lieutenants Paul and Schwatka were in the saddle.

"Forward!" shouted the colonel, and forward we went.

A company of the 2d Cavalry was extended among the timber on the left, to cover the attack upon the bluffs. In a minute our charging companies were half wading, half swimming, through Tongue river, which is swift and broad at that point. The musketry continued to rattle and the balls to whiz as we crossed. Partially screened by cottonwood trees in the bottom-land, we escaped unhurt. In another minute we had gained the base of the bluffs, when we were ordered to halt and dismount, every eighth man holding the horses of the rest. Then we commenced to climb the rocks, under a scattering fire from our friends, the Sioux. The bluffs were steep and slippery, and took quite a time to surmount. Company A had the extreme right; M, the right center; E, the left center, and I, the extreme left. We reached the plateau almost simultaneously. The plain extended about 1,000 yards north and east, at which distance there arose a ridge, and behind that, at perhaps the same distance, another ridge. We could see our late assailants scampering like deer, their fleet ponies carrying them as fast as the wind up the first ascent, where they turned and fired. Our whole line replied, and the boys rushed forward with a yell. The Sioux gave us another salute, the balls going about 100 feet above our heads, and skedaddled to the bluff further back. There, nothing less than a long-range cannon could reach them, and we could pursue them no farther, as the place was all rocks and ravines, in which the advantage lay with the red warriors. The latter showed themselves, at that safe distance, on the east of the ridge, and appeared to take delight in displaying their equestrian accomplishments. I borrowed a field-glass and had a look at them. Not more than a dozen were in view, although at least fifty must have fired upon us in the first place. Those that I saw were dressed in a variety of costumes. One fellow wore what seemed to be a tin helmet, with a horse-hair plume. Another chap wore a "war bonnet," but most of them had the usual eagle feathers. To say the truth, they did not seem very badly scared, although they got out of the way with much celerity when they saw us coming in force. Our firing having completely ceased, we could hear other firing on the south side of the river, far to the left, where the 2d Cavalry had their pickets. This, we subsequently learned, was caused by a daring attempt made by the Indians to cross a ford at that point and take the camp in rear, with the object of driving off the herd. They failed signally, and lost one man killed and some wounded. Whether our party killed any of the Sioux I don't know. They did their best, which is all that could be asked of them.

Our casualties were comparatively few, owing to the prompt action of Mills' battalion, but quite sufficient to cure skeptics of the idea that there were no hostiles in the neighborhood. After the Indians retired, Mills' men were withdrawn to camp, and the bluff was garrisoned by Captain Rawolle's company of the 2d Cavalry, who had a most miserable experience, as they did not bring their tents to the other side and had to endure "in the open" a pitiless rainfall all through the night. The evident object of the savages was to "set us on foot" by stampeding our herd.

Many ludicrous stories grew out of this skirmish, and one in particular deserves to be recorded. During the firing, the pipe of Colonel Mills' tent stove had been perforated, greatly to the horror of his colored servant, who was by no means in love with grim-visaged war. The correspondent of a Southern paper—an officer by the way—recorded the fact, and his paper, taking a practical view of the statement, came out in a wise editorial and condemned the colonel's rashness in wearing a stove-pipe hat in the field! When the paper finally reached us, everybody laughed immoderately, and Mills didn't hear the last of that "stove pipe" for a long time.

General Crook began to grow restive under the continued absence of the friendly Indians, and, not liking his position on Tongue river, moved his command, through a fairly fertile country, to Goose, or Wildgoose, creek, about fourteen miles from the scene of the Indian attack and repulse. The creek which bears a name so undignified is really a fine mountain stream, having two branches, known as Big and Little Goose creek, which, diverging near the foothills of the Big Horn, finally come together and empty themselves into the copious waters of Tongue river. This was a thoroughly delightful camping ground, well wooded, watered and supplied with game, while the scenery was all that could be asked for. That fine region, then terrorized by the war parties of the Sioux and shunned by the Caucasian race, is now thickly settled, and several thriving hamlets have been built on the sites of our old encampments. Herds innumerable now feed where only the buffalo roamed as late as 1876.

We got into camp in a pelting rain, which, however, speedily ceased, and the weather became delightful.

CHAPTER VII

INDIANS IN WAR PAINT

Just as we began to give up all hope of ever again seeing our scouts or hearing from our Indian allies, Frank Gruard and Louis Richard, accompanied by a gigantic Crow chief, came into camp at noon on the 14th, and, amid the cheers of the soldiers, rode direct to the General's headquarters. I proceeded there at once and had an interview with the celebrated scout, Gruard, who is half a Frenchman and half a Sandwich Islander. He was brought to this country from Honolulu when a mere boy; ran the mail for the government on the Pacific coast for some years, and, when only nineteen years old, was captured by Crazy Horse's band of Sioux. The chief spared the young man's life, and he lived in the Indian village, having espoused a handsome squaw, for some years. A misunderstanding with his wife's relatives made the village too hot for him, and, being allowed comparative liberty, he took the very earliest opportunity of taking "French leave." He was then about twenty-eight years of age, was familiar with every inch of the country, could speak nearly every Indian dialect, and was invaluable to General Crook, who would rather have lost a third of his command, it is said, than be deprived of Frank Gruard. The scout told the writer that he and his companions had had a hard time of it since they left Fort Reno to search for the Crows. A band of Sioux got sight of them the second day out, and chased them into the mountains. They eluded their pursuers, and, after four days' hard riding, reached the Big Horn river, which they had to swim with their horses. A few miles from that stream they saw an Indian village, full of women and warriors. The latter to the number of about 300, charged down upon them, mounted on ponies. The scouts had a river between them and the Indians—a small river, but sufficient to insure their safe retreat. The red men fired upon them without effect, and then Gruard, by their large, bushy heads, entirely different from the trimmer Sioux, recognized the Crows. He immediately shouted to them in their own language, and very soon the three scouts were in their midst, saluted by a storm of "Hows!" Then they learned that five Crow scouts had started to find our camp. It was this party that attempted to speak to us from Tongue river bluffs previously, but when Arnold spoke Sioux they became alarmed, suspecting a trap, and retreated. They would have come in only that Gruard told them we were going to camp on Goose creek. They saw us leave 'Fort Phil. Kearney, but when we took the Tongue river road they concluded we were not the party they were looking for, and turned back. Gruard soon set matters right, and before many hours had nearly 200 warriors ready for the road.

They were, he said, within ten miles of our camp, but, with true Indian caution, declined to come in until perfectly assured that it would be a safe proceeding. Baptiste Fourier had remained behind with the Indians to give them confidence. Five Snake, or Sho-sho-ne, scouts, sent from their tribe at Sweetwater valley to notify the Crows that they were coming to help us and should be treated as friends, were with the party. Louis Richard, the Indian scout, and Major Burt went back for the Crows. We waited impatiently for their arrival. At six o'clock a picket galloped into camp to notify Crook that his allies were in sight.

Then we saw a grove of spears and a crowd of ponies upon the northern heights, and there broke upon the air a fierce, savage whoop. The Crows had come in sight of our camp, and this was their mode of announcing their satisfaction. We went down to the creek to meet them, and a picturesque tribe they were. Their horses—nearly every man had an extra pony—were little beauties, and neighed shrilly at their American brethren, who, unused to Indians, kicked, plunged and reared in a manner that threatened a general stampede. "How! How!" the Crows shouted to us, one by one, as they filed past. When near enough, they extended their hands and gave ours a hearty shaking. Most of them were young men, many of whom were handsomer than some white people I have met. Three squaws were there on horseback—wives of the chiefs.

The head sachems were "Old Crow," "Medicine Crow," "Feather Head," and "Good Heart," all deadly enemies of the Sioux. Each man wore a gaily colored mantle, handsome leggings, eagle feathers, and elaborately worked moccasins. In addition to their carbines and spears, they carried the primeval bow and arrow. Their hair was long, but gracefully tied up and gorgeously plumed. Their features, as a rule were aquiline, and the Crows have the least prominent cheek bones of any Indians that I have yet encountered. The squaws wore a kind of half-petticoat and parted their hair in the middle, the only means of guessing at their sex. Quick as lightning they gained the center of our camp, dismounted, watered and lariated their ponies, constructed their "tepees," or "lodges," and, like magic, the Indian village arose in our midst. Fires were lighted without delay, and the Crows were soon devouring their evening meal of dried bear's meat and black-tailed deer. In the middle of this repast, we saw several warriors raise their heads and say "Ugh, ugh! Sho-sho-ne." They pointed southward, and, coming down the bluffs in that direction, we saw a line of horsemen, brilliantly attired, riding at whirlwind speed. Crook sent a scout to meet them. Hardly had he time to start forward when the new-comers crossed the creek, and, in column of twos, like a company of regular cavalry, rode in among us. They carried two beautiful American flags, and each warrior bore a pennon. They looked like Cossacks of the Don, but were splendidly armed with government rifles and revolvers. Nearly all wore magnificent war bonnets and scarlet mantles. They were not as large as the Crow Indians, nor as good-looking, but they appeared to be hardy and resolute. The meeting between them and the Crows was boisterous and exciting. Demoniacal yells rang through the camp, and then this wild cavalry galloped down to headquarters, rode around Crook and his staff, saluted, and, following the example of the Crows, were soon bivouacked and deep in their rough and ready suppers. Tom Cosgrove, chief of scouts in the Wind River valley, accompanied them. His lieutenant was Nelson Yurnell, and his interpreter, a young half-breed, called Ulah Clair. The Indian chiefs of the Snakes present were Wesha and Kawkee, with the two sons of old Washakie.

That night an immense lire was kindled near Crook's tents, and there all the chiefs of both tribes, together with our commanding officers, held "a big talk." Louis Richard acted as interpreter, and had a hard time of it, having to translate in three or four languages. A quarter of an hour intervened between each sentence. The chiefs squatted on their heels according to their ancient custom, and passed the long pipe from man to man. Crook stood in the circle, with his hands in his pockets, looking half bored, half happy. Major Randall, chief of scouts, and other members of the staff were with him. The Indians were quite jolly, and laughed heartily whenever the interpreter made any kind of blunder. The Snakes retired from the council first. They said very little. "Old Crow," the greatest chief of the Crow nation, made the only consecutive speech of the night, and it was a short one. Translated, it was as follows: "The great white chief will hear his Indian brother. These are our lands by inheritance. The Great Spirit gave them to our fathers, but the Sioux stole them from us. They hunt upon our mountains. They fish in our streams. They have stolen our horses. They have murdered our squaws, our children. What white man has done these things to us ? The face of the Sioux is red, but his heart is black. But the heart of the pale face has ever been red to the Crow. [' Ugh!' 'Ugh!'

'Hey!'] The scalp of no white man hangs in our lodges. They are thick as grass in the wigwams of the Sioux. ['Ugh!'] The great white chief will lead us against no other tribe of red men. Our war is with the Sioux and only them. We want back our lands. We want their women for our slaves—to work for us as our women have had to work for them. We want their horses for our young men, and their mules for our squaws. The Sioux have trampled upon our hearts. We shall spit upon their scalps. [' Ugh!' 'Hey!' and terrific yelling.] The great white chief sees that my young men have come to fight. No Sioux shall see their backs. Where the white warrior goes there shall we be also. It is good. Is my brother content?"

The chief and Crook shook hands amid a storm of "Ughs "and yells.

All the red men then left the council fire and went to their villages, where they put on their war-paint and made night hideous with a war-dance and barbarous music. They imitated in succession every beast and bird of the North American forests. Now they roared like a bison bull. Then they mimicked a wildcat. All at once they broke out with the near, fierce howling of a pack of wolves; gradually the sound would die away until you might imagine that the animals were miles off, when, all of a sudden, the howling would rise within a few yards, and in the darkness you would try to discern the foul "coyotes "—next to the Indians the pest of the plains. All night long, despite the incredible fatigue they must have endured in coming to join us, the savages continued their infernal orgies. Their music is fitter for hell than for earth. And yet these were not the worst red men existing. These were "the truly good" Indians. Our young soldiers appeared to relish the yelling business immensely, and made abortive attempts to imitate the Indians, greatly to the amusement of those grotesque savages. I fell asleep dreaming of "roistering devils "and lakes of brimstone.

Crook was bristling for a fight. The Sioux were said to be encamped on the Rosebud, near the Yellowstone river, holding Gibbon at bay. "They are numerous as grass," was the definite Crow manner of stating the strength of the enemy.

Some of the officers, who had had charge of different tribes of Indians at their respective agencies, were fond of discussing at the evening camp-fires the characteristics of the various Indian bands or "nations." From what may be termed the consensus of military opinion I learned what follows:

Nearly every Indian, of any note whatever, possessed at that time two equines—one, a pony for pack work, the other, a horse for war and the chase. The latter can go like a meteor, and has wonderful endurance. Mounted upon him, the Indian warrior could secure a retreat from the *Chasseurs d'Afrique* of Macmahon, with all their Arab horses.

The Indian war-horse is not as beautiful a beast as the Arabian, but he has more toughness than an ordinary mule. These combined qualities of strength, speed and "hold out" made him the main stay of the red man of the plains, whether he was Sioux, Cheyenne or Snake. Where the breed came from, or of what blood compounded, nobody seems to know. It is not a mustang, neither is it an Arabian—perhaps a combination of both. It may be for aught we know, indigenous to this continent—a theory sustained by the fact that the Indians can get more work out of such a horse than any other race of men, white, black or yellow.

When Indians kill game on the hunt, they cut out the tongue, liver and heart, and, unless very hungry, leave the carcass to rot upon the prairie. They don't want to load their horses much unless when near their villages, where the squaws can dry the meat, for the average Indian is still unchanged —still the same mysterious, untamable, barbaric, unreasonable, childish, superstitious, treacherous, thievish, murderous creature, with rare exceptions, that he has been since first Columbus set eyes upon him at San Salvador. Whether friendly or hostile, the average Indian is a plunderer. He will first steal from his enemy. If he cannot get enough that way, he steals from his friends. While the warriors are fat, tall and good-looking, except in a few cases, the squaws are squatty, yellow, ugly and greasy looking. Hard work disfigures them, for their lazy brutes of sons, husbands and brothers will do no work, and the unfortunate women are used as so many pack mules. Treated with common fairness, the squaws might grow tolerably comely; their figures being generally worse than their faces. It is acknowledged by all that the Sioux women are better treated and handsomer than those of all other tribes. Also they are more virtuous, and the gayest white Adonises confess that the girls of that race seldom yield to the seducer, The Sioux abhor harlots, and treat them in a most inhuman manner—even as they treat white captive women— when they are detected. If they do not kill them outright, they injure them for life and then drive them from the tribe. Among the married, such as their marriage is— for polygamy is a recognized institution in the tribe—adultery generally means death to the female concerned if she is discovered, while among the interested "braves "it begets a feud that only blood can extinguish. The Sioux hold it a sin against nature—according to their ideas of sin and nature—for a woman to remain unmarried, and they sometimes punish her, if she continues obstinate, in a very cruel and indelicate fashion. Fortunately for the Sioux women, they, for the most part, believe in matrimony and are spared all trouble on the score of their prolonged virginity.

Imagine all the old maids in America being punished because the men of their generation did not have the good taste to woo and marry them! The Sioux will not have any old maids hanging around their wigwams. This is a truly patriarchal way of providing husbands for the fair sex.

The other Indian tribes are more lax in their ideas of female propriety, and care much less whether a woman is married or the reverse. Taken all in all, the Sioux must be descendants of Cain, and are veritable children of the devil. The rest are a very little behind them, except in point of personal appearance and daring, in which the Sioux excel nearly all other Indians. Most of them are greedy, greasy, gassy, lazy and knavish.

In connection with the subject of female Sioux virtue, I am reminded of a story which caused great amusement in military circles several years ago. A certain handsome and dashing cavalry officer, now deceased, was badly smitten with the really pretty daughter of a leading Sioux chief, whose village was situated quite close to the post. Lieutenant paid some attentions to the girl, in order to while away the tedious summer hours, and, one day, remarked casually to a half-breed interpreter that he would like to own the savage princess and take her East as a living curiosity. The half-breed, taking the matter seriously, informed the maiden's warlike sire. The latter took the matter in good faith also, and resolved to make the "giving away" of his daughter in marriage, for that was how he understood it, memorable. The gay lieutenant was then acting adjutant of his battalion, and at the evening parade, just as he had "set his battle in array," heard a most infernal tumult in the direction of the Indian village. The major in command looked both annoyed and astonished and asked for an explanation. The adjutant could give none, but, by order of his superior, rode in the direction of the disturbance to find out, if possible, its meaning. As he approached the village he saw a great cavalcade moving toward him at full speed, with the old chief and his daughter heading the procession. A horrible suspicion dawned upon the mind of the unlucky adjutant, and this was confirmed a moment later, when the half-breed interpreter, and author of all the mischief, rode forward to inform the officer that Spotted Elk was coming up to the post in due order to surrender his daughter into the keeping of Lieutenant as his wife—or one of his wives. Uttering a most heart-felt malediction on the chief, the girl, the interpreter and the whole Indian generation, Lieutenant spurred back to the parade, requested to be relieved on the ground of sudden illness, wrote a note of explanation to his commanding officer, obtained temporary leave of absence, which was afterwards extended, and bade an eternal farewell to the post, and the village and the Indian princess.

Long afterwards, I met the hero of the foregoing adventure, and found him one of the most winning and gifted officers of the army, who, although an American, had all of "an Irishman's heart for the ladies," and all the Hibernian's fondness for getting into love scrapes. Poor ! He died in the flower of his years—died, too, plainly and unromantically, in his bed, and not as he would wish to have died, on the broad field and at the head of charging squadrons.

CHAPTER IX

SCOUT AND BUFFALO HUNT

Our Indian allies kept up their terrible racket during the whole night after their arrival in our camp, but next morning, June 15th, they were up bright and early to receive rations, ammunition and, such as needed them, new government guns. They were an exceedingly picturesque assemblage, painted and befeathered in all the barbaric splendor of the Indian tribes of that day. They sat in a huge semicircle around the tents and wagons of the quartermaster's department, and received their supplies with aboriginal solemnity; often, however, betraying their satisfaction by the inevitable Indian grunt, which has the sound of "ugh!"

The General had determined to mount his infantry on mules in order to expedite their movements when marching against the Sioux. Accordingly the mules destined for this duty, to the number of 200, most of them entirely unbroken to the saddle, were taken to a flat space down by the creek, and a few hundred yards from camp. The unhappy infantry men, who were to mount the animals, were brought there also, while Colonel Chambers, Major Burt, Captain Luhn, and the officers of Crook's staff, aided by several veteran sergeants who had seen mounted service, proceeded to break in the unwilling riders. I subsequently saw those foot soldiers do their duty most heroically, but I am bound in truth to confess, that their bearing on the morning of June 15, 1876, was anything but awe-inspiring. The mules, first of all, were forced to take the regulation cavalry bridle into their unwilling jaws, and then the rather clumsy McClellan saddle, universally used in our service at that period, was placed upon their backs, doubly secured by girth and surcingle. Then the fun began. A cloud of mule-heels, shod in iron, would rise simultaneously in the air, while the shrill neighing and squealing of the brutes displayed the great indignation that possessed them. They were then allowed to quiet down somewhat, and the unused infantry were ordered to mount their rebellious "steeds." Immediately some of the mules ran off, bucking fiercely, and every minute a score of foot soldiers would either stand on their heads or measure their length in the deep, soft grass, which alone prevented their bones being broken. Other mules would "buck" right where they stood, and then a soldier might be seen shooting up in the air like a rocket, and his very "dull thud" would soon after be heard as his body struck mother earth in his fall from among the clouds.

The Indians, attracted by the noise, and full of native devilment, rushed down from the quartermaster's to see the sport, and their deep laughter at every mishap denoted the satisfaction they felt at the discomfiture of the battered and disgusted infantry. Some of the young warriors would seize the runaway mules, jump upon their backs and demonstrate to the whole command what a natural-born equestrian the North American Indian is. The officers persevered in the experiment, and, by noon, most of the foot troops had acquired sufficient mastery over their "mounts" to enable them to keep their saddles with a doubtful degree of adhesiveness.

All day of the 15th was devoted to active preparation for the approaching movement against the hostiles. Arms were cleaned, horses re-shod, haversacks and saddle-bags filled, and ammunition stowed wherever it could be carried. The General determined to move out on the following morning, with his pack train only. The wagons were to be left behind under command of Major and Quartermaster John V. Furey, with one hundred men to guard them, besides the mule-drivers. An island near the junction of Big and Little Goose creek was picked out as a good defensive position, and arrangements were made to occupy it accordingly. The soldiers detailed for wagon guard were greatly disgusted—all but one man, whose face expressed unlimited satisfaction. I had previously noticed his disposition on the day the Sioux attacked our Tongue river camp. He was, I think, about the only constitutional coward in the whole command. I told him that, with such feelings, he had no business to enlist at all, and he replied, most fervently, "They'll never catch me in this fix again, if I have to desert when I get back to the railroad, if I ever do." The unhappy man's delight at escaping the chances of the coming battle was ludicrous to behold.

The great mass of the soldiers were young men, careless, courageous and eminently light-hearted. The rank and file, as a majority, were of either Irish or German birth or parentage, but there was also a fair-sized contingent of what may be called Anglo-Americans, particularly among the non-commissioned officers. Taken as a whole, Crook's command was a fine organization, and its officers, four-fifths of whom were native Americans and West Pointers, were fully in sympathy with the ardor of their men.

General Crook was particular to see that everything was in perfect order before giving the word to march. The wagon train was "parked" in the position already selected. Every man carried four days' rations, and as much ammunition as animal and rider could stand up under. All the tents were left with the wagon train, and then each man knew that he had to sleep under the star-spangled canopy of heaven when his day's march would be over.

Two hours before daylight, on June 16, 1876, the whole encampment was aroused by the loud exhortations—sermons, perhaps — addressed by the "medicine men" and "head soldiers" of the Crow and Snake Indians to the eager warriors of their respective bands. The harangues lasted for nearly an hour, and then the Indians breakfasted to satiety on the government rations issued the previous day, because it is a rule with the savages never to miss a good opportunity of making a meal, especially when on the war path. The bugles of our command were silent, but, notwithstanding, everything worked like magic. Tents were abandoned to the quartermaster, and every man of the expedition, except the hundred detached, was in the saddle, having barely swallowed a tin full of black coffee and a hard tack, as the sun rose redly on the eastern horizon. Our course was north by west, and lay through a fine "buffalo grass" region, on which signs of the bison were recent. The cavalry, fifteen companies of the 2d and 3d, under Royall, Evans, Noyes, Henry, Mills and Van Vliet, led the van. Then followed the splendid mule pack train, commanded by Chief Packer Tom Moore, as bold a frontiersman as ever looked at an enemy through the sight of his rifle; and, in rear, galled, but gallant, rode, on muleback, the 200 hardy infantry, under Col. Alex. Chambers and the brave Major "Andy" Burt. The Indians, with war bonnets nodding, and lances brilliant with steel and feathers, headed by their favorite chiefs, rode tumultuously, in careless order, filled with barbaric pride of arms, on our flanks. I felt a respect for the American Indian that day.

We nearly turned our backs upon the Big Horn range, but its prolonged flank, so to speak, still showed itself through the corners of our left eyes, toward the northwest. We were marching over the finest game country in the world, and soon our advance, under Major Randall, of the 23d Infantry, chief of scouts, came upon a small group of buffalo, which ran like the wind at the sight of our column. "There will be music in the air now, sure," remarked the veteran Captain Andrews to Sutorius. "Wherever you see buffalo, there, too, you will find Indians," and he lifted his glass to view the retreat of the affrighted bisons.

Just then we halted, and, at the remount, the muzzle of my carbine struck the hammer of my revolver, which, by some oversight, was left down upon the cartridge. An explosion followed. I felt as if somebody had hit me a vigorous blow with a stick on the right rear of my pantaloons, and ray horse, a neat little charger, lent me for the occasion in order to spare my own mount, reeled under the shock. The column halted, thinking I was done for, but at the word "Forward !" shouted impatiently by the commanding officer, it began to move. I dismounted quietly, and found that a portion of the cantel of the saddle had been blown off, but the bullet must have lodged in the earth. Lloyd, Captain Sutorius' servant, said, "You were not made to be killed by bullets, or that would have fixed you," and I was congratulated heartily by the soldiers as I remounted and galloped to the head of the column. Just then Colonel Henry, who was in advance, rode back along the line and said he had heard I was hurt. "Is the bullet in your person?" he asked. "I don't know, Colonel," I answered. "Then by Jove, it is about time you found out," said he, and rode away laughing heartily at my state of indecision, which speedily found the rounds of the whole brigade, from the General to the youngest mule packer.

We were moving over an undulating surface, covered with rich grasses and watered by many small, but limpid, streams. The atmosphere was delightful, and the perfume, caused by the trampling of the myriad prairie flowers under the horses' hoofs, delicious. Our cavalcade extended, or seemed to extend, for miles, and all marched in that profound silence peculiar to the regular army of the United States, and particularly to the mounted service. We had begun to enter the great northern hunting grounds, *par excellence*, the country dear to the heart of the doomed savage, and for which he was willing to shed his life blood to the very last drop.

All at once we ascended to the crest of a grassy slope, and then a sight burst upon us calculated to thrill the coldest heart in the command. Far as the eye could reach on both sides of our route, the somber, superb buffalo were grazing in thousands! The earth was brown with them. "Steady men, keep your ranks," was the command of the officers from front to rear, as many of the younger soldiers, rendered frantic by the sight of the noble game, made a movement as if to break from the column in wild pursuit. Then arose on our right and left such a storm of discordant shouts as can come only from savage throats. The Crow warriors on the west, and the Shoshones on the east, throwing off all that might impede them, and leaving the abandoned traps to the care of their docile squaws, dashed off like mounted maniacs, and made for the gigantic herd of bisons. Then rang out the crack of the rifle, the whoop and the yell of triumph, as buffalo after buffalo Went down before the fire of those matchless horsemen and superb shots! The bisons, for great, lumbering, hump-backed, short-headed creatures, ran like the wind, but the fleet Indian ponies soon brought their wild riders within range, and the work of destruction proceeded apace. The iron discipline of the army kept the soldiers in their ranks, but their glowing cheeks and kindling eyes proclaimed the feverish excitement, the Nimrod passion that consumed them. For at least five and twenty miles this strange scene was continued—our dark mass of regulars and mules, moving at quick time through a country green as emerald, their flanks fringed by painted savages, and the motionless, or fast-flying forms of the monster monarchs of the western wilds. I don't think that a buffalo hunt, surrounded by such martial and picturesque features, had previously occurred upon the American plains, and I am certain nothing like it has been seen since. In fact it would be impossible in these days, because the buffalo—that truest brute representative of the America of Columbus—is almost "as extinct as the dodo "—the result of the paltry greed of hide hunters, and of the gross carelessness of Congress in regard to necessary game laws. That wild, romantic, incomparable hunt will never be forgotten by those who witnessed it.

General Crook, who desired to surprise the village of the Sioux, supposed to be situated in the canon of the Rosebud, at the point near its northern debouch called the Indian Paradise, was annoyed by the conduct of his savage allies, which could not help alarming the wary foe with whom he had to contend; but nothing could check the Indians, so long as a buffalo remained in sight and daylight lasted. Contrary to their general custom, the savages killed the animals in sheer wantonness, and when reproached by the officers said "better kill buffalo than have him feed the Sioux!"

The sun was low when we approached the Rosebud valley, but still, in the distance, right, left and in front, we could hear the rapid crackling of the Indian guns, as they literally strewed the plain with the carcasses of the unfortunate bisons. Quiet reigned only when the sun had set, and we went into camp in an amphitheatrical valley, commanded on all sides by steep, but not lofty, bluffs. Pickets were posted along the elevations, and the command proceeded to bivouac in a great circle, with the horses and pack mules in the center, for fear of a sudden attack and possible stampede. The General gave orders that no fires should be lit, for fear of alarming the Sioux, but the Indian allies paid no attention to them, they lit what fires they listed, and proceeded to gorge themselves with fresh buffalo meat, roasted on the cinders. They also, when they had feasted sufficiently, set up one of their weird, indescribable war chants, of which they never seemed to tire. General Crook called upon the Crows and Snakes to furnish men to scout ahead of our camp during the night, but he could induce a few only of the latter tribe to go forward under Tom Cosgrove and Frank Gruard. The General was angry enough to punish the recalcitrant savages severely, but it would never have done to make them enemies at that stage of the game. He, therefore, submitted with characteristic philosophy to the inevitable.

In that northern climate, the nights are about as cold in June as those of Illinois in late October, and the single blanket, which we were allowed to carry, barely kept off the chill of the falling dew. The whole command sank early to repose, except those whose duty it was to watch over our slumbers, and the boastful, howling Indians, who kept up their war songs throughout most of the night. Captain Sutorius, lying on the ground next to me, with saddle for pillow, and wrapped in his blanket, said, "We will have a fight to-morrow, mark my words — I feel it in the air." These were the last words I heard as I sank to sleep.

Let me say, by way of preface to the succeeding chapter, and what I wrote in '76 remains just as true to-day, if there are any hostile red-skins left on the continent, that the position of a newspaper correspondent in an Indian expedition *forces* him to go in with the rest. There is virtually no such thing as "rear," unless with the reserve, which is generally called into action before the fight is over. Besides, if the journalist does not share the toil and the danger, his mouth is shut, for if he presumed to criticise any movement, some officer would say to him, "What the deuce have you to say about it? You were skulking in the rear, and got everything by hearsay. We don't care what you think." Let no easy-going journalist suppose that an Indian campaign is a picnic. If he goes out on such business he must go prepared to ride his forty or fifty miles a day, go sometimes on half rations, sleep on the ground with small covering, roast, sweat, freeze, and make the acquaintance of such vermin or reptiles as may flourish in the vicinity of his couch; and, finally, be ready to fight Sitting Bull or Satan when the trouble begins, for God and the United States hate noncombatants. Thus was I, who am peaceably disposed, placed in the position of an eye-witness, my "mess" being with the 3d Cavalry, which was about to get most of the hard knocks at Rosebud fight.

CHAPTER X

BATTLE OF THE ROSEBUD

Dawn had not yet begun to tinge the horizon above the eastern bluffs, when every man of the expedition was astir. How it came about, I know not, but, I suppose, each company commander was quietly notified by the headquarters' orderlies to get under arms. Low cooking fires were allowed to be kindled, so that the men might have coffee before moving further down the canyon, and every horse and mule was saddled and loaded with military despatch. The Indians, having digested their buffalo hump banquet of the previous night, were quite alert, but prepared to go on with another feast. The General, however, sent his half-breed scouts to inform them that they must hurry up and go forward. The Snakes, to their credit be it recorded, obeyed with some degree of martial alacrity, but the Crows seemed to act very reluctantly. It was evident that both tribes had a very wholesome respect for Sioux prowess. I noticed, among other things, that the singing had ceased, and it was quite apparent that the gentle savages began to view the coming conflict with feelings the reverse of hilarious. They got their war horses ready, looked to their arms, and, at last, in the dim morning light, a large party left camp and speedily disappeared over the crests of the northern bluffs. The soldiers, with their horses and mules saddled up and bridled, awaited the order to move forward, with that warlike impatience peculiar to men who prefer to face danger at once, rather than be on the lookout for it everlastingly. The)' were as cheerful as ever, joked with each other in low tones, and occasionally borrowed, or lent, "a chew of tobacco" in order to kill time. A few of the younger men grasping the pommels of their saddles, and leaning their heads against their horses, dropped off into a "cat nap."

Presently we saw the infantry move out on their mules, and, within a few minutes, the several cavalry battalions were properly marshaled, and all were moving down the valley, in the gray dawn, with the regularity of a machine, complicated, but under perfect control. We marched on in this fashion, the cavalry finally outstripping the infantry, halting occasionally, until the sun was well above the horizon. At about 8 o'clock, we halted in a valley, very similar in formation to the one in which we had pitched our camp the preceding night. Rosebud stream, indicated by the thick growth of wild roses, or sweet brier, from which its name is derived, flowed sluggishly through it, dividing it from south to north into two almost equal parts. The hills seemed to rise on every side, and we were within easy musket shot of those most remote. Our horses were rather tired from the long march of the 16th, and orders came to unsaddle and let them graze. Our battalion (Mills') occupied the right bank of the creek, with the 2d Cavalry, while on the left bank were the infantry and Henry's and Van Vliet's battalions of the 3d Cavalry. The pack train was also on that side of the stream, together with such of the Indians as did not move out before daybreak to look for the Sioux, whom they were by no means anxious to find. The young warriors of the two tribes were running races with their ponies, and the soldiers in their vicinity were enjoying the sport hugely.

The sun became intensely hot in that close valley, so I threw myself upon the ground, resting my head upon my saddle. Captain Sutorius, with Lieutenant Von Leutwitz, who had been transferred to Company E, sat near me smoking. At 8:30 o'clock, without any warning, we heard a few shots from behind the bluffs to the north. "They are shooting buffalo over there," said the Captain. Very soon we began to know, by the alternate rise and fall of the reports, that the shots were not all fired in one direction. Hardly had we reached this conclusion, when a score or two of our Indian scouts appeared upon the northern crest, and rode down the slopes with incredible speed. "Saddle up, there —saddle up, there, quick!" shouted Colonel Mills, and immediately all the cavalry within sight, without waiting for formal orders, were mounted and ready for action. General Crook, who appreciated the situation, had already ordered the companies of the 4th and 9th Infantry, posted at the foot of the northern slopes, to deploy as skirmishers, leaving their mules with the holders. Hardly had this precaution been taken, when the flying Crow and Snake scouts, utterly panic stricken, came into camp shouting at the top of their voices, "Heap Sioux! heap Sioux!" gesticulating wildly in the direction of the bluffs which they had abandoned in such haste. All looked in that direction, and there, sure enough, were the Sioux in goodly numbers, and in loose, but formidable, array. The singing of the bullets above our heads speedily convinced us that they had called on business. I looked along the rugged, stalwart line of our company, and saw no coward blanching in any of the bronzed faces there. "Why the d d don't they order us to charge?" asked the brave Von Leutwitz. "Here comes Lemley (the regimental adjutant) now," answered Sutorius. "How do you feel about it, eh?" he inquired, turning to me. "It is the anniversary of Bunker Hill," was my answer. "The day is of good omen." "By Jove, I never thought of that," cried Sutorius, and (loud enough for the soldiers to hear) "It is the anniversary of Bunker Hill, we're in luck." The men waved their carbines, which were right shouldered, but, true to the parade etiquette of the American army, did not cheer, although they forgot all about etiquette later on. Up, meanwhile, "bound on bound," his gallant horse covered with foam, came Lemley.

"The commanding officer's compliments, Colonel Mills I" he yelled. "Your battalion will charge those bluffs on the center."

Mills immediately swung his fine battalion, consisting of Troops A,E, I and M, by the right into line, and, rising in his stirrups, shouted "Charge!" Forward we went at our best pace, to reach the crest occupied by the enemy, who, meanwhile, were not idle, for men and horses rolled over pretty rapidly as we began the ascent. Many horses, owing to the rugged nature of the ground, fell upon their riders without receiving a wound. We went like a storm, and the Indians waited for us until we were within fifty paces. We were going too rapidly to use our carbines, but several of the men fired their revolvers, with what effect I could neither then, nor afterward, determine, for all passed "like a flash of lightning, or a dream." I remember, though, that our men broke into a mad cheer as the Sioux, unable to face that impetuous line of the warriors of the superior race, broke and fled, with what white men would consider undignified speed. Out of the dust of the tumult, at this distance of time, I remember how well our troops kept their formation, and how gallantly they sat their horses as they galloped fiercely up the rough ascent.

We got that line of heights, and were immediately dismounted and formed in open order, as skirmishers, along the rocky crest. While Mills' battalion was executing the movement described, General Crook ordered the 2d Battalion of the 3d Cavalry, under Col. Guy V. Henry, consisting of Troops B, D, F and L, to charge the right of the Sioux array, which was hotly pressing our steady infantry. Henry executed the order with characteristic dash and promptitude, and the Indians were compelled to fall back in great confusion all along the line.

General Crook kept the five troops of the 2d Cavalry, under Noyes, in reserve, and ordered Troops C and G of the 3d Cavalry, under Captain Van Vliet and Lieutenant Crawford, to occupy the bluffs on our left rear, so as to check any movement that might be made by the wily enemy from that direction. Those bluffs were somewhat loftier than the eminences occupied by the rest of our forces, and Crawford told me, subsequently, that a splendid view of the fight was obtained from them.

General Crook divined that the Indian force before him was a strong body—not less perhaps than 2,500 warriors— sent out to make a rear guard fight, so as to cover the retreat of their village, which was situated at the other end of the canyon. He detached Troop I of the 3d Cavalry, Captain Andrews and Lieutenant Foster, from Mills to Henry, after the former had taken the first line of heights. He reinforced our line with the friendly Indians, who seemed to be partially stampeded, and brought up the whole of the 2d Cavalry within supporting distance. The Sioux, having rallied on the second line of heights, became bold and impudent again. They rode up and down rapidly, sometimes wheeling in circles, slapping an indelicate portion of their persons at us, and beckoning us to come on. One chief, probably the late lamented Crazy Horse, directed their movements by signals made with a pocket mirror or some other reflector. Under Crook's orders, our whole line remounted, and, after another rapid charge, we became masters of the second crest. When we got there, another just like it rose on the other side of the valley. There, too, were the savages, as fresh, apparently, as ever. 'We dismounted accordingly, and the firing began again. It was now evident that the weight of the fighting was shifting from our front, of which Major Evans had general command, to our left where Royall and Henry cheered on their men. Still the enemy were thick enough on the third crest, and Colonel Mills, who had active charge of our operations, wished to dislodge them. The volume of fire, rapid and ever increasing, came from our left. The wind freshened from the west, and we could hear the uproar distinctly. Soon, however, the restless foe came back upon us, apparently reinforced. He made a vigorous push for our center down some rocky ravines, which gave him good cover. Just then a tremendous yell arose behind us, and along through the intervals of our battalions, came the tumultuous array of the Crow and Shoshone Indians, rallied and led back to action by Maj. George M. Randall and Lieut. John G. Bourke, of General Crook's staff. Orderly Sergeant John Van Moll, of Troop A, Mills' battalion, a brave and gigantic soldier, who was subsequently basely murdered by a drunken mutineer of his company, dashed forward on foot with them. The two bodies of savages, all stripped to the breech-clout, moccasins and war bonnet, came together in the trough of the valley, the Sioux having descended to meet our allies with right good will. All, except Sergeant Van Moll, were mounted. Then began a most exciting encounter. The wild foemen, covering themselves with their horses, while going at full speed, blazed away rapidly. Our regulars did not fire because it would have been sure death to some of the friendly Indians, who were barely distinguishable by a red badge which they carried. Horses fell dead by the score—they were heaped there when the fight closed—but, strange to relate, the casualties among the warriors, including both sides, did not certainly exceed five and twenty. The whooping was persistent, but the Indian voice is less hoarse than that of the Caucasian, and has a sort of wolfish bark to it, doubtless the result of heredity, because the Indians, for untold ages, have been imitators of the vocal characteristics of the prairie wolf. The absence of very heavy losses in this combat goes far to prove the wisdom of the Indian method of fighting.

Finally the Sioux on the right, hearing the yelping and firing of the rival tribes, came up in great numbers, and our Indians, carefully picking up their wounded, and making their uninjured horses carry double, began to draw off in good order. Sergeant Van Moll was left alone on foot. A dozen Sioux dashed at him. Major Randall and Lieutenant Bourke who had probably not noticed him in the general melee, but who, in the crisis, recognized his stature and his danger, turned their horses to rush to his rescue. They called on the Indians to follow them. One small, misshapen Crow warrior, mounted on a fleet pony, outstripped all others. He dashed boldly in among the Sioux, against whom Van Moll was dauntlessly defending himself, seized the big Sergeant by the shoulder and motioned him to jump up behind. The Sioux were too astonished to realize what had been done until they saw the long-legged Sergeant, mounted behind the little Crow, known as "Humpy," dash toward our lines like the wind. Then they opened fire, but we opened also, and compelled them to seek higher ground. The whole line of our battalion cheered "Humpy" and Van Moll as they passed us on the home-stretch. There were no insects on them, either.

In order to check the insolence of the Sioux, we were compelled to drive them from the third ridge. Our ground was more favorable for quick movements than that occupied by Royall, who found much difficulty in forcing the savages in his front—mostly the flower of the brave Cheyenne tribe —to retire. One portion of his line, under Captain Vroom, pushed out beyond its supports, deceived by the rugged character of the ground, and suffered quite severely. In fact, the Indians got between it and the main body, and nothing but the coolness of its commander and the skillful management of Colonels Royall and Henry saved Troop L of the 3d Cavalry from annihilation on that day. Lieutenant Morton, one of Colonel Royall's aids, Captain Andrews and Lieutenant Foster' of troop I, since dead, particularly distinguished themselves in extricating Vroom from his perilous position. In repelling the audacious charge of the Cheyennes upon his battalion, the undaunted Colonel Henry, one of the most accomplished officers in the army, was struck by a bullet, which passed through both cheek bones, broke the bridge of his nose and destroyed the optic nerve in one eye. His orderly, in attempting to assist him, was also wounded, but, temporarily blinded as he was, and throwing blood from his mouth by the handful, Henry sat his horse for several minutes in front of the enemy. He finally fell to the ground, and, as that portion of our line, discouraged by the fall of so brave a chief, gave ground a little, the Sioux charged over his prostrate body, but were speedily repelled, and he was happily rescued by some soldiers of his command. Several hours later, when returning from the pursuit of the hostiles, I saw Colonel Henry lying on a blanket, his face covered with a bloody cloth, around which the summer flies were buzzing fiercely, and a soldier keeping the wounded man's horse in such a position as to throw the animal's shadow upon the gallant sufferer. There was absolutely no other shade in that neighborhood. When I ventured to condole with the Colonel he merely said, in a low but firm voice, "It is nothing. For this are we soldiers!" and forthwith he did me the honor of advising me to join the army! Colonel Henry's sufferings, when our retrograde movement began, and, in fact, until—after a jolting journey of several hundred miles, by mule litter and wagon—he reached Fort Russell, were horrible, as were, indeed, those of all the wounded.

As the day advanced, General Crook became tired of the indecisiveness of the action, and resolved to bring matters to a crisis. He rode up to where the officers of Mills' battalion were standing, or sitting, behind their men, who were prone on the skirmish line, and said, in effect, "It is time to stop this skirmishing, Colonel. You must take your battalion and go for their village away down the canon." "All right, sir," replied Mills, and the order to retire and remount was given. The Indians, thinking we were retreating, became audacious, and fairly hailed bullets after us, wounding several soldiers. One man, named Harold, received a singular wound. He was in the act of firing, when a bullet from the Indians passed along the barrel of his carbine, glanced around his left shoulder, traversed the neck, under the skin, and finally lodged in the point of his lower jaw. The shock laid him low for a moment, but, picking himself up. he had the nerve to reach for his weapon, which had fallen from his hand, and bore it with him off the ground. Our men, under the eyes of the officers, retired in orderly time, and the whistling of the bullets could not induce them to forget that they were American soldiers. Under such conditions, it was easy to understand how steady discipline can conquer mere numbers.

Troops A, E and M of Mills' battalion, having remounted, guided by the scout Gruard, plunged immediately into what is called, on what authority I know not, the Dead Canon of Rosebud valley. It is a dark, narrow and winding defile, over a dozen miles in length, and the main Indian village was supposed to be situated in the north end of it. Lieutenant Bourke, of Crook's staff, accompanied the column. A body of Sioux, posted on a bluff which commanded the west side of the mouth of the canon, was brilliantly dislodged by a bold charge of troop E, under Captain Sutorius and Lieutenant Von Leutwitz. After this our inarch began in earnest.

The bluffs, on both sides of the ravine, were thickly covered with rocks and fir trees, thus affording ample protection to an enemy, and making it impossible for our cavalry to act as flankers. Colonel Mills ordered the section of the battalion moving on the east side of the canon to cover their comrades on the west side, if fired upon, and *vice versa*. This was good advice, and good strategy in the position in which we were placed. We began to think our force rather weak for so venturous an enterprise, but Lieutenant Bourke informed the colonel that the five troops of the 2d Cavalry, under Major Noyes, were inarching behind us. A slight rise in the valley enabled us to see the dust stirred up by the supporting column some distance in the rear.

The day had become absolutely perfect, and we all felt elated, exhilarated as we were by our morning's experience. Nevertheless, some of the more thoughtful officers had their misgivings, because the canon was certainly a most dangerous defile, where all the advantage would be on the side of the savages. General Custer, although not marching in a position so dangerous, and with a force nearly equal to ours, suffered annihilation at the hands of the same enemy, about eighteen miles further westward, only eight days afterward.

Noyes, marching his battalion rapidly, soon overtook our rear guard, and the whole column increased its pace. Fresh signs of Indians began to appear in all directions, and we began to feel that the sighting of their village must be only a question of a few miles further on. We came to a halt in a kind of cross canon, which had an opening toward the west, and there tightened up our horse girths, and got ready for what we believed must be a desperate fight. The keen-eared Gruard pointed toward the Occident, and said to Colonel Mills, '; I hear firing in that direction, sir." Just then there was a sound of fierce galloping behind us, and a horseman, dressed in buckskin, and wearing a long beard, originally black, but turned temporarily gray by the dust, shot by the halted command, and dashed up to where Colonel Mills and the other officers were standing.

It was Maj. A. H. Nickerson, of the General's staff. He has been unfortunate since, but he showed himself a hero on that day at least. He had ridden, with a single orderly, through the canon to overtake us, at the imminent peril of his life.

"Mills," he said, "Royall is hard pressed, and must be relieved. Henry is badly wounded, and Vroom's troop is all cut up. The General orders that you and Noyes defile by your left flank out of this canon and fall on the rear of the Indians who are pressing Royall." This, then was the firing that Gruard had heard.

Crook's order was instantly obeyed, and we were fortunate enough to find a comparatively easy way out of the elongated trap into which duty had led us. We defiled, as nearly as possible, by the heads of companies, in parallel columns, so as to carry out the order with greater celerity. We were soon clear of Dead Canon, although we had to lead our horses carefully over and among the boulders and fallen timber. The crest of the side of the ravine proved to be a sort of plateau, and there we could hear quite plainly the noise of the attack on Royall's front. We got out from among the loose rocks and scraggy trees that fringed the rim of the gulf, and found ourselves in quite an open country. "Prepare to mount—mount!" shouted the officers, and we were again in the saddle. Then we urged our animals to their best pace, and speedily came in view of the contending parties. The Indians had their ponies, guarded mostly by mere boys, in rear of the low, rocky crest which they occupied. The position held by Royall rose somewhat higher, and both lines could be seen at a glance. There was very heavy firing, and the Sioux were evidently preparing to make an attack in force, as they were riding in by the score, especially from the point abandoned by Mills' battalion in its movement down the canon, and which was partially held thereafter by the friendly Indians, a few infantry and a body of sturdy mule packers, commanded by the brave Tom Moore, who fought on that day as if he had been a private soldier. Suddenly the Sioux lookouts observed our unexpected approach, and gave the alarm to their friends. We dashed forward at a wild gallop, cheering as we went, and I am sure we were all anxious at that moment to avenge our comrades of Henry's battalion. But the cunning savages did not wait for us. They picked up their wounded, all but thirteen of their dead, and broke away to the northwest on their fleet ponies, leaving us only the thirteen "scalps," 150 dead horses and ponies and a few old blankets and war bonnets as trophies of the fray. Our losses, including the friendly Indians, amounted to about fifty, most of the casualties being in the 3d Cavalry, which bore the brunt of the fight on the Rosebud. Thus ended the engagement which was the prelude to the great tragedy that occurred eight days later in the neighboring valley of the Little Big Horn.

The General was dissatisfied with the result of the encounter, because the Indians had clearly accomplished the main object of their offensive movement—the safe retreat of their village. Yet he could not justly blame the troops who, both officers and men, did all that could be done under the circumstances. We had driven the Indians about five miles from the point where the fight began, and the General decided to return there, in order that we might be nearer water. The troops had nearly used up their rations and had fired about 25,000 rounds of ammunition. It often takes an immense amount of lead to send even one Indian to the happy hunting grounds.

The obstinacy, or timidity, of the Crow scouts in the morning spoiled General Crook's plans. It was originally his intention to fling his whole force on the Indian village, and win or lose all by a single blow. The fall of Guy V. Henry, early in the fight on the left, had a bad effect upon the soldiers, and Captain Vroom's company became entangled so badly that a temporary success raised the spirits of the Indians and enabled them to keep our left wing in check sufficiently long to allow the savages to effect the safe retreat of their village to the valley of the Little Big Horn. Had Crook's original plan been carried out to the letter, our whole force—about 1,100 men—would have been in the hostile village at noon, and, in the light of after events, it is not improbable that all of us would have settled there permanently. Five thousand able-bodied warriors, well-armed, would have given Crook all the trouble he wanted, if he had struck their village.

I am bound to add, for the honor of the journalistic profession, that Mr. McMillan, who accompanied our battalion, showed marked gallantry throughout the affair, which lasted from 8:00 in the morning until 2 in the afternoon, and the officers with the other commands spoke warmly that evening of the courage displayed by Messrs. Strahorn, Wasson and Davenport.

Our wounded were placed on extemporized travois, or mule litters, and our dead were carried on the bucks of horses to our camp of the morning, where they received honorable burial. Nearly all had turned black from the beat, and one soldier, named Potts, had not less than a dozen Indian arrows sticking in his body. This resulted from the fact that he was killed nearest to the Indian position, and the young warriors had time to indulge their barbarity before the corpse was rescued.

One young Shoshone Indian, left in rear to herd the horses of his tribe, was killed by a small party of daring Cheyennes, who, during the heat of Royall's fight, rode in between that officer's left and the right of Van Vliet. The latter supposed that the ad venture-las savages were some of our red skins, so natural and unconcerned were all their actions. The Cheyennes slew the poor boy with their tomahawks, took his scalp, "leaving not a wrack behind," and drove away a part of his herd. Van Vliet, as the marauders were returning, had his suspicions aroused, and ordered Crawford's men to fire upon them. This they did with such good effect that the raiders were glad to drop the captured ponies and make off in a hurry, having lost one man killed — we found the body next day — and several wounded.

During the severest portion of the conflict General Crook's black charger was wounded under him. Lieutenant Lemley's horse was also hurt and rendered unfit for further service. Lieutenants Morton and Chase, of the 3d Cavalry, did good service throughout the conflict, and narrowly escaped death while riding from one point of the line to the ether. Lieutenant Lemley came near losing his scalp by riding close up to a party of hostile Indians, whom he supposed were Crows. His escape was simply miraculous. In fact, in most cases it was difficult to tell our red-skins from those of Sitting Bull. There is a strong family resemblance between all of them.

We went into camp at about 4 o'clock, and were formed in a circle around our horses and pack train, as on the previous night. The hospital was established under the trees down by the sluggish creek, and there the surgeons exercised their skill with marvelous rapidity. Most of the injured men bore their sufferings stoically enough, but an occasional groan, or half-smothered shriek, would tell where the knife, or the probe, had struck an exposed nerve. The Indian wounded—some of them desperate cases—gave no indication of feeling, but submitted to be operated upon with the grim stolidity of their race.

General Crook decided that evening to retire on his base of supplies—the wagon train—with his wounded, in view of the fact that his rations were almost used up, and that his ammunition had run pretty low. He was also convinced that all chance of surprising the Sioux camp was over for the present, and perhaps he felt that even if it could be surprised, his small force would be unequal to the task of carrying it by storm. The Indians had shown themselves good lighters, and he shrewdly calculated that his men had been opposed to only a part of the well-armed warriors actually in the field.

During the night a melancholy wailing arose from the Snake camp down by the creek. They were "waking" the young warrior killed by the Cheyennes that morning, and calling upon the Great Spirit for vengence. I never heard anything equal to the despairing cadence of that wail, so savage and so dismal. It annoyed some of the soldiers, but it had to be endured. The bodies of our slain were quietly buried within the limits of the camp, and every precaution was taken to obliterate the traces of sepulture. The Sioux did not disturb us that night. There was no further need for precaution as to signals, and at 4 o'clock on the morning of Sunday, June 18th, the reveille sounded. All were immediately under arms, except the Snake Indians, who had deferred the burial of their comrade until sunrise. All the relatives appeared in black paint, which gave them a diabolical aspect. I had been led to believe that Indians never yielded to the weakness of tears, but I can assure my readers that the experience of that morning convinced me of my error. The men of middle age alone restrained their grief, but the tears of the young men, and of the squaws, rolled down their cheeks as copiously as if the mourners had been of the Caucasian race. I afterward learned that the sorrow would not have been so intense if the boy had not been scalped. There is some superstition connected with that process. I think it had reference to the difficulty of the admission of the lad's spirit, under such circumstances, to the happy hunting-grounds.

A grave was finally dug for the body in the bed of the stream, and at a point where the horses had crossed and re-crossed. After the remains were properly covered, a group of warriors on horseback rode over the site several times, thus making it impossible for the Sioux to find the body.

This ceremony ended, our retreat began in earnest. Our battalion was, as nearly as I can remember, pretty well toward the head of the column. Between us and the 2d Cavalry came the wounded, on their travois, and behind them came the mounted infantry. Looking backward occasionally, we could see small parties of Sioux watching us from the bluffs, but they made no offensive movement. As I rode along with Sutorius and Yon Leutwitz, I observed a crowd of Crow Indians dismounted and standing around some object which lay in the long grass some distance to our right. The lieutenant and I rode over there, and saw the body of a stalwart Sioux warrior, stiff in death, with the mark of a bullet wound in his broad bosom. The Crows set to work at once to dismember him. One scalped the remains. Another cut off the ears of the corpse and put them in his wallet. Von Leutwitz and I remonstrated, but the savages only laughed at us. After cutting off toes, fingers and nose, they proceeded to indecent mutilation, and this we could not stand. We protested vigorously, and the captain, seeing that something singular was in progress, rode up with a squad of men and put an end to the butchery. One big, yellow brute of a Crow, as we rode off, took a portion of the dead warrior's person out of his pouch, waved it in the air, and shouted something in broken English which had reference to the grief the Sioux squaws must feel when the news of the unfortunate brave's fate would reach them. And then the whole group of savages burst into a mocking chorus of laughter that might have done honor to the devil and his angels. I lost all respect for the Crow Indians after that episode. I concluded, and I think with justice, that they are mostly braggarts in peace and laggards in war.

As we continued our march, having rejoined the head of the column, we heard a great rattling of small arms in the rear, and concluded we had been attacked. The whole command halted, and then we saw what the trouble was. A solitary and much frightened antelope had broken from cover far toward the rear, and ran directly along our flank for more than a mile. Although at least five hundred men fired at the nimble creature, it ran the gauntlet in safety, and at last found refuge in the thick timber of a small stream, which we were obliged to cross. Owing to the condition of the wounded, we were ordered to halt in an excellent camping place several miles from our wagon train. We were all pretty tired, and the whole command, except the pickets, lay down to rest early in the evening. During the night we were disturbed by some shots fired by our sentinels at what they supposed to be prying Sioux, but nothing serious resulted.

Next day we were *en route* very soon after sunrise, and reached our wagon train on Goose creek in good season. The officers and men left behind were glad to see us, and Major Furey, guessing that we must feel pretty thirsty, as well as hungry, did all that a hospitable warrior could be expected to do for his famished comrades. That night, after having refreshed ourselves by a bath in the limpid waters of Goose creek, we again slept under canvas, and felt comparatively happy. We learned during the night that the General had determined to send the wagon train, escorted by most of the infantry, to Fort Fetterman for supplies, and that the wounded would be sent to that post at the same time. He had sent a request for more infantry, as well as cavalry, and did not intend to do more than occasionally reconnoiter the Sioux until the reinforcements arrived. This meant tedious waiting, and Mr. McMillan, whose health had daily grown worse, was advised by the surgeons to take advantage of the movement of the train and proceed to Fetterman also. "Mac," thinking there would be no more fighting, finally acquiesced, and, greatly to the regret of the whole "outfit," left with the train on the morning of Wednesday, June 21st. We all turned out and gave Colonel Henry and the other wounded three hearty cheers as they moved out of camp. It was the last we were to see of them during that campaign.

CHAPTER XI

IN THE SHADOW OF THE MOUNTAINS

It is impossible to make any reader, who is unfamiliar with active military life, feel what our command, from General to bugler, felt after the departure of the wagon train, when everybody knew that a period of inaction was to follow our recent exciting experiences. To add to the general monotony, our Indian allies suddenly made up their minds that it would be good medicine for them to go home. The Crows, as usual, set the example and left us about the same time as the wagon train, leaving their wounded and a few squaws with us. The Snakes decamped a few days later, but with assurances of the strongest kind that they would rejoin before the new campaign opened. They also left their wounded behind. In fact, most of the latter were too badly injured to be removed. In order to break the sameness of the new condition of things, the General moved us every day or so nearer to the base of the Big Horn mountains. We had. therefore, grass, water, wood and brook trout in ever increasing abundance. The days, from 11 o'clock until four, became intensely hot, but the nights were deliciously cool. Fishing and hunting were about our only recreations, and even the most daring of hunters did not venture much beyond the limits of our picket posts, as Indian signs were abundant on all sides of us. Captain Vroom and Lieutenant Paul were the two literary men of the outfit, and their small, paper-covered circulating library found the rounds of the encampment, greatly to the detriment of the volumes. Schwatka's mind, then, as since, ran on science, He had no love for light literature, and he lay awake of nights thinking of the north pole and Sir John Franklin's bones. Lieut. L , newly married, was still desperately in love, and saw his adored one in every flower that sprang "by fountain shaw or green." He was a most delightful companion at that period of his life. Bourke, always entertaining, occasionally condescended to tell us about his Arizona experiences, while brave old Lieutenant Lawson, eccentric, but beloved, would nod drowsily over the camp fire, and, having listened to the narratives of the other warriors, without attempting to conceal his indifference, would yawn out dismally, in the midst of some heroic recitation of adventure—"Did you now?" Then the young officers would start him on his exploits in the Kentucky brigade during the Civil War, and, stealing off, one by one, unperceived by the old man, would enjoy his discomfiture when he finally realized the situation. There was not in the camp a bottle of beer, a glass of whisky or even a cigar, but there was plenty of government tobacco, and this was about all the luxury the command could boast of at that time.

Perhaps my feelings about this period may be best described by the following passages from a letter written to the paper I represented from Cloud Peak Camp:

"The days run into one another unmarked, except for their length. In your civilized world Sunday chapters off the time—gives you a weekly beginning and end—freshens you up, as it were, every seventh day; but here that day is like every other — sultry, lazy, lonely and cheerless. No 'Charley O'Malley' or other 'Irish dragoon' could ever flourish in an atmosphere so irksome. Indian solemnity appears to oppress everybody, and the fierce, solemn-browed old hills appear to frown reproach on all that is light, or gay, or happy. Sad, desolate old hills, that have no history, old as the Pillars of Hercules, massive as the Apennines, snow-robed like the Alps, and yet without a memory save that of the nomadic Indian, with his hideous painted visage, his wolfish howl and his vermin-garrisoned wigwam. Around their gigantic figures are no gleams of the heroic past; no Hannibal with his mighty oath and mightier achievement; no Scipio with his Roman genius and terrible revenge; no Caesar with his devouring ambition and swarming legions—nor Horace, nor Virgil, nor Tasso, nor

Dante with their deathless symphonies and souls of poetic fire; nor Rienzi with his eloquence ; nor Angelo with his creative glory; nor Bonaparte with his eagle pinions, catching on their golden plumage the fame of the ancient world. These mountains that we look upon to-day are mere heaps of rock, sand and clay, destitute of all that can appeal to the imagination from the magic lights and shades of antique story. But despite the historic barrenness, our mountains are not without their natural attractions, pine-tree forests, foaming cataracts, gloomy canons, and towering pinnacles, showing almost at every step

A red deer's wild and rocky road;

An eagle's kingly flight.

"Besides, they have that mysterious gold-concealing reputation which charms the adventurers, and which Las led many a would-be Monte Cristo to 'sail 'neath alien skies and tread the desert path' in pursuit of the world's ignis fatuus, only to find a tomb in the bowels of the wolf and the raven, or leave his miserable bones, those ghastly land-marks of mortality, to grin solemn warning at those who may follow his fatal 'trail.' But thousands will follow that 'trail,' even though they tread on skeletons at every step. The love of gold is stronger in men than the fear of death.

"Yesterday we received the first mail that has reached us since May 29th. It was rather small—no newspapers whatever having come, except a few for headquarters, and even these were old. Dearth of reading matter is the greatest deprivation we endure. Nobody expected that Crook was going to make an all-summer affair of this campaign, but it looks very like it now. Our wagons are to bring supplies for four months, which looks somewhat tedious. Meanwhile a kind of informal 'post' will be established here, or in this vicinity, under the name of 'Camp Cloud Peak' (Goose creek is not sufficiently heroic it would appear), so that our scouting parties can draw for supplies whenever they get run ashore, which will be pretty often. Everybody sighs for a renewal of active work, as the time then will not appear so long. Loafing hangs heavily upon us, for, unlike nearly all other campaigners, we are utterly cut off from the feminine world, which means civilization, and will be until we return to Fort Fetterman. Mars, when coming on this campaign, left Venus at home to look after the house."

On the morning of the 23d of June, a party of four or five men, mounted and having a couple of pack mules, heavily laden, with them, were challenged by the pickets on the south side of the camp. They proved to be Lieutenant Schuyler—a brother of the Hon. Eugene Schuyler of diplomatic fame—of the 5th Cavalry, a couple of orderlies, a packer and an old miner, named Captain Graves, who had come all the way from Fort Fetterman to join us—traveling generally at night. They had met our wagon train and the wounded *en route*, and, therefore, had little trouble in finding us. The lieutenant was then serving on Crook's staff, and brought some interesting information. He told us, among other things, that General Merritt, with the 5th Cavalry, had been ordered to observe the Cheyennes at the agencies and prevent them from joining their friends already in the field. Nothing, he said, had been heard from General Terry's brigade since Custer left Fort Lincoln at the head of the 7th Cavalry. Alas! Custer was even then, as Schuyler told us the news over a tin full of coffee, marching up the Rosebud, from the landing on the Yellowstone, to his death! He had started from that point at noon on the 22d, and the first act in the immortal tragedy of the Little Big Horn had begun. But we knew nothing of all this at the time, and were, accordingly, happy.

On Saturday, June 24th, the General moved the command still nearer to the mountains, so that a musket shot could easily reach the camp from the foothills. It was a delightfully romantic spot—nothing more beautiful, at least at that season, this side of Paradise. We reveled in the crystal water, and slept beneath the grateful shade of the trees that fringed the emerald banks of those beautiful tributaries of Tongue river, that winding Daughter of the Snows.

Col. Anson Mills, ever restless and enterprising, made an informal reconnoissance from camp on the afternoon of Sunday, June 25th. He went up some distance in the foothills with a small party, and, returning to camp, reported a dense smoke toward the northwest, at a great distance. He called the attention of several to it, and all agreed that it must be a prairie fire, or something of that kind. It was a prairie fire, sure enough, but it was kindled, as we knew afterward, by the deadly, "far-sweeping musketry "of the vengeful savages who annihilated Custer and his devoted band on the banks of the Little Big Horn! Even while we gazed, perhaps, the tragedy was consummated, and the American Murat had fought his last battle.

But the monotony of camp, despite the beauty of the surroundings, became more intolerable than ever. Officers, who, in times of excitement, would take no notice of trifles, became irritable and exercised their authority over their subordinates in a decidedly martinetish manner. This, as a matter of course, produced friction and occasional sulking. One field officer became particularly morose, and another, criticising him, used to say "Major is the most even tempered man in this whole brigade—he's always in bad humor!"

On the 28th of June, in a letter to my paper, I relieved my mind on this branch of the subject as follows: "To banish dull care, we are advised to go fishing. Oh, Isaac Walton—gentle, complacent old fraud ! even your patience would become exhausted sitting on the pebbly banks of Goose creek, rain dripping from your garments, your teeth chattering, 'waiting for a bite.' Even Nimrod's pastime grows monotonous in this vastness of mammoth desolation and preternatural silence. So oppressive, when away from camp, is the latter sensation, that I fancy a shot fired by the man in the moon would be heard among these mountains. We virtually pine for something to read and would not cast away even a dime novel, a 'poem' by Walt Whitman, a lecture by Deacon Bross, or a tract by Brother Moody. Rather than this should last, welcome anything— 'tornado, earthquake, flood or storm.'

"To a man used to the bustle of a great city, camp-life, inactive, is the most infernal of bores.

I have been astonished at the few amusement resources displayed by the officers of this outfit. Only for the occasional 'rubbing up' given them by 'commanding officers,' subalterns would sink into a Van Winklish lethargy, and be eternally lost to 'glory' and the 'service.' Nowhere does 'the little brief authority' of man display itself in such 'capers before high heaven' as in the regular army of this republic. In sooth, a man to be either an officer or private in Uncle Sam's legions, must say: 'Becalm—be calm, indignant heart' almost every day of his life; must muzzle his tongue, quell his spirit, and hug to his breast that granite idol, 'discipline.' In military parlance, the corporal 'sits down' upon the private; the sergeant upon the corporal ; the lieutenant upon the sergeant; the captain upon the lieutenant ; the major upon the captain; the lieutenant-colonel upon the major; the colonel upon the lieutenant-colonel; and the General upon the whole pile. Thus, the nethermost man gets pretty well flattened out, if the others are in bad humor, and at no time are 'commanding officers' so 'cross and contrary' as when lying around camp, tormented by 'blue devils,' and nothing to do.

"A more unromantic looking set of military heroes, the eye never rested upon than ours. Dust, rain, sun and sweat have made havoc of the never very graceful uniforms. The rear portions of the men's pantaloons are, for the most part, worn out. The boots are coffee-colored. Such a thing as a regulation cap is not to be seen in the whole camp—everybody from the General down, wearing some kind of a *sombrero*, picturesque enough, but rather unmilitary. Every face is parched—nearly every beard unshorn, and the eye is wearied by the unending display of light-blue pants and dark blue shirts, all in a more or less dilapidated condition. Our hours are regulated by the bugle, our only means of ascertaining the time. The mornings are chilly, the days hot and the nights wondrously cool for the latter part of June. But we generally have a lovely mountain breeze, highly invigorating, and vastly agreeable, except when it grows unruly and blows down our tents. I wish some enterprising company would lift these superb mountains en masse, move them to Chicago, and plant them for all time on the northwestern prairie, say five miles from Lawndale. How grand it would be to have the Big Horn giant scanning his tremendous countenance in the resplendent mirror of Lake Michigan."

But more stirring days were rapidly, and all unknown to us, approaching. Some half-breeds came into camp on June 30th, and reported that Indian runners had told them of a fight between the hostiles and "pony soldiers" (cavalry), in which the latter had been wiped out. We imagined that the story had reference to our own fight on the Rosebud, and our officers, long familiar with the Indian habit of exaggeration, paid little or no attention to the second-hand intelligence. Yet, as it turned out, the Indian story was absolutely correct. The "pony soldiers," under the ill-fated Custer, had been, indeed, wiped out.

The General, ever inclined to be active, determined to organize a party to enter the Big Horn mountains, for the double purpose of hunting and exploring. Thus was my desire to penetrate those picturesque ranges to be gratified.

CHAPTER XII

ACROSS THE SNOWY RANGE

On Saturday morning, July 1st, General Crook, with Colonel Mills, Major Burt, Lieutenants Bourke, Schuyler, Carpenter, Lemley, half a dozen packers and some newspaper correspondents, left the camp on a hunting and exploring expedition into the mountain ranges. The entire party were mounted on mules, and went provisioned for four days. The weather was very fine, and we were not annoyed by the heavy rain-storms which prevail there at that season. Two hours' ride brought us to the plateau of the eastern slope, and we found a rich table land, carpeted thick with grass, begemmed with countless flowers and watered by innumerable ice-cold streams. Thick pine forests covered most of the ground, but there were numerous natural parks, laid out by the hand of nature with a grace and beauty seldom seen in the artificial works of landscape gardeners. From the plateau we could see three or four snowy ranges, the breezes from which rendered the July atmosphere cool and bracing as the early May zephyrs in less elevated latitudes. Not a man of the party had ever been two miles into the mountains previously, and we followed the trail left by the Snake Indians after they left us for Wind River valley, on June 19th. This led us into the very roughest parts of the Big Horn range, for the Snakes took the most inaccessible route in order to avoid the hunting parties of the Sioux, who periodically go into the mountains to cut lodge-poles and kill game. Our mules, nevertheless, were equal to all emergencies, and by 3 o'clock in the afternoon of our first day out, we reached a lovely dell on the main branch of Goose creek, where we went into camp until the dawn of Sunday. Starting forward again, we reached the beginning of the snowy range about 10 o'clock, and were considerably impeded in our course by the melting snows, which converted the mountain valleys into so many quagmires, in which our animals floundered at about every step. As we ascended higher, we noticed several immense layers of quartz, some of which gave indications of gold, but not in quantities sufficient to justify a rush of people in that direction with the expectation of growing rich in a day or a week. In fact, the gold indications were no greater than those to be observed in almost every great chain of mountains on the continent.

A gentleman of our party, who had traveled much in Europe, particularly in Switzerland, said that the canon through which we moved reminded him in almost every feature of the St. Gothard pass. Below us were the dark, green woods and golden streams, above us and around us were the eternal snows and the tremendous rocks, from which and through which burst and thundered a thousand cascades, forming the headwaters of the splendid rivers that fertilize the slopes of that mountain region throughout its entire extent. Picturesque lakes, none of them completely frozen over, and all of immense depth, so far as we could judge, met the eye at almost every half mile, so that there was no difficulty in recognizing the inexhaustible reservoirs that fed the countless torrents which swell the volume of the Big Horn and Tongue rivers.

At 3 o'clock in the afternoon we reached the highest pinnacle of the snowy range, almost on a level with Cloud Peak, and saw several other immense ranges toward the west and north, which, however, looked more like cloud banks than the mountains of Idaho, Utah and Montana. Resting on this crest for half an hour, we began to descend, the western slope, and struck into one of the loveliest canons that can be imagined, indented by a glorious stream, and garnished by groves of cedar through all its extent. In the middle of this wild paradise we halted and went into camp. General Crook and Lieutenant Schuyler shot a couple of mountain sheep, genuine "big horns," so that our commissariat was well supplied.

We had along three or four pack mules, which carried the heavier portion of our bedding and subsistence. The mosquitoes bothered us terribly while the sun continued visible, but at night the intense cold compelled them to cease their labors and allow us repose.

The General felt anxious to get back to camp by the Fourth, so he announced that he would allow us until noon the next day to prospect for gold and do such hunting as we felt disposed for, after which our homeward march would begin.

At 5 o'clock, on Monday morning, Colonel Mills, Lieutenant Lemley, Messrs. Wasson, Davenport and the present writer left the camp and rode down the canyon to the west, until we reached a point six miles distant from where Crook had established his headquarters. There the party got separated in an unaccountable manner, and Colonel Mills and myself found ourselves alone. We supposed that the others had ridden forward to a prominent mountain peak about six miles further on, and we determined to proceed in that direction. As we advanced, the valley progressed in beauty. We passed lake after lake and stream after stream. The trees increased in size and in variety, and the vegetation assumed a tropical richness. We saw hundreds of bear, elk and buffalo tracks, indicating that the country was full of large game, but the beasts kept successfully out of sight. Dozens of American eagles rose majestically from the rocks and soared proudly above us, screaming with all their might, for, doubtless, they had never seen white men before. We kept on until we reached the base of the mountain, which was our objective point, but still we saw nothing of our late companions, which very much surprised us. Having gone so far, we determined to ascend the peak, the lower part of which was covered with large juniper trees — the crest being a bare rock which rose several hundred feet above the forest. We tied our mules to the trees about two-thirds of the way up the hill, and then scaled the remainder of the almost perpendicular ascent. Thoroughly exhausted with the heat and climbing, we finally reached the summit, and each of us uttered an involuntary exclamation of astonishment. We had actually crossed the range, and stood upon the westernmost outpost of the Big Horn mountains. Below us, to the west, lay the tremendous valley of the Wind river and Big Horn bounded by a wall of mountains, half covered with snow, while two other ranges, of similar character, rose beyond it. 'We observed the great river winding around to the northwest, where it meets the Yellowstone, while the Grey Bull and countless other streams, running from east and west, were distinctly discernible. Along the Big Horn river, for fifteen miles on either side, appeared a strip of rough, sterile lands, similar to what I had already seen in Wyoming, but the western slope of the mountains and the mouths of the canon were natural gardens, studded with evergreen groves and beautified by parks, in which the grass appeared to be several feet high, looking rich as green velvet. The water courses ran from every rock, and the noise of the rushing waters could be heard in the sublime solitude — the only sounds that broke the awful stillness of that beauteous desert.

The lakes studding the valleys looked like pieces of the blue sky which had fallen from the heavens, as if to contrast their ethereal beauty with the lovely earth beneath. My enthusiasm was aroused, and looking down the slope and along the canon, I said to Colonel Mills, "Bring along your Italy." The Colonel laughed, but acknowledged that even in his extensive experience, he had never looked upon anything so picturesque. He pointed out to me several ledges of quartz, and remarked that gold almost invariably accompanied that peculiar geological formation. He also took a sketch of the locality for the benefit of the service. Then we took a last lingering look at the scene, and prepared to descend to where the mules were tied to the juniper trees, a thousand feet below where we stood.

Having found the animals, we faced toward the camp, Colonel Mills acting as guide. We had not proceeded down the slope very far, when, on reaching an opening in the forest, we saw two huge bull buffalo grazing at some distance, and the killing instinct common to masculine humanity immediately suggested the beasts as victims. The mules were tied up again. We approached the edge of the wood, leveled our rifles, and in a minute both bisons were wounded. Mills killed his at the first shot, but, being a young hunter, it took three cartridges to settle my buffalo. Then we cut out their tongues, as we had no means of carrying any other portion, and proceeded on our journey. We reached our camp in the canon at 3 o'clock, and found that Crook had been gone some hours, but had left one of his scouts behind to show us his trail, as he struck out a new route over the mountains, which we found much more practicable than the one we first came over. We overtook the rest of the party at 6 o'clock, and went into camp for the night. Then we learned that Lieutenant Lemley and Mr. Davenport had missed us in the woods and turned back, supposing that we had done the same, while Mr. Wasson's mule was so tired that he could urge it no further and he was obliged to return. Thus, by accident, Colonel Mills and I had the honor of being about the first pale faces that ever crossed the Big horn range completely from the eastern to the western slope. Had we known that the rest had turned back, to confess the honest truth, we should have done the same. The gold prospectors examined some of the streams and lakes, but found no great encouragement, although there were plenty of "indications." We saw some Indian trails, but none of very recent appearance. Next morning, after experiencing a July snow-storm during the night, we resumed our march, and, without further adventure, reached camp about noon on the centennial Fourth. We had nothing but coffee wherewith to drink to the memory of George Washington, but we had a banquet on elk, deer, and mountain sheep, killed by Crook and his officers during the time that Mills and I were wandering through the cedar canon. Taken altogether, the trip was a delightful experience.

Captain Graves, of Montana, with a company of some thirty miners, followed our trail into the mountains, determined to decide the gold question once for all. The captain told me that his party had explored every stream on the eastern slope of the range, from Crazy Woman's creek to Tongue river, and had not found a single grain of gold. He thought that if the precious metal existed in that region at all, it must be in the Wind River valley, where the streams from both mountain ranges converge. Reports since made by prospectors, government surveying parties and others have confirmed the statements of this experienced miner, who first broke ground with the '49ersin California. Several men, experienced in mining, have tried their hands at prospecting, but nothing, except disappointment, has come of it.

Apart, however, from this question of gold, there is no richer tract of country in America, and scarcely any more beautiful than the portion skirting those mountains and contained in their valleys. The summer season is short, it is true ; the winters are long and rather cold, but an industrious population would soon conquer the difficulties produced by these circumstances. Hundreds of thousands of cattle could be raised there, grain could be grown in abundance with powerful streams in such profusion, manufactories would soon spring up, and prosperity would be unlimited. These were about the sum total of my observations at the time, and most of my humble predictions have since been fulfilled. No gold, in paying quantities, has been discovered. There are, as yet, no manufactures, but cattle now graze on those ranges by the myriad, and agriculture has grown apace. The land is no longer a howling wilderness

CHAPTER XIII

THE SIBLEY SCOUT. A CLOSE CALL

The day after the return of Crook's party from their hunt, the General, who expected the wagon train and reinforcements from Fetterman to appear every moment, determined to send out a reconnoitering party along the base of the mountains, northwestward, to locate, if possible, the Indian village, and to take a general observation of the country. Lieut. Frederick W. Sibley, of Troop E, 2d Cavalry, with twenty-five picked men, drawn from the regiment, was detailed to accompany the scouts, Frank Gruard and Baptiste Pourier, on the reconnoissance. John Becker, a mule packer, who had had some experience as a guide, was also of the party. The scouts had ventured forward on our projected route, about twenty miles, two nights previously, but, having seen several parties of Sioux, returned to camp and made their report. An officer came around to my tent on the morning of Thursday, July 6th, and informed me of the plan. He said that the party would proceed toward the Little Big Horn river, and if no Indians were discovered there, they would proceed still further, feeling their way as cautiously as possible. As I was sent out to see the country and write it up, and not to dry rot around camp—something insupportable to most newspaper men—I made up my mind to accompany Lieutenant Sibley, who was, at that time, as fine a type of the young American officer as could be found in the service, and I know that he has not gone backward since. His father, Colonel Sibley, a retired army officer, had died in Chicago, and several members of the family still reside in that city. I had, of course, to obtain General Crook's permission to accompany the party. The General seemed somewhat surprised at my request, and hesitated about letting me go. However, he finally consented, but warned me that I might get into more trouble than, perhaps, I anticipated. Lieutenant Bourke asked me what kind of an epitaph I would like him to write for me, and the other officers rallied me good-naturedly about my proposed trip. I felt elated at having obtained leave to go, and hastened to inform Sibley, who expressed himself much pleased at my resolution. Grim Captain Wells only said to his orderly—" Bring Mr. Finerty a hundred rounds of Troop E ammunition." This command was much more eloquent than an oration.

The party mustered at noon, beyond the creek, each man took a double supply of cartridges, and as much food a? would last for some days. I think it was a mistake to start in daylight, but the scouts seems anxious to get forward, as the General was impatient for definite information of the Sioux. The scouts led us to camp on Big Goose creek, distant about thirteen miles from Crook's headquarters, and there we remained until about sundown. After we had saddled up, Fourier thought he observed a horseman watching us from a shallow ravine. Gruard started off in hot pursuit, but was unable to come up with the suspicious object, which ran off like the wind, and was soon lost sight of in the increasing gloom. The incident rendered the scouts rather uneasy, but they finally reached the conclusion that the object they saw was a stray elk. We moved forward rather circumspectly through the long grass, and I can still remember how we startled scores of sage hens from cover as we advanced. All kept strict silence. Wo marched, for the most part, over the old Fort C. F. Smith trail, Gruard keeping a sharp lookout from every vantage point ahead. The full moon rose behind us at about 8 o'clock, rendering every object as distinct as if it had been daylight. 'We looked like a phantom company marching through that great solitude, with the lofty sierra of the Big Horn looming up grandly on our left flank. We continued thus to ride, in almost dead silence, save for the occasional crunching of our horses' hoofs over the pebbles in the watercourses we had to cross, until, perhaps, 2 o'clock in the morning. Then we halted at a point supposed to be only a few miles from the valley of the Little Big Horn, at least forty miles from Crook's main body, and bivouacked among some small, grass-covered bluffs. Our horses were half lariated, and pickets were posted on the heights to prevent surprise by the Indians, who, we rightly calculated, could not be very far off.

Early on the morning of Friday, July 7th, we were again in the saddle, pressing on cautiously toward where the scouts believed the Indian village to be. When we had reached a point several miles from our late bivouac, and close to the Little Big Horn river, Gruard, motioning us to halt, ascended a rocky mound directly in our front, leaving his horse slightly below the crest. We observed the intrepid scout's movements with some interest, because we knew we were in the enemy's country, and might encounter Indians at any moment. Scarcely had the scout taken a first cautious look from the crest of the ridge, when a peculiar motion of his hand summoned Baptiste Pourier to his side. Baptiste dismounted also, leaving his pony below the crest.

He joined Gruard, and both scouts keenly observed the country from between the rocks on the summit of the bluff, through their glasses. Their observations finished, they mounted their ponies and came galloping back to us in hot haste. "Be quick, and follow, me for your lives," cried Gruard. We mounted immediately, and all followed his lead. He led us through bluffs of red sandstone, which formed, as it were, the footstool of the mountain chain, and we were obliged, sometimes, to make our horses leap down on rocky ledges, as much as six or seven feet, perhaps, in order to follow his course. We soon reached a bluff of sufficient size to conceal our horses on its westerly side, while those of us who were provided with field-glasses—namely, Sibley, Gruard, Pourier and myself—went up into the rocks and waited to see what was coming.

"What did you see, Frank?" asked Sibley of the scout, after we had settled down to make our observations.

"Only Sitting Bull's war party," Frank replied. "I knew they would be here around the Little Big Horn without coining at all."

We did not have long to wait for confirmation of his words. Almost as he spoke, groups of mounted savages appeared on the bluffs north and east of us. Every moment increased their numbers, and, scattered out in the Indian fashion, they seemed to cover the hilly country far and wide. Most of them were in full war costume, which added greatly to the picturesque character of the scene.

"They appear not to have seen us yet," observed Gruard. "Unless some of them hit upon our trail of this morning, we are comparatively safe." Gradually the right wing of the war party approached the ground over which we had so recently ridden. We watched their movements, as may be supposed, with breathless interest. Suddenly an Indian, attired in a red blanket, halted, looked for a moment at the ground, and then began to ride around in a circle. "Now we had better look out," said Gruard. "That fellow has found our trail, sure, and they will be after us in five minutes."

"What, then, are we to do?" asked the young officer in a calm, steady voice.

"Well, we have but one chance of escape," said Gruard, "let us lead our horses into the mountains and try to cross them. But, in the meantime, let us prepare for the worst."

Then we left the rocks and went down among the soldiers, who, poor fellows, seemed ready to face any fate with manly courage.

Lieutenant Sibley said to them: "Men, the Indians have discovered us. We will have to do some fighting. If we can make an honorable escape, all together, we will do it. If retreat should prove impossible let no man surrender. Die in your tracks, because the Indians show no mercy."

"All right, sir," was the simple and soldierly reply of the men, and, without more ado, the whole party followed the officer and the scouts up the rough mountain side which, at that point, was steep and difficult to a discouraging extent. The Indians must have seen us by that time, because they were scarcely more than a mile distant, and numbers of them had halted and appeared to be in consultation.

We continued to retreat until we struck an old Sioux hunting trail on the first ridge of the mountains. "This path leads to the snowy range," said Gruard, who had hunted in that region when a captive among the Sioux. "If we can reach there without being overtaken or cut off," he continued, "our chances are pretty fair." Most of the trail was fairly good, and we proceeded in a direction west of north at a brisk trot. Having traveled five miles or so, and seeing no Indians following us up, Gruard came to the conclusion that the savages had given up the pursuit, or else did not care about attacking us among the mountains, as they are not much accustomed to the more elevated ranges. Our horses were pretty badly used up, and some of the men were suffering from hunger and thirst. Therefore, it was deemed best for us to halt, make coffee and allow our horses to recuperate on the abundant herbage around. We selected a shady spot, and were glad to stretch our weary limbs under the umbrageous trees. But, a very little later on, we came near paying with our lives for the privilege of brief repose. Our halt lasted an hour—possibly longer, because we had begun to believe that the Indians would not follow us into the recesses of the mountains, and grew, for the time being, rather careless. It was afternoon, I think, when we again saddled up and pushed forward, feeling much invigorated. We crossed what Gruard thought was the main branch of Tongue river, or else a tributary of the Little Big Horn, flowing clear, cold and deep through the mountain valleys, and were within full view of the superb snowy range. The same splendid type of scenery that I had observed when out with Crook's hunting party, further southward, was visible on every side. The trail led through natural parks, open spaces, bordered by rocks and pine trees, on the mountain sides. At times the country grew comparatively open. We were riding in single file, the scouts leading, and kept tolerably open order. Suddenly John Becker, the packer, and a soldier who had lingered somewhat in rear, rode up to the lieutenant, exclaiming, "The Indians! the Indians!"

Gruard and the rest of us looked over our right shoulders, and saw a party of the red fiends, in their war bonnets, riding rapidly along that flank at no great distance. We had reached a sort of narrow plain in the mountain range, with woods upon our left, woods upon our front, and high rocks and timber on our right. "Keep well to the left, close to the woods," said Gruard to Lieutenant Sibley. Scarcely was the warning uttered, when from the rocks and trees upon our right, distant, perhaps, 200 yards came a ringing volley. The Indians had fired upon us, slightly wounding the horses of two or three of the soldiers, and also the animal which I rode. "Fall back on the woods!" cried the scout, and every horse was wheeled toward the timber on the left. My horse stumbled from the shock of the bullet, but recovered its feet almost immediately, and bore me in safety to the edge of the timber, under the rapid Indian fire, which, fortunately for us, did not at the moment possess the essential quality of accuracy. There was no need to urge our horses to cover, because they were badly stampeded by the firing, after the manner of most American horses, and we were soon dismounted in the edge of the woods. Lieutenant Sibley, before we tied the animals, made some of the soldiers fire upon the Indians, which had the effect of confining them to the rocks. The savages did not come up to their ordinary marksmanship during this affair, for not a man of ours was seriously wounded, although they succeeded in injuring several other horses by their subsequent volleys, some fatally. We soon had such of the horses as could keep their feet tied to the trees, near the verge of the wood, where, also, Lieutenant Sibley formed us into a semi-circular skirmish line, and matters soon became exceedingly hot in our front. The trees and fallen timber, particularly the latter, served us admirably for breastworks, and we blazed away for some time with right good will. The Lieutenant warned us not to waste our lead, and we slackened fire somewhat. We could see, occasionally, the Indian leader, dressed in what appeared to be white buckskin, and wearing a gorgeous war bonnet, directing the movements of his warriors. Gruard thought he recognized in him White Antelope, a Cheyenne chief famed for his enterprise and skill. He led one charge against us, and every man on the front of the skirmish line fired upon him and his party. We did not know until long afterward that our volley put an end to his career, but so it was. White Antelope led no more charges after that day. His death was a fortunate thing for us, because it damped the spirits of his men, and rendered them more cautious than they would have otherwise been. But he did not fall until he had made it exceedingly interesting for our little party, battling there in the edge of the woods. The Indians lay low among the tall rocks and pine trees, and kept up an almost incessant lire upon our position, filling the trees around us with their lead. I could hear their bullets rattling against the pine tree trunks like hail-stones on the roof of a barn, and it was not comfortable music either. Not a man of our party expected to leave that spot with life, because all well knew that the noise of the firing would bring to the attack every Sioux and Cheyenne within reach, while we were fully fifty miles from any hope of reinforcement. The savages evidently aimed at our horses, thinking that by killing them all means of retreat would be cut off from us.

Meanwhile their numbers continued to increase, and they seemed to swarm on the open slopes of the hills within the range of our vision. We could distinctly hear their savage, encouraging yells to each other, and Gruard said that Sioux and Cheyennes were allied in the attacking force, all of whom appeared to be in great glee at the prospect of a scalping entertainment at our expense. They had evidently recognized Gruard, whom they heartily hated, because they called him by his Sioux name, Standing Bear, and one savage shouted to him, "Do you think there are no men but yours in this country?"

The Indians were prodigal of their ammunition, but we reserved our fire until a savage showed himself. Then we would let him have it without stint. Thus we fought and kept them at bay—for Indians rarely ever seriously attempt to take by storm a position such as we occupied—for several hours, but we could tell by the extension of their fire from our front to the right and left flanks that they were being reinforced from the villages in the neighborhood of the Little Big Horn, and we felt that unless a special providence interfered, we could never carry our lives away from that spot. We were truly looking death in the face, and so close that we could feel his cold breath upon our foreheads and his icy grip upon our hearts.

Nevertheless, I remember that, in one of the intervals of the firing, doubtless the one that followed the fall of the Cheyenne chief, I picked a few specimens of the mountain crocus and forget-me-not growing within my reach and placed them between the leaves of my note-book, where they are preserved, almost perfectly to this day. And yet I felt anything but indifferent to the fate that seemed to await me, and would have given the world, did I have the power of its bestowal, to be back safe and sound in Crook's camp again. Life seemed particularly sweet throughout that eventful day. Close acquaintance with death is not a pleasing sensation.

As the volume of the Indian fire seemed to increase, "no surrender" was the word passed from man to man around the thin skirmish line. Each one of us would, if we found it necessary, have blown out his own brains rather than fall alive into Indian hands. Doubtless, if we had remained long enough, the Indians would have relieved us of all responsibility on that score. A disabling wound would have been worse than death. I had often wondered how a man felt when he thought he saw inevitable, sudden doom upon him. I know it now, for I had little or no idea that we could effect our escape, and, mentally at least, I could scarcely have felt my position more keenly if an Indian knife or bullet had wounded me in some vital spot. So, I think, it was with all the command, but nobody seemed, therefore, to weaken. It is one thing, however, to face death in the midst of the excitement of a general battle. It is quite another thing to face him in almost cold blood, with the certain prospect of your dishonored body being first mutilated in a revolting manner, and then left to feed the wolf or the vulture among the savage mountains. After a man once sees the skull and cross bones as clearly as our party saw them on the afternoon of Friday, July 7, 1876, no subsequent glimpse of grim mortality can possibly impress him in the same manner.

Well, the eternal shadows seemed to be fast closing around us; the Indian bullets were hitting nearer every moment, and the Indian yell was growing stronger and fiercer, when a hand was laid on my shoulder, and Rufus, a soldier who was my neighbor on the skirmish line, said, "The rest are retiring. Lieutenant Sibley tells us to do the same." I quietly withdrew from the foot of the friendly pine tree, which, with a fallen trunk that lay almost across it, kept at least a dozen Indian bullets from making havoc of my body, and prepared to obey. As I passed by Sibley, who wanted to see every man under his command in the line of retreat before he stirred himself, the young officer said, "Go to your saddle bags, with caution, and take all your ammunition. We are going to abandon our remaining horses. The Indians are getting all around us, so we must take to the rocks and thick timber on foot. It seems to be our only chance of escape." I did as directed, but felt a pang at leaving my noble animal, which was bleeding from a wound in the right side. We dared not shoot our surviving horses, for that would have discovered our movement to the enemy.

Gruard advised this strategy, saying that as the Indians occupied the passes east, west and north of us—all of them being difficult at the best—we could not possibly effect a retreat on horseback, even if all our animals had escaped unwounded. If the grass had happened to be a little bit dryer, and it would not take long to dry, as there had been only a light thunder shower during the afternoon, the Indians, in Gruard's opinion, would have tried to burn us out of the timber. He bluntly told the Lieutenant that the position was untenable, at such a distance from

Crook's camp, and even if a man could succeed in getting through to the General, we could not expect timely relief, and all would be over with us long before an attempt at rescue could be made. Therefore, Gruard said, if Lieutenant Sibley did not choose to take his advice, upon the officer should rest the responsibility of whatever might happen.

There was no time to be lost if we meant to get away at all, and certainly there was nothing to gain, but everything to lose, by remaining where we were. Sibley, although very averse to retreating, finally yielded to the calm advice of the scout, whose great experience among the Sioux rendered him familiar with all the methods of Indian warfare. The arguments used by Gruard were warmly seconded by Baptiste Pourier, one of the most reliable scouts on the frontier, who was acquainted from childhood with the subtle tactics of the savages.

When the retreat was decided on, we acted with an alacrity which only men who have, at some time, struggled for their lives can understand. A couple of scattering volleys and some random shots were fired, to make the savages believe that we were still in position. As we had frequently reserved our fire during the fight, our silence would not be noticed immediately. We then retired, in Indian file, through the trees, rocks and fallen timber in rear of us. Our horses were, evidently, plainly visible to the Indians—a circumstance that facilitated our escape. We retreated for, perhaps, a mile through the forest, which was filled with rugged boulders and the trunks of fallen pine trees, through which no horse could penetrate, waded one of the branches of Tongue river up to our waists, and gained the slippery rocks of the great mountain ridge, where no mounted Indians, who are as lazy on foot as they are active on horseback, could pursue us. Then, as we paused to catch our breath, we heard, in the distance, five or six ringing volleys in succession. It was most likely the final fire delivered by the Indians before they charged our late position, with the hope of getting our scalps.

"That means we are safe for the present," said Gruard, "but let us lose no time in putting more rocks between us and the White Antelope." We followed his advice with a feeling of thankfulness that those only who have passed through such an ordeal can appreciate. How astonished and chagrined the reinforced savages must have been when they ran in upon the maimed horses and did not get a single scalp! Even under such circumstances as we were placed in, we could not help indulging in a laugh at their expense. But we had escaped one danger only to encounter another. Fully fifty miles of mountain, rock, forest, river and canon lay between us and Crook's camp. We were unable to carry any food upon our persons. The weather was close, owing to the thunder-shower, and we threw away everything superfluous in the way of clothing. With ravening Indians behind us, and uncounted precipices before us, we found our rifles, and what remained of our 100 rounds of ammunition each, a sufficient load to carry. The brave and skillful Gruard, the ablest of scouts, seconded by the fearless Pourier, conducted our retreat through the mountain wilderness, and we marched, climbed and scrambled over impediments that at any other time might have been impossible to us, until about midnight, when absolute fatigue compelled us to make a halt. Then we bivouaced under the projections of an immense pile of rocks on the very summit of some unknown mountain peak, and there witnessed one of the most terrible wind and hail storms that can be imagined. The trees seemed to fall by the hundred, and their noise, as they broke off and fell, or were uptorn by the roots, resembled rapid discharges of field artillery. To add to our discomfort, the thermometer suddenly fell several degrees, and, being attired in summer campaign costume only, we suffered greatly from the cold.

Almost before dawn we were again stumbling through the rocks and fallen trees, and, about sunrise, reached the tremendous canon cut through the mountain by what is called the southern branch of Tongue river. Most of the men were too much exhausted to make the descent of the canon, so Gruard, finding a fairly practicable path, led us to an open valley down by the river, on the left bank, as hard as we could walk, for if discovered there by any considerable body of Indians, we could only halt, and, worn out as most of the little band were, die together. Fortune favored us, and we made the right bank of the stream unobserved, being then, according to the calculations of the scouts, about five and twenty miles from Crook's encampment. In our front, toward the east, we could see the plain through which Tongue river flowed, where, no doubt, as it was then a fine game country, hostile Indians abounded, while our only safe avenue of escape was to cross the stream and climb the enormous precipice that formed the right side of the canon. But the dauntless Gruard was equal to the emergency. He scaled the gigantic wall diagonally, and led us along what looked like a mere squirrel path, not more than a foot wide, with an abyss of, perhaps, 500 feet below, and a sheer wall of rock, 200 feet high, above us. After about an hour's herculean toil, we gained the crest and saw the point of mountain, some twenty miles distant, where lay our camp and comrades. This, as may well be imagined, was a blissful vision, but we were half dead from fatigue, and some of us were almost famine stricken. Yet the indefatigable Gruard would not stop until we reached the eastern foot-hills, where we made, so to speak, a dive into the deep valley to obtain water—our only refreshment on that hard, rugged road. The leaves from the pine trees made the hillsides as slippery as glass, and where there was neither grass nor tree, the broken stones and "shale" made walking absolutely painful. Scarcely had we slaked our thirst when Gruard led us up to the hills again, and we had barely entered the timber belt, when the scout uttered a warning "hush," and threw himself upon the ground, motioning us to do the same. He pointed toward the north, and there, wheeling around the base of the point of the mountain we had doubled so shortly before, appeared another strong party of the Sioux in open order. The savages were riding along quite leisurely, and, although fairly numerous, were evidently only the advance or rear guard of some larger party. This sight made us desperate. Every man examined his carbine and looked to his ammunition. We all felt that life would be too dearly purchased by further flight, and, following the example of the brave young Sibley and the gallant scouts, we took up a position among the rocks on the knoll we had reached, determined, if called upon, to sell our lives as dearly as possible.

"We are in pretty hard luck, it would seem," said Sibley addressing me, "but d them, we'll show the red scoundrels how white men can light and die, if necessary. Men," he said, addressing the soldiers, "we have a good position; let every shot dispose of an Indian!"

At that moment not a man among us felt any inclination to get away. Desperation and a thirst for vengeance on the savages had usurped the place of the animal instinct to save our lives. In such moments mind rises superior to matter and soul to the nerves. But fortune spared us the ordeal of another fight in our weakened condition. Our position, as the lieutenant had said, was a good one. On the left, or north of us, there was a difficult precipice, which hung above the stream of whose waters we had just drunk to satiety. The woods grew quite thinly on our front, toward the east, and south of us was an almost open slope. Our rear was well secured by an irregular line of huge boulders, and rocks of good size afforded us fair shelter in nearly all directions. There was also some fallen timber, but not enough to make a serious blaze if the enemy should try their favorite maneuver of burning us out. The Sioux, fortunately for them, and, no doubt, for us, too, failed to observe our party, and did not advance high enough on the hills to find our trail. They kept eastward, following a branch of Tongue river.

The excitement over, we all again felt thoroughly worn out, and fell asleep, all except the tireless and ever vigilant scouts, and awoke at dark feeling somewhat refreshed, but painfully hungry. Not a man of us, whatever the risk, Sioux or no Sioux, could endure the mountain route longer, so we took our wearied, jaded lives into our hands, and struck out for Crook's camp across the plains, fording Big Goose creek up to our armpits at 3 o'clock in the morning, the water being as cold as the melting mountain snows could make it. Two of the men, Sergeant Cornwell and Private Collins, absolutely refused to ford the creek, as neither could swim, and the current was exceedingly rapid. Sibley threatened and coaxed them alternately in vain, but those men, who could face bullets and tomahawks without flinching, would not be induced to cross that stream. They begged to be allowed to hide in the bushes on the north side of the creek, until horses could be sent after them. Sibley, after providentially escaping so many dangers, could not sacrifice the rest of his command for two obstinately foolish men, and the scouts urged him to push on. This he did reluctantly, but there was no alternative. We judged that our main camp must still be some dozen miles away on Little Goose creek, but every step, chiefly because of the toil attending the previous mountain journey, became laborious. My readers can judge for themselves how badly we were used up, when it took us four hours to accomplish six miles. The rocks had broken our boots and skinned our feet, while starvation had weakened our frames. Only a comparatively few were vigorous enough to maintain a decently rapid pace. About 5 o'clock we saw some more Indians toward the east, but at some distance. We took no pains, whatever, to conceal ourselves, which, indeed, would have been a vain task on the nearly naked plain; and the savages, if they saw us, which is highly probable, must have mistaken us for an outlying picket, and being only, comparatively speaking, a handful, kept away. At about 0:30 o'clock we saw two horses grazing on a little knoll, and the carbines glittering in their "boots" on the saddles proclaimed the riders to be cavalry men. Presently the men rose out of the long grass and made for their guns, but we hailed them and they recognized us. They were men of the 2d Cavalry, who had obtained permission to go hunting, and who were bound for Tongue river, where they would have certainly fallen in with the Sioux. Lieutenant Sibley sent them into camp for horses and some rations, and also told them to ask for an escort to proceed as far as Big Goose creek for the two men who had stopped there. Most of Sibley's men threw themselves on the ground, unable to move further, and awaited the arrival of the horses. Within an hour and a half Captains Dewees and Rawolle, of the 2d Cavalry, came out to us with led horses and some cooked provisions. They greeted us most warmly, and, having aided us most kindly, proceeded to pick up Sergeant Cornwell and Private Collins, who were found all safe, concealed in the thick undergrowth of Big Goose creek, and who reached camp a few hours after ourselves. It was 10 o'clock Sunday morning, July 9, 1876, when we rode in among the tents, amid congratulations from officers and men alike.

Thus, after passing through scenes of great peril and privation, our little band found itself safe in Camp Cloud Peak, surrounded by devoted and hospitable comrades. After we had somewhat recovered from our great fatigue, and refreshed ourselves by a most welcome bath in the creek, we were obliged to relate our experiences again and again for the benefit of the entire "outfit." All agreed that Frank Gruard, for his good judgment and the skill with which he managed our retreat, deserved to take rank among the foremost of scouts and plainsmen. Nor did quiet, intrepid Baptiste Fourier lack admirers around the campfires of Crook's brigade. The oldest among Indian fighters, including such officers as Colonel Royall and Lieutenant Lawson, concurred in saying that escape from danger so imminent and so appalling, in a manner so ingenious and successful, was almost without a parallel in the history of Indian warfare. It was fortunate, they said, for our party that an officer possessing the coolness and good sense of Lieutenant Sibley had command of it. A rash, bull-headed commander would have disregarded the advice of Gruard and Fourier, and would thus have brought ruin and death upon all of us. Colonel Roy all, in the absence of General Crook, who was in the mountains on a hunt, was kind enough to say that while a spare horse remained in his regiment, it would be at my disposal, in lieu of the one I had lost in the Sibley Scout, as the reconnoissance has ever since been called by the American army.

CHAPTER XIV

THE CUSTER MASSACRE

When we returned to camp, General Crook was, as I have said, up in the mountains over our camp, on another hunt. Colonel Royall, who had heard further reports of a massacre of our cavalry by Indians, and rendered doubly careful by the late unpleasant experience of Sibley's party, sent a few companies of the 3d after the General. They met him and his followers returning to camp, fairly laden to the earth with elk, deer and mountain sheep, which proved a great blessing to our people. Crook received all the news with his customary placidity, and then set about cleaning himself up after his long turn in the mountains. He felt morally certain, however, that some dire disaster had befallen a portion of Terry's command, and he feared the impetuous Custer was the victim. His fears were sadly realized on Monday morning, July 10th, when Louis Richard and other halfbreeds came in from Fetterman with the official account of the catastrophe. With it came a characteristic despatch from General Sheridan to Crook, in which the former said, referring to Rosebud fight, "Hit them again, and hit them harder!" Crook smiled grimly when he read the telegram, and remarked, "I wish Sheridan would come out here himself and show us how to do it. It is rather difficult to surround three Indians with one soldier!" And this was all he said upon the subject then.

The official story of the Custer disaster was put into a few words, but no account that I have heard or read, either on or off the plains, equals in clearness and succinctness the story of the Crow Indian scout. Curly, who alone of the immediate command of General Custer survived the memorable disaster of June 25, 1876. The following is the gist of Curly's statement:

"Custer, with his five companies, after separating from Reno and his seven companies, moved to the right around the base of a high hill overlooking the valley of the Little Horn, through a ravine just wide enough to admit his column of fours. There were no signs of the presence of Indians in the hills on that side (the right) of the Little Horn, and the column moved steadily on until it rounded the hill and came in sight of the village lying in the valley below them. Custer appeared very much elated, and ordered the bugles to sound a charge, and moved on at the head of his column, waving his hat to encourage his men. When they neared the river, the Indians, concealed in the undergrowth on the opposite side of the stream, opened fire on the troops, which checked the advance. Here a portion of the command were dismounted and thrown forward to the river, and returned the fire of the Indians. During this time the warriors were seen riding out of the village by hundreds, and deploying across Custer's front and to his left, as if with the intention of crossing the stream on his right, while the women and children were seen hastening out of the village in large numbers in the opposite direction.

During the fight at this point, Curly saw two of Custer's men killed who fell into the stream. After fighting a few moments here, Custer seemed to be convinced that it was impracticable to cross, as it only could be done in column of fours exposed during the movement to a heavy fire from the front and both flanks. He therefore ordered the head of the column to the left, and bore diagonally into the hills, down stream, his men on foot, leading their horses. In the meantime the Indians had crossed the river (below) in immense numbers, and began to appear on his right flank and in his rear; and he had proceeded but a few hundred yards in the new direction the column had taken, when it became necessary to renew the fight with the Indians who had crossed the stream. At first the command remained together, but after some minutes' fighting it was divided, a portion deploying circularly to the left, and the remainder similarly to the right, so that when the line was formed, it bore a rude resemblance to a circle, advantage being taken, as far as possible, of the protection afforded by the ground. The horses were in the rear, the men on the line being dismounted, fighting on foot. Of the incidents of the fight in other parts of the field than his own, Curly was not well informed, as he was himself concealed in a deep ravine, from which but a small part of the field was visible.

The fight appeared to have begun, from Curly's description of the situation of the sun, about 2:30 or 3 o'clock P. M., and continued without intermission until nearly sunset. The Indians had completely surrounded the command, leaving their horses in ravines well to the rear, themselves pressing forward to the attack on foot. Confident in the great superiority of their numbers, they made several charges on all points of Custer's line; but the troops held their position firmly, and delivered a heavy fire, which every time drove them back. Curly said the firing was more rapid than anything he had ever conceived of, being a continuous roll, or, as he expressed it, "like the snapping of the threads in the tearing of a blanket." The troops expended all the ammunition in their belts, and then sought their horses for the reserve ammunition carried in their saddle pockets.

As long as their ammunition held out, the troops, though losing considerably in the fight, maintained their position in spite of all the efforts of the Sioux. From the weakening of their fire toward the close of the afternoon, the Indians appeared to believe that their ammunition was about exhausted, and they made a grand final charge, in the course of which the last of the command was destroyed, the men being shot, where they lay in their positions in the line, at such close quarters that many were killed with arrows. Curly said that Custer remained alive throughout the greater part of the engagement, animating his men to determined resistance, but about an hour before the close of the fight he received a mortal wound.

The Crow said, further, that the field was thickly strewn with the dead bodies of the Sioux who fell in the attack— in number considerably more than the force of soldiers enframed. He was satisfied that their loss exceeded 200 killed, besides an immense number wounded. Curly accomplished his escape by drawing his blanket around him in the manner of the Sioux, and passing through an interval which had been made in their lines as they scattered over the field in their final charge. He thought they must have seen him, for he was in plain view, but was probably mistaken by the Sioux for one of their own number, or one of their allied Arapahoes or Cheyennes.

In most particulars the account given by Curly of the fight is confirmed by the position of the trail made by Custer in his movements and the general evidences of the battle field. Only one discrepancy is noted, which relates to the time when the fight came to an end. Officers of Reno's battalion, who, late in the afternoon, from high points surveyed the country in anxious expectation of Custer's appearance, and who commanded a view of the field where he had fought, say that no fighting was going on at that time—between 5 and 6 o'clock. It is evident, therefore, that the last of Custer's command was destroyed at an earlier hour in the day than Curly relates."

Much doubt was expressed at the time as to the truth of Curly's tale, but the famous Sioux chief. Gall, who had an important command among the hostiles during the battle, on being taken over the field in 1888, by the officers at Fort Custer, confirmed the statement of the Crow scout. Custer, according to Gall, did not succeed in crossing the river. He saw at a glance that he was overpowered, and did the only thing proper under the circumstances, in leading his command to higher ground where it could defend itself to some advantage. Even in that dread extremity, his soldier spirit and noble bearing held the men under control, and the dead bodies of the troopers of Calhoun's and Keogh's companies, found by General Gibbon's command lying in ranks as they fell, attested the cool generalship exhibited by the heroic leader in the midst of deadly peril. It had always been General Custer's habit to divide his command when attacking Indian villages. His victory over Black Kettle on the Washita was obtained in that manner, but the experiment proved fatal to Major Elliott and a considerable squad of soldiers. It was the general opinion in Crook's command at the time, that had an officer of more resolution been in Major Reno's place, he would have attempted to join Custer at any cost. Reno was, no doubt, imposed upon by Indian strategy, and his retreat to the bluffs was, to say the least of it, premature. But, in the light of after events, it does not seem probable that he could have reached the fatal heights upon which Custer and his men perished. Had Custer taken his entire regiment into the fight he might still have sustained a repulse, but would have escaped annihilation. It is always a tactical error to divide a small command in face of the enemy. This was Custer's error. Applying the same principle on a larger scale, Napoleon erred when he detached Grouchy after Ligny. That fault cost him his crown and liberty. Reno, at the Little Big Horn, was Custer's Grouchy.

Some prominent army officers, and others, have held that Custer did not obey the order of General Terry. This point has given rise to controversy, and I think it only fair to reproduce the commanding officer's instructions to General Custer, issued on the day that he marched from Rosebud landing. The order was as follows:

"The Brigadier-general commanding directs that as soon as your regiment (the 7th Cavalry) can be made ready for the march, you proceed up the Rosebud in pursuit of the Indians whose trail was discovered by Major Reno a few days since. It is, of course, impossible to give any definite instructions in regard to this movement, and, were it not impossible to do so, the department commander places too much confidence in your zeal, energy and ability to wish to impose upon you precise orders which might hamper your action when nearly in contact with the enemy. He will, however, indicate to you his own views of what your action should be, and he desires that you should conform to them, unless you shall see sufficient reason for departing from them. He thinks you should proceed up the Rosebud until you ascertain definitely the direction in which the trail above spoken of leads. Should it be found, as it appears to be almost certain that it will be, to turn toward the Little Big Horn, he thinks that you should still proceed southward, perhaps as far as the head waters of the Tongue river, and then turn toward the Little Big Horn, feeling constantly, however, toward your left, so as to preclude the possibility of the escape of the Indians to the south, or southeast, by parsing around your left flank. The column of Colonel (General) Gibbon is now in motion for the mouth of the Big Horn. As soon as it reaches that point, it will cross the Yellowstone and move up at least as far as the forks of the Big and Little Big Horn. Of course its future movements must be controlled by circumstances as they arise; but it is hoped that the Indians, if upon the Little Big Horn, may be

so nearly inclosed by the two columns that their escape will be impossible. The department commander desires that on your way up the Rosebud you should thoroughly examine the upper part of Tulloch's creek, and that you should endeavor to send a scout through to Colonel Gibbon's column with information of the result of your examination. The lower part of that creek will be examined by a detachment of Colonel Gibbon's command. The supply steamer will be pushed up the Big Horn as far as the forks of the river are found to be navigable for that space, and the department commander, who will accompany the column of Colonel Gibbon, desires you to report to him there, not later than the expiration of the time for which your troops are rationed, unless, in the meantime, you receive further orders."

Custer marched only twelve miles up the Rosebud on June 22d. On the succeeding day he made thirty-three miles. Then Indian signs began to show themselves, and the trail became hot. On June 24th Custer marched twenty-eight miles, halted and waited for reports from his scouts. At 9:25 o'clock that night, according to Reno's report, Custer called his officers together, and told them that, beyond a doubt, the village of the hostiles had been located by the scouts in the valley of the Little Big Horn. It would, therefore, he said, be necessary to cross the divide between the Rosebud and the Little Big Horn, and, in order to effect this without being discovered by the Indians, a night march would be necessary. The command resumed its march, and began crossing the divide at 11 o'clock p. m. Three hours later the scouts informed Custer that the divide could not be crossed before daylight, so the command halted and made coffee. The march was resumed at 5 A. M., the divide was crossed at 8 o'clock, and the command was in the valley of one of the branches of the Little Big Horn. Some Indians had been seen, and, as all chance of surprising the village was, therefore, at an end, Custer resolved to march at once to the attack.

Commands were assigned on the march, and Reno had Troops M, A and G placed under his orders; Colonel Benteen received command of Troops II, D and K; Captain McDougall with Troop B escorted the pack train, and Custer took with himself the fated Troops C, E, F, I and L.

Reno claimed that he received no definite orders from Custer, but moved with the companies assigned to him along with the rest of the column, and well to its left. He saw Benteen moving with his battalion still further to the left, and the latter officer told Reno that he had orders to sweep everything before him. He did not see Benteen again until 2:30

o'clock, when the survivors of both battalions, together with Captain McDougall's troop, rallied on the bluffs above the Little Big Horn river.

Custer carried his battalion to the right, and in this order all moved down the tributary creek to the Little Big Horn valley. When Custer saw all the signs of the presence of a large village, previous to the division of his command, he became greatly elated, and, waving his hat above his head, he, according to the statements of some of the soldiers who were detached with Reno and Benteen, shouted: "Hurrah!

Custer's luck!" But luck turned its back on the hero of sixty successful charges that bloody day. His long, yellow locks had been cut shorter than was his wont, for the sake of convenience, and, after the tragedy, some of the officers who survived likened the dead hero to Samson. Both were invincible while their locks remained unshorn.

Horned Horse, an old Sioux chief, whose son was killed early in the fight, stated to the late Capt. Philo Clark, after the surrender of the hostiles, that he went up on a hill overlooking the field to mourn for the dead, as he was too weak to fight, after the Indian fashion. He had a full view of all that took place almost from the beginning. The Little Big Horn is a stream filled with dangerous quicksand, and cuts off the edges of the northern bluffs sharply near the point where Custer perished. The Indians first saw the troops on the bluffs early in the morning, but, owing to the abruptness and height of the river banks, Custer could not get down to the edge of the stream. The valley of the Little Big Horn is from half a mile to a mile and a half wide, and along it, for a distance of fully five miles, the mighty Indian village stretched. Most of the immense pony herd was out grazing when the savages took the alarm at the appearance of the troops on the heights. The warriors ran at once for their arms, but by the time they had taken up their guns and ammunition belts, the soldiers had disappeared. The Indians thought they had been frightened off by the evident strength of the village, but again, after what seemed quite a long interval, the head of Custer's column showed itself coming down a dry water course, which formed a narrow ravine, toward the river's edge. He made a dash to get across, but was met by such a tremendous fire from the repeating rifles of the savages that the head of his command reeled back toward the bluffs, after losing several men, who tumbled into the water, which was there but eighteen inches deep, and were swallowed up in the quicksand. This is considered an explanation of the disappearance of Lieutenant Harrington and several men whose bodies were not found on the field of battle. They were not made prisoners by the Indians, nor did any of them succeed in breaking through the thick array of the infuriated savages.

Horned Horse did not recognize Custer, but supposed he was the officer who led the column that attempted to cross the stream. Custer then sought to lead his men up to the bluffs by a diagonal movement, all of them having dismounted, and firing, whenever they could, over the backs of their horses at the Indians, who had by that time crossed the river in thousands, mostly on foot, and had taken the General in flank and rear, while others annoyed him by a galling fire from across the river. Hemmed in on all sides, the troops fought steadily, but the fire of the enemy was so close and rapid that they melted like snow before it, and fell dead among their horses in heaps. He could not tell how long the fight lasted, but it took considerable time to kill all the soldiers. The firing was continuous until the last man of Custer's command was dead. Several other bodies besides that of Custer remained unscalped, because the warriors had grown weary of the slaughter. The water-course, in which most of the soldiers died, ran with blood. He had seen many massacres, but nothing to equal that. If the troops had not been encumbered by their horses, which plunged, reared and kicked under the appalling tire of the Sioux, they might have done better. As it was, a great number of Indians fell, the soldiers using their revolvers at close range with deadly effect. More Indians died by the pistol than by the carbine. The latter weapon was always faulty. It "leaded "easily and the cartridge shells stuck in the breech the moment it became heated, owing to some defect in the ejector. It is not improbable that many of Custer's cavalrymen were practically disarmed, because of the deficiency of that disgracefully faulty weapon. If they had been furnished with good Winchesters, or some other style of repeating arm, the result of the battle of the Little Big Horn might have been different.

What happened to Custer, after he disappeared down the north bank of the river, has already been told in the words of Curly and Horned Horse. Not an officer or enlisted man of the five troops under Custer survived to tell the tale. The male members of the Custer family, George

A., Colonel Tom and Boston, were annihilated. Autie Reid, a young relative of the General, who, like Boston Custer, accompanied the command as a sightseer, was also killed. Mark Kellogg, of the St. Paul and Bismarck press, the only correspondent who accompanied the Custer column, nearly succeeded in making his escape. The mule he rode was too slow, however, and he was finally overtaken and shot down. Had he succeeded in getting away, his fame would have rivaled that of the explorer, Stanley.

Among the many distinguished people who fell in that dreadful conflict was Brevet-colonel Keogh, who had previously fought for the pope under Lamoriciere, in Italy, and who attained the rank of colonel in the volunteer service, because of gallant and meritorious conduct throughout the Civil War. He was a noble-hearted gentleman—the *beau ideal* of a cavalry commander—and the very soul of valor. There also died Captain Calhoun, Custer's brother-in-law; Captain Yates, Col. W. W. Cook, the regimental adjutant; Lieutenants Crittenden, Smith, Riley, Harrington, McIntosh and several others.

Reno crossed the Little Big Horn, accompanied by some of the scouts, and charged down the valley a considerable distance. He finally halted in the timber and was, as he subsequently claimed, attacked by superior numbers. He remained in position but a short time, when he thought it advisable to retreat across the river and take up a position on the bluffs. This movement was awkwardly executed, and, in scaling the bluffs, several officers and enlisted men were killed and wounded. The Indians, as is always the case when white troops retreat before them, became very bold, and succeeded in dragging more than one soldier from the saddle. Captain De Rudio, an Italian officer, exiled from his country for political reasons, and a scout, unable to keep up with Reno's main body, concealed themselves in the brush, and the Indians passed and repassed so close to them that they could have touched the savages by merely putting out their hands. They were fortunate in remaining undiscovered, and joined Reno on the 27th, after the arrival of Terry and Gibbon.

Col. F. W. Benteen, now retired and residing at Atlanta Ga., has, at the request of the author, given the following statement relative to the movements of his battalion after parting from the main command:

"There was to have been no connection between Reno, McDougall and myself in Custer's order. I was sent off to the left several miles from where Custer was killed to actually hunt up some more Indians. I set out with my battalion of three troops, bent on such purpose, leaving the remainder of the regiment, nine troops, at a halt and dismounted. I soon saw, after carrying out the order that had been given me by Custer, and two other orders which were sent to me by him, through the sergeant-major of the regiment and the chief trumpeter, at different times, that the Indians had too much 'horse sense' to travel over the kind of country I had been sent to explore, unless forced to; and concluded that my battalion would have plenty of work ahead with the others. Thus, having learned all that Custer could expect, I obliqued to the right to strike the trail of the main column, and got into it just ahead of McDougall and his pack train.

I watered the horses of my battalion at a morass near the side of the road, and the advance of McDougall's 'packs' got into it just as I was 'pulling out' from it. I left McDougall to get his train out in the best manner he could, and went briskly on, having a presentiment that I'd find hot work very soon. Well, *en route*, I met two orderlies with messages—one for the commanding officer of the 'packs' and one for myself. The messages read: 'Come on. Be quick' and 'Bring packs;' written and signed by Lieutenant Cook, adjutant of the regiment. Now, knowing that there were no Indians between the packs and the main column, I did not think it necessary to go back for them—some seven or eight miles—nor did I think it worth while waiting for them where the orders found me, so I pushed to the front at a trot and got there in time to save Reno's * outfit.' The rest you know."

Reno, Benteen and McDougall, having effected a junction, fortified themselves on the bluffs and "stood off " the whole Indian outfit, which laid close siege to them, until the 27th. Several desperate charges of the savages on the position were handsomely repulsed. The troops, especially the wounded, suffered terribly from thirst, and during the night a few daring soldiers succeeded in getting some water out of the river in their camp kettles, at the peril of their lives. One of those brave men was Mr. Theodore Golden, then of the 7th Cavalry, and now a resident of Janesville, Wisconsin.

The situation of the closely beleagured troops was growing desperate, when the infantry and light artillery column of General Gibbon, which was accompanied by General Terry, came in sight on the morning of the

27th. The soldiers of Reno, at this inspiring vision, swarmed out over the rough-and-ready breastworks, cheering the heroes of Fort Fisher and Petersburg vociferously. Many wept for joy and the chivalrous Terry and the gallant Gibbon did everything in their power to cheer up the wearied soldiers in their hour of misfortune. The Indians did not attempt any further attack after the rescuing party arrived. They, too, were tired out, and had expended a vast quantity of ammunition. They drew off toward the mountains, first burning such irremovable impedimenta as remained in their village. A part of their tepees had been burned in the fight with Custer. General Gibbon, after a brief rest, set out to see what had become of that officer. Reno's men felt certain that something dreadful had happened to their comrades, because during the afternoon of the 25th and the morning of the 26th they had recognized the guidons of the 7th Cavalry, which the savages were waving in an ecstasy of triumph. General Gibbon had to march several miles before he came upon the field of blood. The sight that met his eyes was a shocking one. The bluffs were covered with the dead bodies of Custer's men, all stripped naked, and mostly mutilated in the usual revolting manner. The General's corpse was found near the summit of the bluff, surrounded by the bodies of his brothers and most of the officers of his command. The Indians, who had recognized his person, and who respected his superb courage, forebore from insulting his honored clay by the process of mutilation. The 7th Infantry, General Gibbon's regiment, buried the gallant dead where they fell, marking the graves of all that could be identified. Custer's remains, and those of his relatives, together with those of most of the officers, have since been removed. The brave General is buried at West Point, from which he graduated, and on which his glorious career and heroic death have reflected immortal luster.

Three hundred and fifteen enlisted men, and seventeen commissioned officers, together with several civilians, scouts and others, perished in this unfortunate battle. Charley Reynolds, the scout, whose name is still a household word upon the plains, fell dead by the side of his beloved chief.

After performing the sad duty of burying the dead, the wounded were placed on mule litters, and Generals Terry and Gibbon, slowly and sadly, retraced their way to Rosebud landing, on the Yellowstone, where, like Crook, they awaited reinforcements, and made no forward movement until August.

CHAPTER XV

MERRITT'S FIGHT ON THE WAR BONNET

On July 12th the Snake Indians, 213 men, commanded by their grand old chief, Washakie—an Indian who greatly resembled the Rev. Robert Collyer, except for the darkness of his complexion—and his two sons, rejoined us, according to promise. They were welcome, as we had been seriously annoyed every night, owing to the enfilading of our camp by small parties of Sioux from the woods in the foot-hills. They did little damage, but they rendered the herding of our horses and mules more difficult. One night a Sioux warrior, more daring than his comrades, stole in between our pickets and attempted to run off some horses. He was discovered in time. Several shots were fired. The whole camp was alarmed, and there was a rattle of fire-arms, in the dead hour of night, from one end of our lines to the other. But the nimble Sioux escaped in the darkness, leaving his hunting-knife behind him. He got none of our animals.

On July 13th our wagon train arrived from Fetterman, escorted by seven companies of infantry from the 4th, 9th and 14th Regiments. These, with the companies that had remained with Crook, made a respectable battalion of well-seasoned foot soldiers. Among the officers who joined us with this detachment was Captain Burke, of the 14th, a very popular man. But with the wagon train there also came the devil, in the shape of a peddler who sold whisky. Two abandoned females, disguised as mule drivers, also came into camp. Such of the soldiers as had money got drunk with amazing promptitude; but they were not many. General Crook got angry when he learned what was going on, ordered, the whisky barrels seized and the harlots put under arrest, to be sent back with the first train. A captain got intoxicated on duty, neglected to place his pickets properly, was tried in the field, deprived of his command, and ordered, under arrest, to Fort Fetterman. This gallant but unfortunate soldier, for whom I entertained a sincere regard, was subsequently dismissed from the service, that being the finding of the field court martial. I suppose there was no way out of it, but I have always considered the sentence too severe. The pickets are always commanded, in the immediate sense, by good sergeants, and our non-commissioned officers are the best in the world. Therefore the danger from the captain's neglect was not great; but, of course, discipline had to be maintained. I wish the court martial had had the power to order the whisky peddler flogged. He was the greater culprit of the two. The severity in the case mentioned had the effect of restoring order, and thenceforth no officer touched whisky, chiefly because there was none to touch except what the surgeons had in their medicine chests. At this time I changed my mess to Troop A, 3d Cavalry, then commanded by First Lieutenant Joseph Lawson, an Irish Kentuckian, and as gallant an old gentleman as ever drew a sword. He was an original in every way, and joined the Union army, on principle, at a time when nearly all his neighbors of fighting age were donning the rebel gray. Lawson was absolutely without fear, but his many peculiarities induced his brother officers to quiz him when they had nothing else to do. He bore it all with supreme good nature, and, on the day of battle, showed the whole brigade that an officer need not always hail from West Point in order to gain that place in the affections of his soldiers which dauntless courage alone can win.

It was, I think, on July 14th that General Crook was surprised by the appearance in his camp of a sergeant named Bell, and two private soldiers, named Evans and Stewart, of the 7th Infantry, who came with despatches from General Terry. They also brought details of the Custer fight, with which we were already familiar. Those brave men traveled at night and lay by in the day time, so as to avoid any parties of the

Sioux who might be prowling around the country. They had come from Rosebud landing, on the Yellowstone, where Terry's force then lay, and had crossed no large Indian trail, of recent formation, while *en route*. This convinced the General that the main body of the hostiles was still in the locality where Custer had fallen, and where the Sibley Scout had located them. Crook was very reticent at this period of the campaign, but, judging by subsequent events, I think he delayed moving against the Sioux until the 5th Cavalry could arrive to reinforce him, or, perhaps, he had arranged some combination with Terry, as the latter's three soldiers were sent back with despatches, two days after their arrival in our camp. I was glad to learn, subsequently, that they reached their destination without misadventure.

The General employed his scouts and Indians in reconnoitering the enemy, whose hunting parties they could see down Tongue river nearly every day. Crook was very impatient to attack, but our cavalry horses were, for the most part, in poor condition, and he wished to have the assistance of General Merritt's fresh and splendid regiment, before making a forward movement, which he wished to be decisive. I know that General Crook afterward regretted this delay, because the brilliant General Merritt, with his 5th Cavalry, was detained by an unexpected movement of the Cheyennes at Red Cloud agency, and had to do battle with them on War Bonnet creek. Maj. T. H. Stanton, of the pay department, brought information to Merritt, on Saturday, July loth, that eight hundred warriors of the band mentioned, fully armed and equipped, would leave the agency early on Sunday morning for the purpose of joining the hostiles in the Big Horn region.

Captain Charles King, U.S.A., then with the 5th Cavalry, thus clearly defines the situation in his excellent description of the operation: "To continue on his (Merritt's) march to Fort Laramie and let them go would have been gross, if not criminal, neglect. To follow by the direct road to the reservation, sixty-five miles away, would have been simply to drive them out and hasten their movement. Manifestly there was but one thing to be done, to throw himself across their path and capture or drive them back, and to do this he must, relatively speaking, march over three sides of a square while they were traversing the fourth, and must do it undiscovered."

Well, General Merritt did it undiscovered. He is a man of quick decision, and soon had seven troops of his gallant regiment in rapid motion to intercept the enterprising Cheyennes at their favorite crossing on War Bonnet creek. Buffalo Bill accompanied him as chief of scouts. After a difficult night march, Merritt had his command in position at dawn, and succeeded in keeping it perfectly concealed. Lieutenant Hall, his quartermaster, marched all night to overtake him, and his wagons were plainly visible, some miles away, at sunrise. A large body of Indians, watching the wagons, was visible also. The train drew nearer, the Indians following it up behind the bluffs, so as to be out of view, but this action on their part inadvertently exposed them to Merritt, of whose presence they were utterly unconscious. The General waited for the proper moment to strike, and it came when two mounted couriers, evidently detached from the train, came riding along the trail not far from where he was lying in wait. The Indians, impatient for blood, swooped down upon the two soldiers, but Merritt was too quick for them. He sent forward a small party to check the charge of the Cheyennes. Buffalo Bill was in the van, and reaped the brightest laurels of his adventurous life that morning, by slaying Yellow Hand, the Indian leader, in single combat. The other Cheyennes came on rapidly to the assistance of their friends, and then Merritt, unmasking his whole force, under Carr and Mason, hurled it upon them like a thunderbolt. The savages were taken totally by surprise, and were driven back upon the agency in wild disorder. They thought Merritt must have dropped from the clouds. He followed them to the agency and placed them under an effective guard, after which he renewed his march to reinforce General Crook.

Merritt's action on the War Bonnet was worthy of his well-won fame as a general, but it prevented him from joining Crook's command until the beginning of August, and by that time the Sioux, having exhausted nearly all the game at the base of the mountains, made a general break for the north, scattering themselves over many trails so as to confuse pursuit.

About July 20th General Crook sent a man named Kelly —a hanger-on of the pack train—with despatches to General Terry, informing the latter, as I was told, of his probable future course of action, and leaving it optional with him to make a junction of the two commands or not. The

General offered Kelly a small escort, but he declined with thanks and told me, afterward, that nothing less than a regiment would be of any use, whereas by going alone and on foot, he could travel all night, sleep in the undergrowth on the streams he would follow in the daytime, and thus reach his destination in safety. "You see," said Kelly, "I am fairly familiar with the country, and can guide myself, when it ain't cloudy, by the stars. When I can't see the stars, I can follows the canons, and I cannot run into an Indian village, because their dogs always bark at night and so give warning of their whereabouts. Indians never keep watch on dark nights, leastways the Sioux don't, and I know what I'm talking about. Another thing, I won't be bothered with a horse, or a mule either. More men have lost their lives on this frontier through their horses whinnying to the Indian ponies, out of cover, or through the mules braying than through any other cause. Then an Indian will go to hades after a horse, but when it's a man afoot, and he carries a good gun, Mr. Indian is not so eager to follow him up, because the man afoot has the advantage of cover. Of course if I ran into a whole heap of Indians, that would be a different matter. I'd get through all right anyhow, never you fear.

Kelly was an eccentric fellow, young, tall and well built. He was to receive good pay for his mission, but it took him a day or two to fully make up his mind. He started out one evening, wearing only moccasins on his feet, but the cacti pierced the deer hide and he returned for his shoes. He started again, Gruard accompanying him some distance. At last Kelly saw, or thought he saw, an Indian on a bluff ahead of him. "What am I going to do with that fellow?" he inquired of Frank. "Better go up there and ask him," replied the scout. Kelly turned back again, but he made a third attempt, and nobody expected him to succeed in it; yet he did. He followed out his own programme—marched down the Rosebud canon in the night time, and slept during the day. Finally, after dodging some Indian villages, he reached the Yellowstone, and, aided by a log, floated down to where General Terry's camp was situated and delivered his despatches. This I learned after we met General Terry in August. I inquired for Kelly, whom I found with the wagon train, cleaning a rifle, and he succinctly related, as given above, the story of his remarkable adventure. He had determined, if he fell by accident into the hands of the Sioux, to play off as a madman, because the savages rarely ever injure a maniac, whom they regard as being under the special protection of the Great Spirit. Kelly, in my opinion, was near enough to the crazy line to play the role to the entire satisfaction of the Indians.

We learned with no little dismay, about the end of July, that General Crook, when he would resume the campaign, intended to abandon his tents and bivouac his command during the remainder of the season. He would also rely upon his pack train only, allowing no man to carry more than a single blanket, and limiting clothing of every kind to the most meager dimensions. Toward the end of the month four Crow Indians came in from Terry's camp, and reported the Sioux still in strong parties around the Little Big Horn and the northern tributaries of Tongue river. General Crook, at this news, became very impatient to attack, and immediately made a movement some ten miles to the northwestward, along the foot-hills of the great range. The scouts saw several outlying parties of Indians, but not the main body. The General became convinced that the savages were playing some trick, and, seemingly, determined to attack them with his inferior forces. He became very restless, and, quite evidently, was much annoyed by the slow advance of Merritt, for which he could not then account. Merritt, as has already been shown, was not in fault, but, on the contrary, had, by his bold diversion on War Bonnet creek, prevented a most potent reinforcement of the hostiles by the discontented Cheyennes of the agencies. No advices concerning General Merritt's action had reached our camp, so that we were all profoundly ignorant at that period of the great service which he had rendered.

General Crook, under the circumstances, appeared to be greatly exasperated. He seemed to swing, like a pendulum, between a desire to fight at and cost and an innate feeling that to risk a battle with an outnumbering band of savages so recently and signally victorious, would be very rash, and might, as in the case of the gallant Custer, result in disaster. Orders were actually given to march directly on the Little Big Horn and engage the Sioux, when, on the afternoon of August 2d, a courier from Merritt arrived announcing that he was approaching rapidly at the head of ten troops of the excellent 5th Cavalry. This courier was Charley White, the familiar friend of Buffalo Bill, a tall, stout, fair-complexioned, long-haired, pock-marked man of about thirty-five, whose chief desire was to imitate the celebrated "Bill" in every particular. Buffalo Bill was a great favorite with General Sheridan, and generally accompanied that immortal hero whenever he went to hunt, or scout, upon the plains. On one occasion Sheridan was annoyed to find that "Bill" had gone East to arrange for the exhibition which has since become world famous as the Wild West Show. Charley White appeared instead. "Who the are you?" asked Sheridan, in his abrupt, impetuous way. "When Cody is not here," replied Charley, "*I* am Buffalo Bill."

"The d you are!" cried Sheridan. Buffalo Chip, you mean!".

Charley felt crushed, and the unfortunate nickname clung to him until the day of his gallant death at Slim Buttes.

After delivering his message to our General, Charley White rode around our camp and was hailed by soldiers, packers and train men by the title bestowed upon him by Fighting Phil.

"You fellows look as if you didn't have any chuck (the frontier word for rations) in a month," said he to Tom Moore.

"Get off your horse," said Tom, "and we'll relieve your famine in a pair of minutes."

White accordingly dismounted, and we all surrounded him. He related the whole of Buffalo Bill's exploit with great glee, and made us think that the days of Achilles and Hector had been renewed in Merritt's fight en War Bonnet creek. Poor fellow! Buffalo Bill seemed to him "a big. ger man" than all the generals of the United States army.

The courier from Merritt had met Crook's brigade on the northernmost branch of Tongue river—about one good march from the field where Custer died. It was understood in the camp, but on what authority I now forget, that Crook had arranged a rendezvous with Terry on that stream for the very day on which Merritt's advance was reported. But the hero of Fort Fisher failed to keep the tryst. The Sioux scouting parties had hovered around us, at a safe distance, for days. They avoided fighting, but fired the mountains and the plains, for miles upon miles, making it next to impossible to observe any object, however prominent, through the thick and pungent cloud of smoke. The scouts of our command found it difficult to determine whether the hostiles had retired into the Big Horn fastnesses or retreated toward the British possessions. Finally those experts of the wilderness came to the conclusion that Sitting Bull had adopted the latter alternative. They had located one broad and well defined trail, which led toward the north, but they also suspected that the hostiles had left a strong war party near the mountains to observe our movements and gather up what game they could find in that fecund region.

General Crook, impatient to form a junction with Merritt, and feeling sure that the Indians were trying to outwit him, moved out with all his force from Tongue river camp on the morning of August 3d, and fell in with Herritt's column on Goose creek, after a march of twenty-five miles, that evening. This movement raised our force to nearly 2,000 fighting men, most of them in excellent condition. Our wagons, including those of General Merritt, amounted to160, and it was determined to park them all, and place them under command of Major Furey, with orders to retire on Forts Fetterman and Laramie by easy marches. The General decided not to detail any troops to guard the wagons, as the discharged soldiers, drivers and hangers-on, all well armed, numbered fully 200 men—sufficient to defend the train against any ordinary party of hostile Indians.

Orders were issued that no man should take with him a change of clothing, but each person was allowed to carry 100 rounds of ammunition and four days' rations on his horse or person. A single blanket and a saddle blanket, with a poncho, if he were lucky enough to possess one, must serve for covering. The saddle always constitutes the pillow of the cavalryman, and the knapsack of the foot soldier, on the plains. Lieutenant Bubb, chief of the commissariat, with Tom Moore, chief packer, as assistant, was placed in command of the pack train. It carried fifteen days' rations for each soldier and all the reserve ammunition.

It blew great guns on the night of August 3, 1876, and more than half the tents were leveled to the ground, greatly to the discomfort of the weary troops. It was to be our last night under canvas for some time, and rude old Boreas made us feel his power. A terrible red glow lit up the clouded midnight sky, and, looking westward in amazement, we saw the whole front of the Big Horn mountains on fire! Although the conflagration was many miles distant from our camp, the strong west wind bore the pungent timber smoke upon us in blinding volumes, and countless wild animals, driven frantic by fear, careered through the fiery darkness, like beings of another world, some of them uttering weird sounds of unreasoning terror. It was a superb, if awe compelling, scene. The prairies, ignited by the burning brands from the sierra, were also in a flame, and preparations were made to fight fire with fire, in Indian fashion, if it became necessary. Our Indian allies burned over a large belt of prairie west of our camp early in the evening, so that we felt comparatively secure. But the smoke and cinders were stifling, and few could sleep in comfort under such conditions.

Generals Crook and Merritt, together with the various battalion commanders, held a long consultation during the evening. I had had time to observe the new arrivals in the course of the day, and they impressed me favorably. General Merritt was quite tall, rather spare and nearly beardless. He had a florid complexion, keen eyes, of grayish hue, and small, but comely and resolute, features. General Carr, then lieutenant colonel of the 5th Cavalry, was short, fairly stout, full bearded, and lavish, while in conversation, of graceful and energetic gestures. The other officers, I learned subsequently, took very little part in the deliberations. Before the council broke up, Buffalo Bill, the Hon. W. F. Cody, was summoned by the General in command. He was then in the prime of a matchless manhood. In form, as in face, he had hardly his peer on the American continent. He was dressed in full frontier costume—buckskin breeches, long riding boots, blue shirt, colored neckerchief and broad, white sombrero, with the usual "snake" band. His long, silky brown hair, with a suspicion of dark auburn glinting through it, fell over his shoulders in graceful profusion, and his dark, exceedingly expressive and handsome eyes seemed to blaze with martial ardor. As the meeting of the officers was a council of war, I could not get within privileged ear shot, and I knew military etiquette too well to make myself intrusive; but I met Cody immediately after adjournment, and had quite a long talk with him. He would not, of course, say anything about what had passed in the General's tent, but I remember that he felt doubtful of striking any Indians with the force we then had.

"If they want to find Indians," said he, "let them send

a battalion, which I am willing to guide, and I'll engage we'll have our fill of fighting before reaching the Little Missouri. The hostiles will never face this outfit, unless they get it in some kind of a hole, and there are plenty of them in this country. Crook ain't going to run into them? though. He served in Arizona too long for that."

"Have you scouted here before?" I asked of the formidable frontiersman.

"Not exactly here," said he," but a man who is educated to prairie life is at home anywhere. Lieutenant Lawson, there, can tell you how I once guided him correctly through a country I had never set eyes on before."

Mr. Lawson nodded a cordial assent, and Bill retired to find such repose as he could under the circumstances.

CHAPTER XVI

MARCHING IN DARKNESS

Daylight came at last, accompanied by the usual shrill bugle-call, and the hoarse harangue of the Snake "head-soldier "as he roused the sleeping savages from their lairs to look after their neighing ponies. Clouds partially obscured the sun as we tightened our horse girths, or swallowed our scanty allowance of ration coffee, bacon, and hardtack. All our superfluous baggage was rolled into bundles and turned over to Major Furey, while we, like the highwaymen of old, had nothing except what we had on our frames and what we could impose on our sorry-looking steeds. The poor horses looked supremely miserable. Even those of the newly arrived 5th were completely played out by the scout in pursuit of the Cheyennes—the very thing that allowed the main body of the enemy to escape from the Big Horn without a battle. As for the animals of the 2d and 3d Cavalry, they had had no grain or corn since the beginning of June, and at least a third of them looked well fitted for the boneyard.

The infantry, under Colonel Chambers, appeared stout and soldierly and moved off at a swinging step three hours ahead of us. General Merritt became chief of cavalry. Royall retained his old command of the 2d and 3d, and Carr led the 5th. The twenty-five companies were formed into five battalions, the 3d and 5th being strongest, having two each and the 2d one. At 7 o'clock we were all in the saddle and moved in three columns *via* Prairie Dog creek to Tongue river, following the track of the guides and the infantry.

Frank Gruard and Buffalo Bill were in. advance with a select body of scouts. Colonel Stanton, paymaster, had chief command of the irregulars, while Major Randall, with the Chief Washakie, directed the Snake Indians. 'We made about twenty miles that day, passing over the old campground of June 9th, where the Sioux gave us that first salute. Everything around the place looked desolate, and it seemed to me as if years had elapsed since I saw it last. Since Merritt joined we had adopted the plan of forming a circular camp, with our horses picketed in the center during the night; so that in case of an attack no stampede of our stock could be effected.

To detail all the incidents of a march, would be very tiresome, both to me and to my readers, so I will glance only at the chief features of our second northward pilgrimage. We marched twenty-five miles further down Tongue river on August 6th, crossing that sinuous stream—perhaps "the crookedest in the world—no less than seventeen times, which made the march tell severely on our admirable infantry, who, nevertheless, got into camp just as soon as we did. Our course lay through Tongue river canon, one of the most rugged and dangerous passes in that land of difficult and interminable defiles. The sun was hotter than on any march during the campaign, and the thermometer must have ranged at 105 in the shade from 8 A. M. to sundown.

The men converted Tongue river into a bathing reservoir, for our soldiers lost no opportunity in the way of keeping their bodies clean, especially when they marched without even a change of underclothing.

Failing to cut across the Sioux trail at that distance down the Tongue, Crook determined to move westward, through a dry canon, to Rosebud creek, and move down that rivulet some distance, as the southern part of the valley was a favorite Indian resort. This gave us another twenty-five mile march over a very broken country, full of rocky bluffs and clumps of pine trees, and having hardly sufficient water to refresh our already used-up horseflesh. Finally, after halting innumerable times, because of the intolerable heat and dust, which nearly asphyxiated man and beast, we reached again the famous Rosebud, some six miles north of our fighting ground of June 17th, and about a mile and a half from the point in the canon to which Mills' battalion of the 3d Cavalry penetrated on the day of the conflict. Subsequent investigation showed what a dreadful fate we escaped by obeying Crook's order to file out of the trap by our left flank. Immense piles of felled trees in our path and on the sides of that savage ravine showed where the Sioux had lain in ambush for our approach. Half a mile further on and not a man of our battalion would have come out alive. The five companies of the 2d, following to support us, would have been massacred without fail, for there was no room to deploy or to rally. The Indians held the timber barricades in front and flank. They would have closed upon our unguarded rear, and another horror would have been added to the long and ghastly catalogue of Indian-American warfare. However, a miss is as good as a mile, and we felt duly thankful that we escaped being the awful example of that unfortunate campaign. We camped in a most beautiful valley, hemmed in by thickly timbered hills, which were blazing like so many volcanoes, the Indians having fired the woods, either by accident or design. That portion of the Rosebud vale is called "the Indian Paradise," and truly, for many miles, it deserves that heavenly name. Two miles north of where we bivouacked we found the site of the mammoth Indian village, to protect which Sitting Bull fought on the 17th of June. It was situated in an expanse of the valley two miles square, and protected by steep, rock-guarded eminences on every side. Crook's force could never have captured and held such a position, defended as it must have been, judging by the number of lodges, by at least 3,500 fierce, desperate, and well-armed warriors.

The scouts went down the Rosebud fifteen miles, and returned in the evening with intelligence of a fresh Indian trail, leading diagonally from the Little Big Horn river toward the Yellowstone. This cheered us up somewhat, and we lay down to sleep with the hope of a speedy encounter and a quick return, victorious, of course, to civilized existence. But, as usual, "man proposes and God disposes." When the reveille sounded on the morning of the 8th, no man could see his neighbor, owing to an abominable alliance between the fog and smoke. We felt our way down through the old Indian village for a few hours, and then Crook ordered a halt, hoping for a gale to clear away the atmospheric obscurity. We lay by until 6 o'clock that evening, when an obliging breeze sprang up, and everything came out of the gloom smiling and picturesque. We knew that we had a night march before us to make up for lost time; so when the orderlies came galloping along the lines with orders to saddle up, we were not taken by surprise. Still following the Rosebud, we marched at dark, the cavalry on the flanks and the infantry and pack train in the center, but not far in advance, so that all might be within supporting distance. The moon did not rise for some hours, and the evening was dark as Erebus. Intense silence pervaded the line of march, and not a sound was heard but the solemn tramp of the cavalry columns, advancing through the gloom, except when a solitary jackass, attached to the pack train, gave vent to his perturbed feelings in a bray, which, amid the mountain echoes, sounded like the laughter of a legion of mocking devils. The lonesome donkey repeated his performance so often and so loudly that he had to be muzzled, as he appeared determined to apprise the Sioux, if any were within hearing, of our approach. The mules were heard from occasionally, but, on the whole, their conduct was decorous and patriotic. Does any reader remember his experience during a night march in total darkness? Of course thousands of my readers marched with Sherman and with Thomas, and know all about it. But a night march in the Indian wilderness of the North is one of the most impressive incidents of war. It is weird, *outre*, awe-inspiring. The vastness of untamed nature is around you, and its influence is insensibly felt. You are on the track of a mysterious enemy. The country over which you are marching is to you an unread chapter. You see something like a black shadow moving in advance. You are conscious that men and animals are moving within a few paces, and yet you cannot define any particular object, not even your horse's head. But you hear the steady, perpetual "tramp—tramp —tramp "of the iron-hoofed cavalry, broken by an occasional stumble and the half-smothered imprecation of an irate trooper; the jingle of carbines and sling-belts, and the snorting of the horses as they grope their way through the eternal dust, which the rider can feel in his throat, like the thick, stinking vapor of a champion London fog. Once in a while a match, struck by a soldier to light his pipe, would flash in the gloom, like a huge fire-fly, and darkness would again assert itself. In this manner we proceeded for quite a time, when, all of a sudden, a tremendous illumination sprang up from behind us and lit almost the whole line of the valley. Reflected in it, we could see the arms glistening as our battalion moved steadily along, and the bluffs, left and right, seemed like giants keeping watch and ward upon the pass. We turned in our saddles to observe the phenomenon, and beheld a flood of flame, which, rushing like a charging battle-line storming some fated town, burst over the mountain crest behind us, twenty miles away, flinging its lurid banner to the very arch of the firmament, almost as if the gates of hell had been flung open to allow "the demons down under the sea" to throw defiance at the power which hurled them from the heavens during the apocryphal battle which the genius of a Milton has portrayed in immortal words. I have seen some magnificent freaks of fire in my time, including the Chicago disaster and the conflagrations in the Big Horn range, but that sudden outburst of flame in the Plutonian gloom of Rosebud valley surpassed, in lurid splendor, anything that I have ever imagined or beheld. It was something to be witnessed only once in a lifetime. Soon afterward the moon rose on our right, and its chaste luster tamed down the infernal glow on the southward hills. We pressed forward until 2 o'clock, when we halted and lay down under our single blankets to catch the hasty sleep of Indian campaigners.

CHAPTER XVII

CROOK AND TERRY MEET

Next day we made twenty miles through one of the roughest countries I ever traveled over, still following the Rosebud. It looked like the bottom of an extinct lake. We were pursuing the Indian trail, but the Sioux had burned almost every blade of grass behind them, so that our horses were nearly starved. That entire section of the valley is a huge coal-bed—one of the most extensive in America, and this accounts for the peculiar sterility of the surface soil. We saw huge lumps of coal sticking out of the sides of the canyon, while the ground in many places was black as ink from genuine coal dust. Someday, I thought, when the Sioux are all in the happy hunting grounds, this valley will rival the Lehigh of Pennsylvania. But my observations of coal did not blind me to the fact that the weather had taken a change for the worse. A cold, disagreeable rain, accompanied by a chilling north wind, set in, and, after a tramp of twenty-two miles, we halted in a cross canon, where, fortunately, some grass remained, lit fires amid the gigantic rocks, cut into fantastic columns and corners by the action of waters which had subsided countless ages ago, and made ourselves as comfortable as it was possible to be in the most inhospitable looking country outside of Iceland or Siberia. Honestly, that part of the world looked utterly unfinished, just like a half-built house, raw, dirty and cheerless. Darwin might have been able to find that "missing link" somewhere along the Rosebud. Soon after we halted, Capt. Jack Crawford (Buffalo Bill's friend) and Captain Graves, of Montana, rode up to our dismal, smoky camp fire, and handed me some private letters, for which I was duly grateful. The gallant fellows left Fort Fetterman with despatches for Crook, on July 28th, reached our wagon train four days later, and, despite every warning, had followed our tortuous trail by Prairie Dog, Tongue river, the dry canon and Rosebud, until they came up with us in that home of storms. The night came on, cold as midwinter, and we, provided with only summer outfit, shivered like palsy patients. It seemed to me as if the combined winds from "a' the airts" had concentrated on that wretched spot, to give us sinners a foretaste of the inferno. Heat and dust are bad; but cold and mud take the vim out of a fellow, and make him think of houses and stoves. We had seen neither since May 29th. Nevertheless, the morning of August 10th, dawned on a comparatively happy set of mortals, for we were nearing the famed Yellowstone river, and that would, at least, be a change of scene. We had marched only twelve miles, however, when some of the scouts rode back to inform the General that the Sioux trail had suddenly diverged toward Tongue river. We were then marching over a portion of the route followed by Custer on his last fatal scout. His trail was cut deep into the soil and still looked fresh. We halted on some high, grassy ground above the creek, at the point where it turns due north, where we allowed the horses to have a lunch. Then we moved northward, and had not proceeded more than a mile, when we observed a mighty column of dust, indicating a large body of men and animals in motion, in our front, about three miles down the Rosebud. "They are Sioux!" exclaimed some of our officers. "If so, you will immediately hear music," others replied. Just then "a solitary horseman "separated himself from our vanguard, and rode like the devil in a gale of wind down the river. It was Buffalo Bill, the most reckless of all frontiersmen. "He's going to reconnoitre," remarked Colonel Royall. "That's Bill's style, you know." At this point a handsome young Shoshone Indian—the only one of the reds for whom I entertained a shadow of liking—rode up and ejaculated. "How?" He looked down the road, and his piercing eyes glittered like jet in the sunbeams. "What's that?" I asked, pointing to the pillar of dust. "Heap pony-soldier (cavalry). No Sioux—Sioux far off—run when pony soldier and good Indian come strong—heap strong now. Sioux no good—run away. Ugh!" and the young savage, with a ferocious grin distorting his comely features, lashed up his pony and disappeared over the ridge. Within a few minutes Buffalo Bill, his long hair streaming on the wind, came galloping madly back to our lines. "What is it, Bill? "asked Colonel Royall. "Terry and his outfit," replied the scout. "He's got wagons enough to do an army corps. Were we going to catch Indians with such lumber as that?" and he dashed off to see Crook. It was true. Terry had been three days marching from the Yellowstone, thirty miles from where we halted. Crook immediately ordered us into camp, and Terry who, mistaking us for Sioux, because of the panic of his Crow scouts who saw some Snake Indians in our van, had formed line of battle, continued to advance. The General and his staff rode up first and joined Crook and his officers. It appeared to be a cordial meeting, although I am rather of opinion that Crook intended to operate alone, and met Terry "just by chance." General Terry was then a fine looking man, about fifty years of age. He had a genial face, but looked like a fighter.

The principal thing that attracted my attention, and that of all our force, was the remnant of the 7th Cavalry. It came in, formed into seven small companies, led by Major Reno — a short, stout man, about fifty years old, with a determined visage, his face showing intimate acquaintance with the sun and wind. The horses were all in splendid condition, having been grain-fed all along; but many of the officers and men looked tired, dirty and disgusted — just as most of Crook's column had appeared for many weeks. The 2d Cavalry, four companies, called the Montana Battalion, under Maj. J. S. Brisbin, and a crowd of rather green infantry — most of them recently from Detroit — followed, and after them came a light field battery of four guns and a huge wagon train. The men of the respective commands saluted each other cordially, but there was no cheering or undue excitement of any kind. Every one felt that there was naught to cheer about. When you have seen one regiment of our soldiers in the field, you have seen all. There is hardly any difference in the calibre of the men, and, as for uniform, the absence thereof is a leading characteristic of the service. Perhaps this is all the better, for a more disfiguring costume than the fatigue dress of the United States army the imagination of the most diabolically inclined of existing tailors could not conceive. Our Indian allies, on the other hand, with their beautiful, glossy, abundant black hair, their ornamented "leggings," and flowing, richly -colored blankets, together with their sleek, fat forms, presented a most picturesque aspect. To be sure they were more or less troubled with parasites, but so we became in a few weeks, without a change of underclothes. It is a comfort to reflect that, probably, Julius Caesar, Pompey and Mark Antony picked "gray-backs" off their togas in olden times; that "the Little Corporal" certainly amused himself in driving the crawling enemy from his shirt about the morning of "Lodi's murderous bridge," and that General Grant, with characteristic phlegm, routed them from his body, by aid of blue ointment, when he started "the Rebs" out of Vicksburg. As a correspondent, I was doubly consoled to know that only one insect got into Washington from Manassas before "Bull Pun Russell," and that was the bug which occupied his hat when it was blown off his head while crossing the celebrated Long bridge. Excuse this chapter on vermin, but Scotia's favorite bard devoted one of his neatest sonnets to the same subject. When a young lady, full of romance, is inclined to fall in love with a dashing soldier, let her conjure up this picture: A summer morning in the wilderness. A hero with a single shirt, 300 miles from a laundress. A willow tree and the warrior depopulating said garment in the shade thereof.

The Crows, Snakes and Rees, when they met, had a grand howl in concert, their enthusiasm being in striking contrast with our indifference. In fact, the shadow of a coming fizzle was already upon us. Terry and Crook had a "big talk" that evening. The former did not wish to deprive Crook of command. The latter insisted that the senior should take his proper place. Finally he of Fort Fisher agreed to accept "the glory" thrust upon him, but said that General Crook should always share in his councils. The commander of our column looked the picture of disgust. "This command is now too large," he observed to a friend. "We shall find no Indians while such a force sticks together."

Among the newspaper men who either came up with or followed Terry's command, were James J. O'Kelly, now member of the British Parliament, of the New York *Herald*; "Phocion" Howard, of the Chicago *Tribune*, and Charles S. Diehl, of the Chicago *Times*. They accompanied Terry's column after it parted with ours on Powder river.

General Terry, impressed with Crook's idea of campaigning in light marching order, retaining his pack train, sent all his wagons back to

Rosebud landing, under the escort of General Nelson A. Miles and the 5th Infantry.

The combined columns, about 4,000 effective men, horse and foot, were ordered to march eastward to Tongue river, on the Indian trail, at daybreak. We marched, accordingly, about fifteen miles, reached Tongue river, and went into camp in one of the beautiful valleys that abound in that region. We found the skeleton of a murdered miner—a bullet-hole through his skull and shoulder-bone—and buried it. The man had been killed about the beginning of June, and coyotes had eaten the body, the clothing being quite fresh, and the hair on the head showing the mark made by the Sioux scalping knife. The hapless man's dead pony, which had been shot also, lay near him in a state of most offensive putrefaction. Such was the fate of him who sought for fortune in that demon-peopled land. That night a terrific storm of wind and rain came up. We had no tents, and had to sleep in the puddles. You can imagine how we passed the night. Water saturated us at every point, and the rain kept pouring down until the afternoon of the succeeding day, retarding our inarch, and making every man of the command feel as if possessed of a devil. This, however, is "glory," and no one must complain. Officers and men slept in rain and dirt, drank coarse coffee, and ate hardtack and raw bacon. All this is the concomitant of war and fame. The rays of the star of "glory "are made up of filth, hardship and disappointments. Fighting is the least of the evils attendant on a military career. And yet, the worst feature of a summer campaign is paradise itself compared with the untold miseries suffered by our troops when engaged in a winter hunt after Indians. But, after all, the best time to strike the savages is when snows are deep and pony locomotion almost impossible. To give some idea of the severity of the fall and winter in that region, let me recall the fact that General Connor, when operating against the Sioux in that same territory, in 18G0, had 300 horses frozen to death on the picket lines, the night of September 7th.   On August 12th and 13th we continued our northward march on the Tongue, losing horses every mile of the way. When we reached Pumpkin creek, about forty miles from the Yellowstone, we switched eastward toward Powder river. The rain and mud made the marching terrible, and some of Terry's young infantry lay down exhausted in the dirt. Many of them bad to be placed on pack-mules or carried on travois.

Even' company, almost, of the 2d, 3d and 5th Cavalry had to abandon or shoot used-up horses. We made fully thirty miles, over a most infernal country, before halting. Chambers "astonishing infantry," as Napier would have called them, made the full march, and not a man fell out of the ranks. In fact they reached camp, and were in bivouac, before ourselves. The Roman legions or the army of Austerlitz never made better time than the splendid detachments of the 4th,14th and 9th Infantry. They and their gallant officers deserve unstinted praise for their magnificent foot work. This so-called creek was a miserable stream, full of alkali, and about the color of the mud on city street crossings after a rainy spell. There was very little wood, and we had to sleep at night in pools of water and were thankful to get a chance to lie down even in that way.

We marched all day Tuesday, August 15th, along Pumpkin creek through a terrible section. The soil looked like the surface of a non-atmospheric planet, hard, repulsive, sterile. It made one's heart sick to look at the place. But there were strong marks of mineral wealth, especially iron and coal, along the route. I am convinced that all that part of Montana is a tremendous coal region, which, one day, will yield untold wealth to some enterprising corporations. This kind of land continued until we struck the Powder River valley, which, like all the valleys of the larger streams, is extremely fertile. But our animals were so exhausted that we hardly made more than a couple of miles an hour, on the average. The horses staggered in the columns by scores, and most of the men had to lead their animals during three-fourths of the march. Very frequently a played-out horse would fall, as if shot, and the rider was compelled either to abandon the equipments or pack them on a mule. All the led horses were in use, owing to frequent deaths of the line animals, and dozens of dismounted cavalrymen toiled painfully along, over steep, rugged hills, in the rear of the column. Our whole line of march from the Rosebud to the Powder and Yellowstone rivers was dotted with dead or abandoned horses. Some of the newly-enlisted infantry grew desperate—their feet bleeding and their legs swollen from the continuous tramp—and refused to move a step. They had to be mounted on the ponies of the friendly Indians and carried along. One man, an officer's cook, without saying a word to anyone, lay back under a tree to die. He was not missed for twelve hours, when General Terry, who is very kind hearted, sent back the Crow Indians and some cavalry to see what had become of the poor fellow. They found him a raving maniac, and bore him into camp strapped to an extra pom'. Many of the young foot-soldiers seemed injured for life. Some of Terry's men could not keep up at all. Gibbon's veterans marched like Romans. Chambers' men rivaled O'Leary and Weston. Taken all in all, Crook's column had the tougher material, except as regards horses. What chance had we of catching Indians with such beasts? The animal I rode was a fair specimen. His shoulder was a mass of scabs and blood. He stumbled at every step, and I had to lead him more than half the time. When I got on his back I made a bargain with him—he was to carry me and I was to keep him from falling and breaking both our necks. Yet this poor devil of a horse was a superb, prancing, fiery, and most untamed, steed compared with the ghastly skeletons that disfigured most of our cavalry companies. Such is Avar in the wilderness. Our government ought to have had a supply of fresh horses on the Yellowstone, so that we might follow hot on Sitting Bull's trail, which led direct to the Little Missouri river.

All Wednesday and Thursday we kept moving at snail's pace northward, along the glorious valley of Powder river, thickly timbered and covered with grass knee high. It has a uniform width of about four miles—the country on either side being sterile, except as regards mineral products. Finally, at 3 o'clock on the afternoon of August 17th, we sighted the famed Yellowstone, a majestic stream, wide and deep, and camped on the angle made by the junction of Powder river, (the left bank) with that fine inland water-thoroughfare. From that grand river the part of Montana and Wyoming good for anything will, undoubtedly, be settled. At 5 o'clock the steamboat "Far West" came up from Tongue river, and the soldiers ran, like a flock of overgrown children, to see it. The poor fellows had not seen steam since May 18th, and this glimpse of civilization reminded them of home. Some fresh, well dressed infantry were on board, together with a couple of cannon. Also there was a colored cabin girl—another reminder of "the States." Dinah modestly covered her eyes when she saw all of the soldiers who were not on picket or on the river bank, about half the command, nude in the water. Lieutenant Von Leutwitz, of the 3d Cavalry, had just got on his shirt, and was standing with his back toward the boat, when the waves, caused by the motion of the vessel, flew over him, swept away half his clothing and wet him thoroughly. He received a thundering cheer from "the boys," and ran up the bank *a la Adam* before the fig leaves, swearing strange German oaths and damning the Yellowstone from the bottom of his heart. Every man who marched from Rosebud and Goose creek washed his shirt, etc., allowed the garments to dry in the sun, and put them on without ironing. There was one great drawback to the common laundry—a dearth of soap. Despite of this, I felt comfort in knowing that I was a little less like a ground-hog. Why do not our gallant militia, when in their summer camps, practice the noble art of washing without soap for a few days?

In concluding a letter to the paper I represented, about August 18th, I said:

"I think I mentioned the fact that Crook insisted on Terry assuming command while the two expeditions hung together. Terry is, therefore, responsible. Crook feels awfully disgusted. Sitting Bull has played all of us a shabby trick. Like a greedy gambler, he has won a large stake, and then, when the chances are about equalized, he draws out and leaves us in the lurch. Probably I am disappointed in Mr. Bull, but he knows his own business best. I went to see Crook and his staff last night. Having no tents, it is rather difficult to discover the whereabouts of any one. After a long chase, I finally came upon a group of seedy-looking fellows—having all the appearance of brigands—sitting on the wet grass under a cottonwood tree. They were Crook and his staff. I interviewed them, but could not obtain much information. The general idea was to follow the trail to the Little Missouri, and then nobody knew where. This makes the affair extremely unpleasant for all concerned. I think the game is up, and that there will be little, if any, fighting. I close this letter with a feeling of disgust and disappointment.

"Incertitude is the order of the day at present. Many camp-followers, including some of the correspondents, are leaving the expedition. I have not yet made up my mind what is best for me to do. I hate to leave at this stage of the futile campaign, and yet, by remaining, I shall see very little else than mud, misery and rough country. One good battle and a decent wind up to this wretched business would just suit me now. But I fear very much that the last shot of this section of the campaign has been fired. This comes of the official imbecility which, at the outset, sent an insufficient force to fight a powerful enemy, and, in the end, sent green troops to impede our movements, and left us cavalry horses fit only for the purposes of a glue factory."

CHAPTER XVIII

UNDER A DELUGE

We were drying our saturated clothes on the bank of the Powder river, the filthiest stream in America or elsewhere, on the morning of August 24th. Thunder and "everlasting wet" had pursued us all the way from Tongue river camp, but the night of August 23, 1876. was the most utterly miserable so far experienced. Unfortunately, our camp had to be moved in order to give the horses fresh grass, and our temporary shelters had to be abandoned in the midst of a torrent of rain. There was no very dire necessity for the move, as General Terry had supplied our horses with grain for a few days, but the soldiers were obliged to follow the orders of the battalion commander all the same. The movement was attempted to be countermanded when too late to do any good, and we went into camp about 200 yards from our first bivouac, in some lowlands under a range of sand hills, flooded with water, and fully a mile from wood. Clothing and blankets were thoroughly soaked, and, having neither tents nor camp fires, most of the troops were in a most unenviable situation.

To keep dry was impossible, and to keep warm was equally so; for a cold north wind set in at nightfall as if to drive the water more mercilessly into our bones. The officer with whom I messed and myself made a desperate effort to sleep, but met with almost utter failure. Our one army blanket and leaky poncho were no protection against the solid sheet of rain fulling from the opaque clouds, and the eternal, infernal rat-tat-tat, growing faster and heavier each second, on the gum covering made us think that the devil was beating his famous tattoo for our especial benefit. Cold may be warded off. Heat can be modified in some way, but, without canvas, it is impossible to combat the terrible rainstorms of that region. The oldest of the soldiers, men who had served all through our great war and some of the wars of Europe, declared that they had experienced nothing more distressing, either under Havelock in India, Von Moltke in France and Germany, or Sherman in Georgia and the Carolinas. Vivid flashes of lightning, followed by tremendous peals of thunder, added satanic grandeur to the misery. All the artillery in the world could hardly have produced such an indescribable uproar. The horses drew their picket-pins from the sodden soil and stampeded, plunging helplessly around in the swamps. Something that felt like an elephant walked over my "bunk." I punched the creature with my carbine, and by the vigorous kick which it gave my saddle in return, I became aware of the presence of a scared pack-mule. The lightning revealed the wretched troops gathered on the sheltered side of the low hills, huddled in groups and vainly trying to keep up some animal heat. A few of their remarks came fitfully to my ears, and served to amuse me in some measure. One fellow had had enough of glory, and would either desert or secure his discharge before coming on another Indian campaign. Another damned whisky for leading him into the army.

"Now, George," said an Irish soldier, "wouldn't you just wish you had a little drop to mix with all this water?"

"No fear of you mixing it, Tim," George answered, "you always take it straight in Ireland."

"Bad luck to the ship that brought me over thin," Tim replied. "If I had taken my poor owld mother's advice and remained in Cashel it isn't like a drowned rat I'd be this night."

"Ooh, be J , this is the most G— damnablest outfit I ever struck in my twenty-five years of sarvice," said a Milesian veteran, in disgusted tones. "Divil shoot the ginerals and the shoulder-straps all around. Shure they have no more compassion on a poor crayture of a soldier than a wolf has on a lamb!"

"A tough old lamb, you are, Jerry, sure enough," said another warrior. "A wolf would have to howld his head a long way from the wall afore he could eat you."

"We can't have even coffee, and must eat our bacon raw to-night," lamented a native American. "The confounded sage-brush won't burn, and the d—d rain wont' let it."

In the midst of these flying remarks I suddenly fell asleep, and a woke, perhaps an hour later, to find water running over, under and all around me. To get up was useless, so I lay and soaked in my clothes until morning came, gray, cold and cheerless. Then I looked at Lieutenant Lawson, bundled up in his blanket beside me. He was just as badly off as I was, so we rose with great unanimity and made a break for Captain Meinhold's camp-fire, where we struggled with the rain-fiend for more than an hour. Everybody looked tired and haggard, but the situation was not without its ludicrous features. At about 7 o'clock the weather cleared a little, and then, seated on a stone, a captain could be seen wringing out his shirt tail, a lieutenant wrestling with his one pair of stockings, and the non-commissioned officers and privates helping each other to dry their overcoats and saddle-blankets. As for underclothing and shoes being wet, they were too well used to that to mind it much. I had slept in the rain several times on the trip, but the experience of that night was the nearest approach to hell upon earth that I have known.

At 10 o'clock, our fifteen days' rations being all packed, the order to march came, and Crook's column turned its back upon the Yellowstone. We marched up the west bank of Powder river, through unending coal-fields, about ten miles, and went into camp on high ground. General Terry had resolved to cut loose from us and cross to the left bank of the Yellowstone. Crook had determined to follow the Indian trail to the Little Missouri river, and as much farther as it might lead. The Snake and Crow Indians, appalled by the hardships which they clearly saw in store for them, abandoned the column the moment we faced up the Powder river. They knew they were safe in going home, because the Sioux and their allies had evacuated the Big Horn country. Buffalo Bill, who had theatrical engagements in the East, and three newspaper correspondents, who did not relish so much water on the outside, forsook us also, and started down the Yellowstone on the steamer. "Ute John," an Indian partially civilized, was the only redskin who remained with us, but all Crook's white, and most of his half-breed, scouts continued faithful.

The weather continued abominable as we resumed our march. We made another short march up Powder river on the 25th, and next day crossed to its right bank, and marched twenty miles toward the Little Missouri, halting on a branch of O'Fallon creek, which is distinguished by running through the most adhesive mud on the American continent. We were following the Indian trail discovered on the Rosebud, which our junction with General Terry's column prevented us from pursuing with greater alacrity. We reached O'Fallon creek proper on the 27th, and went into bivouac under a pelting shower. Several officers and soldiers began to show signs of approaching sickness, and a few cases of rheumatic and neuralgic fever were reported. The exposure told mostly on the older men, and several of these — notably Captains Andrews and Meinhold — did not long survive the hardships of that campaign. I was hardy enough, and felt very little inconvenience, except a sense of being abominably dirty. The rain and the heat of the bivouac fires had so shrunken my boots that I could not remove them. In fact, I was afraid to do so, even if I could, because I would have been unable to get them on again. This was a common experience on that trip. Several men did not have their boots off for two weeks, at least.

Our march on the succeeding day brought us to Cabin creek, why so called nobody can tell, as nothing more substantial than an Indian tepee was ever erected thereon. That night we had thunder, lightning and a deluge. We gave up the idea of rest, and were glad to keep even moderately warm. The horses sank in the mud to their kneejoints, and soldiers' shoes were pulled off in trying to drag their feet through the sticky slime. "Can hell be much worse than this?" said an officer to me next morning. He was cleaning about twenty pounds of wet clay from his boots with a butcher-knife. His clothes were dripping, his teeth chattering, and his nose a cross between purple and indigo. IC looking like tho devil could make a man fit for the region he inquired about, that young lieutenant was a most eligible candidate.

The scouts reported the Indian trail growing fresher, so Ave moved ten miles further east, and encamped among a detached section of bluffs, chiefly cone-shaped, which were very picturesque. 'We found that the Indians were following the Sully trail of 1864, which leads at that point directly to the Missouri. General Crook thought that the village might be on the headwaters of either the Glendive or Beaver creeks, and sent out the scouts, who remained absent over thirty hours, which compelled us to lie over for one day. On the morning of August 31st they reported no Indians at the point designated, and we marched to Leaver creek, about a dozen miles, so that the troops might have their bi-monthly muster for pay. Beaver creek is called the Indian branch of the lesser Missouri, and runs through a lovely champaign country. How General Hazen, in his famous report, could call the section of territory from Powder river to that stream "a desert" passes comprehension and excited general surprise. A finer locality for either grazing or till-age purposes could hardly be imagined. With few exceptions, the tract indicated is an unbroken meadow-land. Timber is scarce, but coal abounds in marvelous quantities. Every cut made by the water, and the sides of every bluff, large or small, showed immense blocks or veins of that mineral, thus settling the fuel supply question beyond cavil. Our troops lit some fires made of this material, and found them admirable. We saw two burning coal ledges. The coal is bituminous on the surface, but, doubtless, all the other varieties can be found when mines are opened there, which must be the case in the not remote future.

If inexhaustible supplies of coal, water and grass cannot make a country rich, the Americans have lost their renowned enterprise, and the pioneer spirit which, more even than the rifles of the continentals, "made a gigantic nation spring from the waters of the Atlantic and converted a fettered colony into a proud republic, prosperous, limitless and invincible," is no more. We expected to find a Sahara, and we entered a land of promise. Our animals appreciated this fact as much as we did, for the starved creatures filled themselves to satiety with the succulent grasses of the Montana plains.

CHAPTER XIX

HALF-RATIONS AND HORSE MEAT

We made two marches north on Beaver creek, about thirty-two miles, and, finding no Sioux, moved up Andrew's creek, nearly due east, about twenty miles. Crook became satisfied that the Indians had crossed to the Little Missouri, and, on September 4, we marched to that river on Custer's trail of 1874, perhaps eighteen miles east, and crossed it at 2 o'clock in the afternoon. The stream is sullen and muddy, like its large namesake, and has tremendous bluffs or "buttes," which are filled with coal and iron veins on both sides. Wild cherries, plums, and "buffalo berries "grow in profusion on the banks, so our soldiers had quite a feast that evening. Many men were suffering from internal ailments, and this timely fruit supply checked sickness of that nature to a great extent. It rained all day, as usual, and made night a thing of horror. We camped where Sully camped in 1802, and where Custer did ten years afterward, and on some of his later scouts. It was an amphitheatrical valley, "rock enchaliced," 'as it were, and would have been an excellent thing for some artist to sketch. By the way, our artistic brethren were not very enterprising on that campaign. A man capable of producing good sketches could have made a small fortune. But hard campaigning, on very coarse food and sometimes insufficient, would hardly enliven the genius of a city man gifted with the artist's magic skill. On the whole, I think the artists were sensible to remain in the land of the civilized. I never appreciated the force of the lines,

O solitude! where are the charms that sages have seen in thy face? until It struck George Crook's Indian-hunting "outfit." "The wild freedom of the plains" sounds well in a comfortable parlor, but does not feel quite as nice when your hide is wet and clammy with rain, like the skin of a frog, and when you have as much mud on your person as would disgrace a stockyards' pig. I have seen an English regiment after returning from the Crimean war, hairy, patched up, and tanned, but so ragged, filthy, folorn-looking a set of men as the soldiers of Crook's expedition I have never beheld. That they were not vermin-eaten is to me a bewildering mystery. Let civilization scratch itself all over when it hears that we had not three pounds of washing-soap in the entire command, and that no man, not even General Crook himself, had a second shirt to his back! I have seen that officer wash his own underclothes in the Yellowstone and sit on the bank to let them dry.

General Gibbon cried out to our column when he passed us the day the junction was effected on the Rosebud : "Why, soldiers, you're even dirtier than my men ! "I should think they were. Terry's men moved with 205 wagons, "Sibley "and "A" tents, together with a pack-train, while Crook's command had only rations on their mules, and all the clothing they possessed on their frames. Terry's troops applied to Crook's a nickname unfit for ears polite, but which unmistakably referred to the dilapidated condition of the rear portion of their pantaloons. If any reader considers this picture overdrawn, I call upon any man in that column, from General Crook to the humblest private, to contradict me. I wish to let the American people know what their gallant army had to undergo in fighting those red scoundrels who have too long been treated as chiefs and equals. Crook is severe, and I'd rather be with Terry, as regards food, shelter, and clean flannel, but he goes for the Indians as one of themselves would do, and has shown that an American army can stand, without much growling or the slightest approach to mutiny, more than any other troops upon this earth. At the same time, I hope that the General, should he ever repeat that experiment, will allow a little more soap and an additional pair of stockings to each man. In referring to the array as American, I do not wish it understood entirely in the native sense, for a large proportion of the rank and file was made up of the material that covered the British arms with glory in the Peninsula—the never war-absent Irish—and of Germans, whose slow bravery solidifies the Celtic ardor with Yankee coolness, and makes the three elements a military body that, to use the words of a dashing American officer who had accompanied the column from the outset, "would go with the Balaklava 'six hundred' into the' mouth of hell' and then brandish their carbines and call upon the ' Light Brigade' to follow them and fight their way out at the other end."

A word about officers. Most of them are high-bred, manly, learned, good-humored, hospitable gentlemen, while a very few are narrow-minded, jealous, punctilious, "swell-headed," irritable, excitable, and generally unfit for anything but retirement into private life. I am glad to say that the percentage of the latter grade is insignificant, and the sooner the army is rid of them the better. The high-toned, chivalric class of officers almost extinguish the others, but one disagreeable "shoulder-strap" is enough to disgust an entire regiment. As for bravery, the quality is so universal in the American army, that no officer gets credit for fearlessness, which is regarded as a matter of course. Judgment, skill and dignified firmness are far more necessary. A hectoring, bullying officer never gains the respect and confidence of his men, were he as bold as Ajax, while the quiet, determined, yet courteous, commander wins the hearts of his subordinates, and, because of his moral influence, is obeyed with all the more alacrity. Personally, I have nothing to complain of; but were I an officer serving under certain other officers, I think I'd feel like occasioning a special court-martial. Nothing appears so unmanly and uncalled for in any soldier as an insulting, snappish tone toward his inferiors, knowing, as he must know, how utterly helpless, according to the humiliating military code, they are. If an inferior officer resents the impertinence of his superior, he may obtain temporary satisfaction, but, in the end, he will be made to suffer. In regard to the privates, they count for so many machines, and have no right to question orders, good or bad.

Theirs not to reason why, Theirs but to do and die,

without resisting the higher power. Their only resource is the disgraceful one of desertion, and no wonder that some of them adopt even that vile mode of breaking their fetters. How a man of spirit, brought to enlist through intemperance or other folly, must burn and long to tear the windpipe out of some official bully, who talks to him as though he were a dog. I admit some of the soldiers are roughs, just fit to be kicked around, but the greater number are good men enough, some of them men who "have seen better days," and some who, in soldiering, have learned a lesson that will reform their lives.

We marched some thirty miles from the Little Missouri to Heart river, on September 5th. We were within 160 miles of Fort Lincoln, and about 200 from the northern edge of the Black Hills. To accomplish either march, we had half rations for two and a half days only. I interviewed General Crook on the subject. This was what occurred:

"You are sending in a courier, General?"

"Yes, to Fort Lincoln. He will carry some mail and telegrams for the command," Crook answered.

"What do you propose to do now, General?"

He paused for a moment, and, pulling his peculiar beard, said very slowly: "We are five full marches from Fort Abraham Lincoln. We are seven, at least, from the Black Hills. By going to the Missouri we lose two weeks' time. By marching on the Hills we gain so much. I march on the Black Hills to-morrow. Between going to and coming back from Fort Lincoln we should lose more than half our horses."

"How much rations have you left?"

"Only two days' and a half half rations, but we must make them last for seven, at least. It must be done. The Indians have gone to the Hills and to the agencies. The miners must be protected, and we must punish the Sioux on our way to the south, or leave this campaign entirely unfinished."

I looked at him in some amazement, and could not help saying: "You will march 200 miles in the wilderness, with used-up horses and tired infantry on two and one-half days' half rations!"

"I know it looks hard," was the reply, "but we've got to do it, and it shall be done. I have sent a telegram for supplies to General Sheridan. The wagons will meet us at Crook City or Deadwood. If not, the settlements must supply our wants. Nobody knows much about this region, but it looks fair. We'll kill some game, too, perhaps, to make up for short rations. Half-rations will be issued after to-night. All will be glad of the movement after the march has been made. If necessary," he added, "we can eat our horses."

This suggestion fell upon me like a splash of ice water.

I could hardly believe, even then, that such an alternative would present itself, but it did, as will be seen, very soon. We were encamped in a bleak and dreary spot. Everybody appeared to be gloomy, and even old Lieutenant Lawson admitted that he had never seen such hard times with his beloved Kentucky brigade.

"As for eating a horse," said he, after I had told him of General Crook's remarks, "I'd as soon think of eating my brother!"

But hunger is a great sauce, and Lieutenant Lawson dined on horse steak, like the rest of us, before many days.

I wrote my despatches that evening under a half blanket, precariously supported by poles cut in the neighboring marsh, while the rain came down as if it had not rained before in several years.

By great exertions, the soldiers collected quite a lot of wood, and by the glare of the camp fires that night, I could see the steam rising from the bivouac as thickly as it rises in a laundry on washing day. The soldiers were too tired to mind the deluge.

The weather did not improve on the three following days, and all the aroyos, or small ravines, were filled with water. The whole country was as wet as a sponge, but without elasticity. Our horses played out by the score, and between two and three hundred dismounted cavalrymen were marching in rear of the wonderful infantry battalion. Every little while the report of a pistol or carbine would announce that a soldier had shot his horse, rather than leave it behind, with a chance of being picked up by straggling Indians. Some of the poor beasts fell dead from the effects of fatigue and want of proper forage, but a majority simply lay down and refused to budge an inch further. My horse became a burden on my hands. Do what I would, I could not induce him to get out of his slow walk, and I tolerated him only because I could not get along without the writing material which was carried in the saddle-bags.

On the night of September 7th, General Crook detached 150 picked men, fifteen from each troop of the 3d Cavalry, in the field, under Col. Anson Mills and Lieuts. Emmet Crawford, A. II. Von Leutwitz and Frederick Schwatka, accompanied by a train of fifty pack mules, with Commissary Bubb and Chief Packer Moore, to make a dash for the Black Hills settlements and bring back supplies to the famishing troops. It was my desire to have accompanied the party, but my horse was useless, and I was compelled to remain with the main command.

Not a stick of wood had we seen for eighty-six miles, and this, added to the cold, ever-falling rain, made life almost unendurable. There was hardly any coffee left, and this could not be cooked, while the poor remains of sugar and salt were absolutely washed out of the pack saddles by the falling flood. Hard tack had disappeared, and nothing remained, on September 8th, but to eat one another or our animals.

While trudging along through the mire on the morning of that day, leading our worn-out steeds, Lieutenant Lawson and I observed a small group of soldiers by the side of the trail busily engaged in skinning a dead horse, and appropriating steaks from its hinder parts. This was the beginning of our horse rations. The men were too hungry to be longer controlled, and the General wisely ordered that as many horses as would be necessary to feed the men be selected by the officers and slaughtered day by day. It was a tough experiment, but there was no help for it, and anything outside of actual cannibalism was preferable to starving slowly to death. Some of the men, before they began to destroy the horses for food, had taken to splitting the fat leaves of cacti, and, when wood was procurable, they roasted them at the camp fires. This induced a species of dysentery, from which a large portion of the command suffered during the remainder of the march.

CHAPTER XX

FIGHTING AT SLIM BUTTES. AWFUL SCENES

As we were about to break camp, on the morning of September 9th, a packer named George Herman rode up in hot haste to General Crook, bearing a dispatch from Colonel Mills, which announced that his detachment had attacked and captured, that morning, an Indian village of forty-one lodges, a large herd of ponies, and some supplies. The Sioux were still fighting to regain what they had lost, and the colonel requested reinforcements. He was then seventeen miles south, at Slim Buttes, on a tributary of Grand river. General Crook at once selected one hundred men, with the best horses, from the 3d Cavalry, fifty from Noyes' battalion of the 2d, and the 5th Cavalry, and, accompanied by his staff and the commanding officers of the different regiments, rode forward to the assistance of his subordinate. Mills, not anticipating an Indian fight, had allowed his men only fifty rounds of ammunition each, and Crook was alarmed lest the Sioux should compel him to expend his last cartridge before assistance could reach him. I accompanied the advance, but my infernal beast broke down completely two or three miles from camp, and I had to lead him the rest of the way. The road was so bad that the cavalry could not go at a very fast pace, so I was lucky enough to reach the captured village very soon after Crook got in. All was quiet then, for the Sioux had withdrawn to procure re-enforcements before Crook arrived, and, as subsequently appeared, did not know of his arrival at all. They fancied that Mills, like Custer, was all alone. Approaching the scene of fight, I saw a small ravine, between gentle hills, in which the captured pony herd was corraled, while our cavalry horses were picketed along the slopes. Several large Indian tepees, covered with canvas or buckskin, were pitched on the east side of the northern slope, and showed the location of the village. A solitary tepee on the north side of the hill was used as a hospital, and there the wounded were placed. I met Mills, as I led in my jaded hack, and he showed me the position. He was surrounded by high, very steep bluffs on all sides but the east, and, consequently, the defeated Indians had a full chance to annoy him. It was noon when I met him, and the fight had closed about 10 o'clock. The capture of the village was but the work of a few minutes. The Indian trail had been struck the previous afternoon, and was followed up to within four miles of the village when Mills went into camp. He reconnoitered with Gruard, and finding the location, determined to attack next morning.

Of course it rained all night, and, while yet dark, the colonel moved forward his detachment, together with the pack mules, two miles. Then he halted the packers, fearing their beasts' braying would alarm the Indians, dismounted all his cavalry, except twenty-five men under Schwatka, and moved forward to "fall on." Capt. Jack Crawford, of Omaha, a well-known scout, and some other guides, went with Gruard and joined in the subsequent charge. Mills arriving in the edge of the ravine where the redskins slept securely, as they thought, sent Lieutenant Schwatka with his twenty-five mounted men, to drive off the pony herd. The ponies were stampeded at once, but rushed for the village and alarmed the Indians.

Von Leutwitz and Crawford, with fifty men each, on foot, surrounded the lodges and charged. There was a ripping of canvas and buffalo hide, as the Sioux had no time to untie the strings of the lodges and, therefore cut the tents with their knives. The soldiers fired a volley which the Indians returned in a desultory way. Almost at the first shot Lieut. A. H. Von Leutwitz, of Troop E, 3d Cavalry, fell with a bullet through his right knee joint. This gentleman had served in the Austrian and Prussian armies, had fought at Montebello, Magenta, Solferino, all through the Italian campaign of '59, had distinguished himself at Gettysburg and other great battles of our war, and had escaped comparatively unscathed. Yet his hour had come, and he fell wounded in a miserable Indian skirmish the very first man. Colonel Mills and Lieutenant Crawford then led on the soldiers and made short work of the village, although the Indians kept up a scattering fire from the bluffs.

When daylight came, the Sioux made matters much hotter, and the soldiers who were much exposed on that bare bluff were almost at their mercy. Mills sent back for his train, which came up with Moore, Bubb and R. A. Strahorn, all of whom behaved in a gallant manner during the skirmishing which followed. Lieutenant Crawford acted with fine judgment, and was spoken highly of by the soldiers who participated in the affair. Schwatka did his work in a thorough manner, and made a mark of which he may well be proud. But Mills is peculiar, and occasionally the reverse of politic, which to some extent neutralizes his undeniable ability as an officer. Yet, for all that, Crook's column can never forget his brilliant dash on September 9, which saved it from much greater privation. He captured a large amount of dried provisions, 2,500 buffalo robes, and many other campaign luxuries which Indians appreciate as much as white men.

One of gallant Custer's guidons, Colonel Keogh's gauntlets, five horses of the 7th Cavalry and several other relics of the fated regiment were among the prizes secured. A party of Sioux, unable to make their escape, took refuge in a sort of deep, brush-covered gully, just above the site of the village, on the eastern slope, dug intrenchments with their hands and knives, and could not be dislodged by Mills' detachment. In an attempt to drive them out, nearly all the casualties occurred. Private John Wenzel, of Troop A, 3d Cavalry was killed, and Sergt. Ed Glass, of Troop E, one of the boldest non-commissioned officers in the army, was shot through the right forearm. Several other soldiers were wounded in attempting to carry this fatal den.

The firing of the Indians from the bluffs compelled the soldiers to throw up temporary breastworks, which saved them from particularly serious damage. The riding mule of Mr. Moore, and a horse belonging to Troop I were shot from the "lava bed" arrangement. Mills, when he sent back for his train in the morning, had the good sense to send for re-enforcements at the same time. Crook arrived a little after 11 o'clock, and immediately attacked the Indian burrow in the gully. In that affair he displayed to the fullest extent his eccentric contempt for danger. No private soldier could more expose himself than did the General and the officers of his staff. I expected to see them shot down every moment; for Charley White, the well-known scout, was shot through the heart, just across the ravine, not ten paces from Crook. Kennedy, of the 5th Cavalry, and Stevenson, of the 2d, were wounded, the one mortally and the other dangerously, beside him, while many other soldiers had hair-breadth escapes. The boys in blue, although unquestionably brave, did not quite relish the idea of being shot in the digestive organs by an unseen and "ungetatable" enemy, but their officers rallied them without difficulty, heading the assault, musket or carbine in hand. Besides General Crook and his staff, Major W. H. Powell and Major Munson, of the infantry, Major Burke, of the same branch of the service; Lieut. Charles King, of the 5th Cavalry; Lieutenant Rogers, and the ever gallant Lieut. W. Philo Clark, of the 2d Cavalry, took desperate chances in true "forlorn hope" fashion. The guide, Baptiste Pourier, already so distinguished for bravery, fought his way into the cavern, and succeeded in killing one of the male Indians, ingeniously using a captive squaw as a living barricade between himself and the fire of the other warriors. He took the scalp of the fallen brave in a manner that displayed perfect workmanship. Scalping is an artistic process, and, when neatly done, may be termed a satanic accomplishment.

Crook, exasperated by the protracted defense of the hidden Sioux, and annoyed by the casualties inflicted among his men, formed, early in the afternoon, a perfect cordon of infantry and dismounted cavalry around the Indian den. The soldiers opened upon it an incessant fire, which made the surrounding hills echo back a terrible music. The circumvallated Indians distributed their shots liberally among the crowding soldiers, but the shower of close-range bullets from the latter terrified the unhappy squaws, and they began singing the awful Indian death chant. The pappooses wailed so loudly, and so piteously, that even the hot firing could not quell their voices, and General Crook ordered the men to suspend operations immediately. Then Frank Gruard and Baptiste Pourier, both versed in the Sioux tongue, by order of General Crook, approached the abrupt western bank of the Indian rifle pit and offered the women and children quarter. This was accepted by the besieged, and Crook in person went to the mouth of the cavern and handed out one tall, fine looking woman, who had an infant strapped to her back. She trembled all over and refused to liberate the General's hand. Eleven other squaws, and six pappooses, were then taken out, but the few surviving warriors refused to surrender and savagely re-commenced the fight.

Then our troops re-opened with a very "rain of hell" upon the infatuated braves, who, nevertheless, fought it out with Spartan courage, against such desperate odds, for nearly two hours. Such matchless bravery electrified even our enraged soldiers into a spirit of chivalry, and General Crook, recognizing the fact that the unfortunate savages had fought like fiends, in defense of wives and children, ordered another suspension of hostilities and called upon the dusky heroes to surrender.

After a few minutes' deliberation, the chief, American Horse—a fine looking, broad-chested Sioux, with a handsome face and a neck like a bull—showed himself at the mouth of the cave, presenting the butt end of his rifle toward the General. He had just been shot in the abdomen, and said, in his native language, that he would yield, if the lives of the warriors who fought with him were spared. Some of the soldiers, who had lost comrades in the skirmish, shouted, "No quarter!" but not a man was base enough to attempt shooting down the disabled chief. Crook hesitated for a minute and then said—" Two or three Sioux, more or less, can make no difference. I can yet use them to good advantage. Tell the chief," he said, turning to Gruard, "that neither he nor his young men will be harmed further."

This message having been interpreted to American Horse, he beckoned to his surviving followers, and two strapping Indians, with their long, but quick and graceful, stride, followed him out of the gully. The chieftain's intestines protruded from his wound, but a squaw—his wife, perhaps —tied her shawl around the injured part, and then the poor, fearless savage, never uttering a complaint, walked slowly to a little camp fire, occupied by his people, about 20 yards away, and sat down among the women and children. The surgeons examined the wound, pronounced it mortal, and during the night American Horse, one of the bravest and ablest of the Sioux chiefs, fell back suddenly, and expired without uttering a groan.

Crook, after the surrender of the chief, took all the survivors under his protection, and ordered the dead and wounded to be taken from their late stronghold. Let the country blame or praise the General for his clemency, I simply record the affair as it occurred. Several soldiers jumped at once into the ravine and bore out the corpses. The warrior killed by Baptiste Pourier was a grim-looking old fellow, covered with scars and fairly laden down with Indian jewelry and other savage finery. The other dead were three squaws—one at first supposed to be a man— and, sad to relate, a tiny pappoose. The captive squaws, with their children, came up to view the corpses. They appeared to be quite unmoved, although a crowd of half-savage camp followers, unkempt scouts and infuriated soldiers surged around them—a living tide. The skull of one poor squaw was blown, literally, to atoms, revealing the ridge of the palate and presenting a most ghastly and revolting spectacle. Another of the dead females—a middleaged woman—was so riddled by bullets that there appeared to be no unwounded part of her person left. The third victim was young, plump, and, comparatively speaking, light of color. She had a magnificent physique, and, for an Indian, a most attractive set of features. She had been shot through the left breast, just over the heart, and was not in the least disfigured.

"Ute John," the solitary friendly Indian who did not desert the column, scalped all the dead, unknown to the General or any of the officers, and I regret to be compelled to state a few —a very few—brutalized soldiers followed his savage example. Each took only a portion of the scalp, but the exhibition of human depravity was nauseating. The unfortunates should have been respected, even in the coldness and nothingness of death. In that affair, surely, the army were the assailants, and the savages acted purely in self-defense. I must add, in justice to all concerned, that neither General Crook nor any of his officers or men suspected that any women or children were in the gully until their cries were heard above the volume of fire poured upon the fatal spot.

That was a peculiar picture of Indian warfare at Slim Buttes. There a dead cavalry horse lay on his side on the western bank of the bloody burrow, while Tom Moore's mule, his feet sticking up in the air, lay on his back about thirty yards nearer to the abandoned tepees. On the southern slope of the embankment, in the line of fire, face downward, the weight of his body resting on his forehead and knees, the stiff, dead hands still grasping the fully cocked carbine, two empty cartridge shells lying beside him, lay John 'Wenzel. He had been shot through the brain—the bullet entering the left jaw from below, and passing out through the top of his head—by either American Horse or Charging Bear, after having fired twice into the gully. He, doubtless, never realized that he had been hit. poor fellow. Wenzel knew more about a horse than, perhaps, any man of Troop A, 3d Cavalry, and used to attend to my animal before he was detailed, for the reason that he was well mounted, to accompany that, to him, fatal advance movement of Colonel Mills. Diagonally opposite, on the northern slope, lay the stalwart remains of Charley White— "Buffalo Chip," as he was called—the champion harmless liar and most genial scout upon the plains. I saw him fall and heard his death cry. Anxious to distinguish himself, he crept cautiously up the slope to have a shot at the hostiles. Some of the soldiers shouted, "Get away from there Charley, they've got a bead on 3'ou 1" Just then a shot was fired, which broke the thigh bone of a soldier of the 5th Cavalry, named Kennedy, and White raised himself on his hands and knees in order that he might locate the spot from whence the bullet came. As he did so, one of the besieged Indians, quick as lightning, got his range and shot him squarely through the left nipple. Charley threw up his hands, crying out loud enough for all of us to hear him, "My God, my God, boys, I'm done for this time!" One mighty convulsion doubled up his body, then he relaxed all over and rolled like a log three or four feet down the slope. His dead face expressed tranquility rather than agony, when I looked at him some hours later. The wind blew the long, fair locks over the cold features, and the eyes were almost perfectly closed. The slain hunter looked as if he were taking a rest after a toilsome buffalo chase. Last, and also least, the slaughtered Indian pappoose, only about two months old, lay in a small basket, where a humane soldier had placed the tiny body. Had the hair of the poor little creature been long enough. "Ute John," I believe, would have scalped it also.

With all this group of mutilated mortality before them, and with the groans of the wounded soldiers from the hospital tepee ringing in their ears, the hungry troopers and infantry tore the dried Indian meat they had captured into eatable pieces, and marched away as unconcernedly as if they were attending a holiday picnic. It was, indeed, a ghastly, charnel-house group—one which, if properly put on canvas, would, more than anything I have read of, or heard described, give the civilized world a faithful picture of the inevitable diabolism of Indian warfare. Most of our dead were hastily buried by their comrades, but the bodies of the Indians, both male and female, were left where they fell, so that their friends might have the privilege of properly disposing of them after we had left. The Sioux Indians, so far as known, never place their dead in the earth, so that leaving the bodies above ground was of no particular consequence in their case. During the afternoon, American Horse, and some of the squaws, informed Gen. Crook, through the scouts, that Crazy Horse was not far off, and that we would certainly be attacked before nightfall. The General, under the circumstances, wished for nothing better.

Sergeant Van Moll, of Troop A, 3d Cavalry, and some soldiers, had carried the dead body of Private Wenzel, the carbine still clutched in the dead hands, to a place convenient to the small camp fire at which Lieutenant Lawson and I were trying to enjoy a tin cup full, each, of coffee, made from some of the berries captured in the Indian village. They had picked the unexploded cartridge from the chamber and then wrested the weapon by main force from the stiff fingers of the corpse, whose face and fair, sandy locks were covered and matted with blood. A grave was being dug, and the lieutenant was preparing to read the service for the dead, when, all at once, we were fired upon from the bluffs, which surrounded us on all sides except the east. To occupy them thoroughly, would have required an army corps, so that nobody was to blame for this second attempt on the part of the Indians to recapture their ponies and get back their tepees and other property.

The buttes called "Slim" are of an extraordinary shape, very lofty, and strongly resemble a series of mammoth Norman castles, or a semicircular range of gigantic exposition buildings. They have tier upon tier of rocks, with the hardy northern pine growing in every crevice, contrasting the green with the gray, and clothing the otherwise bare stern, granite crags with a savage beauty. Along the ledges, and among the pines, the Sioux led their war ponies and began operations. No time was lost by Crook in meeting their attack. With the rapidity of an exploding shell, the brigade, which had nearly all come up, broke into a tremendous circle of skirmishers, forming a cordon of fire around the horses, pack mules and captured ponies. General Merritt was Crook's second in command, and directed the movements of the troops in our section of the field. The Indian bullets whizzed in among us for a few minutes, and the voices of our officers could he heard shouting: "Steady men! Take your proper intervals! Don't fire until you get the range! Forward! Double quick time! D—n it, Reilly, are you firing at the Black Hills? Never waste a shot, boys! ", *etcetera*, as the infantry and dismounted dragoons trotted out to face the enemy.

Colonel Chambers, with his officers and men, made straight for the southern bluff, while General Carr, with the 5th Cavalry, also dismounted, made for the hills on the west and southwest. The 3d Cavalry, under Colonel Royall, took charge of the northern and northwestern heights, while the 2d Cavalry, under Maj. Henry E. Noyes, protected the eastern flank, which was exposed on an open plain, and, being mounted, rode around by the northern end of the bluffs to checkmate any attempt Crazy Horse might make to cut off our rear guard, under Sibley, which was driving the stragglers and used-up horses in before it. The bloodiest battles are not always the most picturesque. The evening fight at Slim Buttes was not particularly sanguinary, as regarded our side, but it was the prettiest battle scene— so acknowledged to have been by men who had witnessed a hundred fights—that ever an Indian war correspondent was called upon to describe.

When our men got within range, their fire opened steadily. First it was the infantry "pop-pop pop," slow but sure; then the livelier racket of the cavalry carbine, and finally, the rapid, ringing discharges of the Winchester repeaters, from the Indian lines, showing that Crazy Horse was neither "dead nor deaf nor dumb." On the infantry front the rattle soon swelled into a well-sustained roar. The 5th Cavalry caught the infection, and the clangor soon spread nearly around the whole field. Our men, supplied with plenty of ammunition, resolved to silence the fire of the Indian enemy. Long wreaths of smoke, held low by the heavy atmosphere, enveloped the skirmish lines, and showed more picturesquely as the evening advanced. Those wreaths gradually crept up from tier to tier on the bluffs as the soldiers continued to ascend. The combatants were finally shrouded in its sulphurous gloom. Through this martial vapor you could observe the vivid flashing of the fire arms— our boys creeping stealthily from ledge to ledge, and the Indians, bold as ever, but utterly confounded, stunned and dispirited, perhaps, by the ceaseless fusillade, retiring before the stronger force, disputing every inch of ground as they retreated. It was a matter of astonishment with every man on that trip how our men came off with such small loss, in the comparative sense. The best explanation is that the Indians of the plains generally fire from horseback, which may, in some degree at least, account for the very common inaccuracy of their aim in battle. Besides, in firing down hill, unless the slope is gradual, and free from serious obstructions, the range cannot be very accurate, while, *per contra*, the party moving upward can see every prominent object clearly defined against the artificial sky line. Every time an Indian got killed, or disabled, his comrades picked him up and carried him off. The infantry must have done great execution, their "long toms"—altered Springfields— reaching the enemy far beyond the range of the carbine. The 5th Cavalry were very warmly engaged, and fired upon the Sioux with great enthusiasm. Driven by the forces named from their original point of attack, the defeated Sioux came out through the ravine in the northwestern angle of the bluffs and charged the position of the 3d Cavalry. Like the Napoleonic cuirrassiers at Waterloo, they rode along the line, looking for a gap through which to penetrate. They kept up perpetual motion, apparently encouraged by a warrior, doubtless Crazy Horse himself, who, mounted on a fleet, white horse, galloped around the array and seemed to possess the power of ubiquity. Failing to break into that formidable circle, the Indians, after firing several volleys, their original order of battle being completely broken, and recognizing the folly of fighting such an outnumbering force any longer, glided away from our front with all possible speed. As the shadows came down into the valley, the last shots were fired, and the affair of Slim Buttes was over.

Our loss in the action was about thirty, all told. Those who died on the field were Private 'Wenzel, of the 3d Cavalry; Private Kennedy, of the 5th Cavalry, and the ill fated scout, Charley White. Most of the soldiers wounded, among them the celebrated sharpshooter, Edward Glass, a sergeant of the 3d Cavalry, and Private Wilson, of the same regiment, were disabled for life. The Indians must have lost quite heavily. Several of their ponies, bridled but riderless, were captured during the evening. Indians never abandon their war horses, unless they should happen to be surprised or killed. Therefore many saddles, to use the Caucasian military phrase, must have been emptied. Pools of blood were found on the ledges of the bluffs, indicating the places where Crazy Horse's warriors paid the penalty of their valor with their lives.

I have heard the number of the Sioux variously estimated, but I cannot presume to verify any of the estimates made. There could not, in my opinion, have been more than from six to eight hundred of their fighting men opposed to us. Had they been of equal number, it is difficult to say how, notwithstanding the unquestioned courage of our troops, the affair might have terminated. They had fresh horses, while ours were entirely used up, and, therefore, the celerity of their movements would have enabled them to fling a superior force on any point of our widely-extended circular skirmish line. I am convinced, however, that no equal force, of any color, could have beaten such men as composed Crook's brigade on the day of Slim Buttes.

Night fell suddenly, and Lieutenant Lawson and I, each the proud and glad possessor of a captured buffalo robe, lay down to sleep, with our half blankets over us, while Sergeant Van Moll and a small party of Troop A proceeded to complete the burial of Private Wenzel, so rudely interrupted in the afternoon by the attack of the Sioux from the bluffs. The brave old Lieutenant—a God-fearing Irish Presbyterian—would have read the prayers over the remains, but he was tired out, and my pious inclinations were utterly subdued by a tendency to sleep, which would have required, at the time, all the horrors of which Indian warfare is capable to overcome. The sergeant and the soldiers, one of them holding some sort of an improvised lantern, scooped out the grave with shovels borrowed from the chief packer, and Van Moll acted as chaplain. They wrapped Wenzel's old overcoat around the body, and laid him to rest as carefully as if he had been a major-general.

No useless coffin enclosed his breast,
Not in sheet or in shroud they wound him; But he lay like a warrior taking his rest, With his martial cloak around him.

American Horse, before he died, gave some information to General Crook about the war. Dr. Mcgillicuddy, who attended the dying chief, said that he was cheerful to the last, and manifested the utmost affection for his squaws and children. The latter were allowed to remain on the ground after the dusky hero's death, and subsequently fell into the hands of their own people. Even "Ute John" respected the cold clay of the brave Sioux leader, and his corpse was not subjected to the scalping process.

We broke camp early on the morning of September 10th, which was raw and drizzling. A gray mist enshrouded the bluffs, and the muddy stream that ran through the battle field was swollen to an uncomfortable depth by the rains that had fallen in the mountains.

The rear guard of the column consisted, that morning, of two troops of the 5th Cavalry, commanded by Captains Sumner and Montgomery, under Gen. E. A. Carr. They remained dismounted, until all the rest of the command had filed by them, bound for "the Hills." Scarcely had they mounted their horses, when they were attacked most determinedly by Indians secreted in the ravines that abound in that region. But they were veterans, and coolly held their ground. They lost many wounded, but none killed outright. The Indians, on the other hand, were unfortunate, and left five warriors gasping upon the sod. Crazy Horse, convinced that Slim Buttes was not the Little Big Horn, drew off in despair, and the remainder of the march was made without molestation.

The rain continued throughout the day, turning the country into a quagmire. We were so used to being wet to the skin that no man who could keep his feet uttered a complaint, but our eyes would often turn compassionately to the long string of travois (mule litters) on which our sick and wounded were being dragged toward civilization. The chill, merciless rain poured upon them constantly, and neither poncho nor blanket could keep it out. The General turned over all the dried meat, coffee and other provisions captured in the Indian village to those *hors de combat*, so that we who were healthy, if otherwise miserable, had to put up as best we could with Indian pony steak which, at least, did not "taste of the blanket," like some of the old cavalry horses we had been previously compelled to devour.

One of the most cheerful men I marched with, amid the pelting rain, was Capt. Charles King, now celebrated as a military novelist, who was then, if I mistake not, a lieutenant and regimental adjutant of the 5th Cavalry. He was full of anecdote, but complained occasionally of the effect of serious wounds which he had received while fighting the Apaches in Arizona and which, subsequently, compelled his retirement from active service.

CHAPTER XXI

MARCHING IN THE MUD

At about noon, on September 11th, we entered a range of bluffs, known as Clay Ridge. The rain fell in unending sheets, as we wound through the serpentine defiles of that abominable sierra, our horses slipping in the mud when we remained on their backs, and our boots absolutely sticking in the rotten soil when we dismounted. The ridge ought to be re-christened "Church Spire Range," because the rocks are fashioned into fantastic pinnacles, resembling the spires which "pierce the clouds" from the summits of sacred edifices. The number of steeples reminded me of Brooklyn, Beecher and "the celebrated case," which then agitated the public mind. At last, we reached the southern edge of Clay Buttes, and saw, through the rising mist, a dark blue wall a long distance in our front. Our guides made out Bear Butte on our left and the lofty peak of Inyan Kara on our right. We were within plain view of the Black Hills. They were not yet entirely visible—only their outposts, but the sight made us feel quite cheerful.

General Crook ordered Colonel Mills with a picked company of fifty men, all mounted on captured Indian ponies, to ride forward to the Black Hills camps and settlements for the purpose of ordering supplies to meet us, after we had cleared the tedious defile of Clay Buttes. Mills was accompanied by Lieutenants Bubb and Chase The intrepid scouts, Captain Jack Crawford and Frank Gruard, were sent in as government couriers.

Our march from Owl creek to Willow creek, on September 12th, was one of the worst of the campaign. We were "on the go" from daylight until after dark, leading our miserable horses most of the way. Colonel Royall, as loyal an old soldier as ever placed foot in stirrup, "hoofed it" beside me mile after mile, never complaining but lightening up the dismal prospect of events with anecdotes of Mexico and the Civil War. We made over thirty-five miles on that march. Our only guide to the position of camp was a fire kindled by the headquarters staff of the General, who had got in ahead. The darkness was so thick that, to use the rude language of the tired soldiers, you could "cut it with a knife." We came up after the 5th Cavalry, but we could hear the commands of the officers of that regiment, as they sought to place their men in position before ordering them to dismount.

Finally our turn came. We were, to all appearance, on the brink of a deep ravine, fringed by trees of some kind. I can hear old Royall's gruff voice yet, calling out, "Colonel Mills, put your battalion in camp beyond the creek." Our troop led that night, and Lieutenant Lawson called out "A Company, right into line!" The order was obeyed. "Don't delay there," shouted Colonel Royall. "Forward!"

"Forward!" repeated the old lieutenant, and, not knowing but what we might be riding down a precipice, we moved ahead. The undergrowth parted before us. My horse made a plunge in the dark. Several other horses and riders did the same, and we all landed, with a flop, in about three or four feet of water, thus adding: to our misery. We quickly spurred up the opposite bank, unsaddled and unbridled our animals, and threw ourselves down on the wet ground to rest. Hunger was forgotten, because indescribable fatigue held us captive for the moment. When, two hours later, the tired orderly, Roberts, made a fire and fried some horse steak, Lieutenant Lawson and I felt in better appetite. But we had to wash down that strange repast with only the alkaline waters of Willow creek.

On the road between Owl and Willow creeks, we had lost seventy horses and had buried in a big pit about the same number of saddles and other equipments. Before quitting the camp at Slim Buttes, General Crook had caused all the immovable property of the Indians to be burned. It was a pity, but it could not have been helped. The order was thoroughly executed by Maj. W. H. Powell, of the 4th Infantry. Some of the soldiers managed to retain a few souvenirs, but the weakness of their horse flesh compelled most of them to abandon their booty on the wayside. The poor dismounted cavalrymen had a terrible time of it, and came straggling into camp until daylight, presenting a most pitiable appearance. What cheered the whole command up was the knowledge that the Belle Fourche was only five or six miles distant, and that, once there, we would be nearing civilization.

We were breakfasting on pony steak the morning of September 13th, when we heard the lowing of oxen, which then seemed sweetest music to our ears. The effect on the troops was electrical. The fatigues and privations of the march were forgotten by the light-hearted and easily-pleased soldiers. "Hurrah for old Crook!" "Hurrah for old Mills," they shouted, like schoolboys who get an afternoon off. Neither of the officers named was very venerable, but when a soldier speaks of his superior as "the old man" you may be sure he is in good humor with him. The arrival of the beef herd, together with some wagon loads of crackers and vegetables from Crook city, on the edge of "the Hills," changed the aspect of affairs and made everybody feel happy. The beeves were speedily shot and butchered, and the soldiers were not long in satisfying their appetites upon the meat, which they roasted, in Indian fashion, on willow wands, that served the purpose of toasting forks. With the exception of what had been secured in the captured Indian village, the command, from General Crook downward, had lived upon horse, or pony, meat for more than a week. Some of the soldiers, who had exhausted all their regular rations in an improvident manner, had begun earlier. As I sampled all kinds of equine meat on the trip, I will give my opinion of that style of diet in brief: Cavalry horse meat, played out, sore-backed subject, fried without salt, stringy, leathery, blankety and nauseating. Cavalry horse, younger than preceding and not too emaciated, produces meat which resembles very bad beef; Indian pony, adult, has the flavor, and appearance, of the flesh of elk; Indian pony, colt, tastes like antelope or young mountain sheep; mule meat, fat and rank, is a combination of all the foregoing, with pork thrown in.

Some of the soldiers were fortunate enough to shoot a few antelope while on the march, but as there was neither bread nor salt, hunger was general, and the horses and ponies were killed, as I have said, by men regularly detailed for that purpose. Indeed, I saw a heap of the hind quarters of Indian ponies in front of the 5th Cavalry headquarters— a few wicky-ups—during the halt on Owl creek, and the late Capt. W. Philo Clark, of the 2d Cavalry, acting as commissary, distributing the "beef" to the soldiers of the different commands. The kind-heartedness of some of the enlisted men was touching. All of his troopers loved Lieutenant Lawson, and, one evening, a private came to his bivouac with one of the hind quarters of a fine, fat Indian pony colt, on which we dined sumptuously, although the old officer made wry faces, and said again that he felt like a cannibal while eating horse flesh. But famine is, indeed, a stern master, and the campaign cured all who participated in it of any tendency toward epicureanism.

After passing Clay Ridge, Sergeant Van Moll and a corporal, named Bessie, obtained leave to go on a hunt for antelope. Mr. Lawson enjoined them not to go too far from the column, for fear of falling in with Indians. Night came, and they failed to return. The lieutenant became uneasy, but nothing could be done until morning. After midnight we heard the sound of horses' hoofs, and, in the struggling, sickly moonlight, Van Moll and Bessie rode up to our bivouac. They had shot an antelope, but came near paying dearly for it. As they were traveling southward to join the column, after night had fallen, they heard the barking of Indian dogs, right in their path. They made a *detour*, but only succeeded in striking an Indian village, through which they had to ride at full gallop — their horses being in fairly good condition. The astonished Indians fired a few shots after them but did not attempt to make pursuit, probably because their ponies were turned loose to graze. The bold sergeant, who was as truthful as he was courageous, declared that he had never had such a scare during all the years of his Indian experience. The Indian village was, doubtless, occupied by some of the savages who had fought us at Slim Buttes, and who were making for the agency because winter and starvation were approaching.

The destruction of the game upon the great plains was about to settle a question that had puzzled the American government for twenty years. The Sioux nation had never been thoroughly whipped in a pitched battle with our troops, but hunger tames the bravest, and no general of the American army was better aware of that fact than George Crook. All other commanders had withdrawn from pursuit after following the hostile train till their horseflesh played out, but Crook resolved to teach the savages a lesson. He meant to show them that neither distance, bad weather, the loss of horses nor the absence of rations could deter the American army from following up its wild enemies to the bitter end, and, in bringing this home to the stubborn mind of Crazy Horse, he achieved the crowning triumph of a campaign that might have, otherwise, seemed almost abortive. This was the reason why he subjected his command and himself to hardships that, under ordinary circumstances, might have been easily avoided. He could not have worn out the obstinacy of the Indians in a more effective manner. But, at the time, he was rather unpopular with the soldiers, while many of the officers did not hesitate to criticise his campaign freely among themselves, in spite of the etiquette which generally restrains their utterances in regard to their commanders. The long absence of vegetables from our scanty supplies told upon the health of many of the troops toward the last, and some cases of scurvy—none of them very severe—were reported. The eyes of the country were at that period fixed upon Philadelphia, where the centennial exhibition was in progress, or the toilsome cross march of General Crook's brigade would have attracted the national attention.

Our march from Willow creek to the Belle Fourche occupied only a couple of hours, and was devoid of any remarkable incident. The river was pretty high, but we crossed to its southern bank and went into camp. I should have said that before the passage of Clay Ridge, General Crook, whose campaign I had freely, but fairly, criticised as a correspondent, seeing that I was dismounted, very kindly lent me one of his own horses—the same that had been wounded under him at Rosebud fight in June, and which had entirely recovered. Otherwise I should have been compelled to tramp it all the rest of the way into "the Hills," something I was quite willing to do if necessary, because there were not enough horses "to go round "in the 3d Cavalry. The regiment had suffered very severely in regard to horse flesh, and so also had the other cavalry organizations. The brigade had abandoned or shot not less than between five and six hundred horses since we broke camp on Tongue river in the beginning of August. I have since heard that some of the apparently played-out beasts, when relieved from carrying their riders, rallied, lived on what they could find, and were finally restored to the regiments to which they belonged, but I don't think they could have numbered very many.

CHAPTER XXII

INVADING THE BLACK HILLS

The order of the lieutenant-general to General Crook, which reached the latter on the Belle Fourche, September 14th, commanded the brigade to march southward, via the Black Hills, and directed the brigadier to meet Sheridan at Fort Laramie without loss of time. The command was turned over to General Merritt, and on the night of the 15th— the expedition being then encamped on Whitewood creek —Crook and his staff, around a huge log fire, drank farewell to their comrades in champagne procured from Deadwood and served in tin cups. Some Black Hillers, of the prominent type, assisted at the ceremony, General Dawson, United States inspector of internal revenue, being the principal person. Next morning Crook's party, consisting of himself and his personal staff, some infantry officers going home on leave, an escort of twenty men under Lieutenant Sibley, and the newspaper correspondents, whose mission ended with the cessation of "war's alarms," and the "Hillers," turned their faces southward and, seeing that the fogs and damps had cleared away, like the idolaters of the Orient, worshiped the sun. Crook City, the northernmost picket of the Hills, was distant sixteen miles, and Deadwood lay about the same distance beyond. We met a regular caravan from the settlements proceeding to the camp, bringing with them onions, cabbages, turnips, potatoes and other vegetables, all of which were grown in the neighborhood of the "cities" already named. Oak groves and gentle uplands, watered fairly, were the chief features of the nearer landscape. Herds of cattle, guarded by grim-looking herders, "armed to the teeth, "of course, grazed with bovine tranquility among the pretty dells of this northern Arcadia. Behind rose the irregular and far from imposing wall of the Black Hills proper —pastoral in their singular beauty, but entirely, at their first view, destitute of that imperial grandeur which marks the mighty range of the Big Horn monarch of the northwestern mountains. Covered thick with pine and fir trees, the Hills have a sable appearance, which, for a wonder, makes their title no misnomer. They are a ring-worm formation on the face of this earth—independent and eccentric in construction—separated by hundreds of miles of prairie or bad lands from all other highlands—and neither the parents of lesser eminences nor the children of greater. Prof. Jenny has expended the harsh vocabulary of science in his report upon those highlands, and I, having a horror of technical verbiage, and a profound belief that too much indulgence in the same leads to thorough mystification and final softening of the brain, refer the geologically curious to that learned person's documents, if they desire more thorough information.

We were not long in reaching Crook city, a rough-and tumble place, situated in the opening of a wooded ravine, on the Whitewood. It contained about 250 houses, all frame or log—the latter style of architecture predominating. An explosion stirred the atmosphere and made the hills shiver with sound as we approached. It was a cannon which some enthusiastic parties fired in honor of the General's visit. This performance was repeated several times, and a fair-sized crowd of hairy men and bilious women thronged around the little cavalcade, and indulged in stentorian or shrill shouts of welcome. We were all forcibly dismounted and led to an attack on Black Hills whisky, which we found more formidable than either Sitting Bull or Crazy Horse. Subsequently dinner was served in the nearest approach to a hotel that the place could furnish, and if Crook City failed in many of the delicacies of the season, it certainly did not fail in warmth of hospitality. There was an appearance of depression about the settlement which showed a lack of prosperity, and some of the houses appeared untenanted. The mining gulches were either deserted or worked in a slow, unsatisfactory manner.

The men loafing around with their hands in their pockets, did not carry upon their faces the light of success. I made some inquiries, and found that Crook City was on the wane. It started up, mushroom like, in May, but the main gulch having been "washed out," it was found impossible to utilize the water in Whitewood creek any further, and the energies of the populace were directed toward the work of turning the water power of Spearfish creek—one of the finest streams in the Hills—into the first-named stream, so as to create the proper sluicing facilities for mining such gold as might exist in that district.

Crook City, according to my best information, has not improved its fortunes much beyond what they were in the fall of the centennial year. More is the pity, too, because its kindly, open-hearted founders deserved all the success that courage and energy should win.

By the time the horses were fed, General Crook was ready to proceed, and, followed by the usual wild cheering, we rode on to Deadwood City, over a well defined and "improved" wagon road, through a wooded tract, just enough undulating to escape being called a timbered prairie. On the right and left, however, rose some lofty pinnacles of rock, and ledges of quartz showed themselves at every step. Heaps of the mineral, thrown around promiscuously, as it were, appeared in the most unexpected places, looking like deposits of petrified snow. Quartz being the concomitant of gold, its presence always indicates the strong probability of the presence of that precious metal, and, as regards quartz, the Black Hills appear to be an irregular mass of that mineral. We encountered a number of horsemen and several wagons on our way to Deadwood. Everybody was armed, and the men all wore huge spurs, which jingled like sleigh bells after the first snow-fall. Some "ranches" appeared at intervals, bearing the legend "saloon" on their dingy fronts. As a rule, it would be better for the traveler to have some Indian lead in his carcass than have a glass of ranch rot-gut in his stomach.

About three miles from "the city" we met a group of equestrians who were well mounted and dressed in neat fashion. Their clean, civilized, respectable aspect made us, by way of contrast, look like white savages—veritable Goths and Vandals. I am free to say that a seedier, more tattered and generally disreputable looking group of cavaliers, from the General downward, than we were, never rode into any town, ancient or modern.

The gentlemen who came to meet us were introduced by General Dawson as Mayor Farnham and the aldermen of Deadwood. Half an hour's ride brought us to the suburbs of the mountain municipality. We passed by several groups of miners hard at work, "panning out" gold dust, which, they told us, ranged from 10 to 85 cents per pan, the latter being very much in the minority. I had always looked with some degree of suspicion on the Black Hills business, and was considerably astonished to find a settlement of such proportions as that we were riding through. First we "struck" Montana" City" and then Lower Deadwood, and then Deadwood "City "—an artillery salute of thirteen guns being fired as Crook's countenance appeared in the latter place. The General acknowledged the universal enthusiasm, nearly all the population being in the main street, cheering, yelling and prancing around as if the day of jubilee had come, by lifting his weather-beaten hat and bowing right and left, after the manner of public men.

We drew up in front of the Grand Central Hotel—a wooden establishment kept by a burly Teuton—*a la* the knights of old returning from a crusade against the Turks and fleas in Palestine. Mayor Farnham did not say to General Crook what a certain mayor of Chicago said to King Kalakaua on the arrival of that dusky monarch in the city —" Now we'll take our leave until you put on a shirt and clean yourself up!" but he designated significantly the public bath house, for such a luxury existed even then in Deadwood, and pointed out the best ready-made clothing establishment in the town. The General took the hint, as did also the rest of us, and, half an hour later, the sluice leading from that bath house looked as if Powder river, of muddy memory, had been emptied into it. When we again appeared in public, our appearance was not quite so forbidding as in the morning, but there was still considerable room for improvement. Deadwood City, in the fall of 1876, presented an appearance which combined, in a singular manner, the leading features of Cheyenne, 'Wyo.; Braidwood, Ill., and McGregor, Iowa, at that period. Like Cheyenne, it possessed a multitude of "variety" theaters and a crowd of brazen and bedizened harlots, gambling halls, drinking "dives" and other moral abominations. Like Braid wood, it had a long, straight frame or log house street—just as it is popularly believed a snipe has one long, straight digestive apparatus, destitute of ramifications. Like McGregor,

Deadwood was shut in by high wooded hills, which seemed to choke off the air currents, and to massively protest against any extension of the city's width. The tendency was to force the place along the ravine and convert it into a geometrical line— length without breadth. A couple of fires and a first-class cyclone, which swept the long street described, have since partially cured Deadwood of its tendency to burrow in the valley. Nuggets and gold dust, quartz and placer mining made up the conversation of those times in what might be called Deadwood society. I was shown specimens of gold in all forms until I felt like a jaundiced patient—everything I looked at turned yellow, and I thought of Midas and the unpleasant fix that gentleman got himself into when he touched any object. The placer mines were already giving signs of exhaustion, and, as most of the experts predicted then, Deadwood had finally to rely upon the quartz mines, and the men with capital enough to work them for such prosperity as she now enjoys.

The arrival of Crook's army in the neighborhood caused quite a flutter among such merchants as had supplies for military needs, and every kind of speculator, from a photographer to a three-card-monte man, was soon on the road to Whitewood creek, where lay Crook's brigade, commanded by the able and gallant Merritt.

After dark, all Deadwood and the surrounding settlements, over 2,000 people, turned out and gave Crook an "ovation." It was very noisy. The General had to address the crowd from the hotel balcony. He made an off-hand speech, which showed intimate acquaintance with the habits and sentiments of the mining fraternity. Neither did he hesitate to crack a few bluff jokes about the Indian troubles, which, as the phrase goes, were "well received." Afterward he was ushered to the Deadwood theater, where he was formally addressed and presented with "the freedom of the city." When that much was disposed of, Crook, who abhors hand-shaking, was subjected to the pump-handle nuisance at the front door of the dramatic temple. He survived it all, not without some wry faces, I imagine. The General appeared to be very much liked by the miners, his long residence on the Pacific coast having familiarized him with hundreds of the brotherhood.

In the evening I took a stroll around the city, and visited everything of interest. Wearing cavalry "pants," and looking altogether like one of

Uncle Samuel's boys out of repair, the hardy and hearty miners took it for granted that I was earning thirteen dollars per month fighting "Injuns." As I wished to "post" myself on the country, I did not undeceive them, but was compelled to swallow enough "forty-rod" to kill an ordinary alderman. The effects of that accursed "beverage" were apparent for a week later, and I was not the only awful example. But as I am now making my own confession I'll say nothing about other people's follies. As Mickey Free would poetically observe, "Their failin's is nothin' tome."

I visited half a dozen "hells," where I noticed some Chicago toughs, all engaged in the noble art of faro or some other thimble-rigging devilment. In that lively time Deadwood "sports" killed off a man or two every night. Between them and the Sioux it was a hard matter to keep the population of the place up to the maximum standard. Women, as in Cheyenne, acted as "dealers" at many of the tables, and more resembled incarnate fiends than did their vulture like male associates. I observed that decided brunettes or decided blondes were more engaged in evil works than their negative fellow-women. Most of the miners would prefer playing "faro" or "monte" with men, for the women were generally old and unscrupulous hands, whose female subtlety made them paramount in all the devices of cheating and theft. I observed one of them —a brunette, either French or Italian, something of the Latin order anyway — with some attention. She had a once-handsome face, which crime had hardened into an expression of cruelty. Her eye glittered like that of a rattlesnake and she raked in the gold dust or "chips" with hands whose long white fingers, sharp at the ends, reminded one of a harpy's talons.

Every gambler appeared to play for gold dust. Nobody took greenbacks, and the gold-scales were in constant requisition. They allowed twenty dollars for every ounce of gold, and placed greenbacks at the regular discount. Not alone in gaming, but also in commercial transactions, was "dust" used. A miner swaggered up to the bar with five or six others, and called for the "drinks." They were supplied, and he tossed his buckskin wallet to the bartender, who weighed out the requisite amount of "dust" and handed back the balance. I am inclined to believe that this display of crude bullion was made a good deal for effect to make people believe that gold was as plentiful in Deadwood as were sands on the seashore.

CHAPTER XXIII

CLOSING THE CAMPAIGN

As nearly every horse-shoer in Deadwood happened to be on a spree the night of Crook's reception, Lieutenant Clark, our acting quartermaster, had to go around with a posse of soldiers and sober up sufficient of the boys to get our horses shod. This operation consumed several hours, and it was nearly daylight before we got to bed. We did not start very early next morning, and, at breakfast, I read a copy of *The Black Hills Pioneer*—a neat little sheet, which contained a very good account of our recent campaign, and of Crook's oratorical effort on the preceding night. It "blew" a little about the hills, and advertised the Cheyenne and Sidney routes in sensational style. I did not notice any politics in its pages. At 8 o'clock we were in the saddle, and *en route* for Custer City. We moved on through a forest road, meeting "ranches" every mile or two, and encountering or overtaking wagon trains moving to and fro between Deadwood and the railroad settlements. We passed by several mining camps, most of which reported fair progress. We met a wagon train from Red Cloud, loaded with supplies for the expedition, on Box Elder creek, escorted by three companies of the 4th Artillery under Major Smith. It seemed strange to meet that branch of the service—nearly always on coast duty—so far inland. Like nearly all soldiers, they were hospitable, and we had a pleasant time for an hour or two. I had not come in contact with the 4th Artillery since June 3, 1866, when I saw them at Buffalo, patroling the Niagara river in order to save Canada from a Fenian invasion. General Crook is a regular "path-finder," and when we started, on Monday, the 18th, after making Castleton, about forty-two miles from Deadwood, we took a regular "cut-off," marching in the direction of Harney's peak. At Castleton we found great preparations being made both for gulch and ledge mining, but matters were in too undeveloped a condition to glean much important information. It was evident, however, that something had been discovered there, or people would not be going to so much trouble. The inhabitants of Castleton numbered about 200, mostly practiced miners. They had some strips of cultivated ground and several herds of cattle. They were people of "great expectations," like nearly all of their class.

Our "cut-off" lay through a superbly parked country resembling the Big Horn foot-hills, over which towered, in craggy sublimity, the haughty crest of Harney's peak. We followed the course of Castle creek and its tributaries— streams that are as transparent as the air on a sweet May morning. The grass and the leaves were green and nature was clothed in loveliness. Birds sang amid the shady groves and trout leaped in the rivulets. The squirrels frisked from tree to tree, and there was an exhilaration in the atmosphere that made us triumph over time and recall the days of happy boyhood, when every leaf and flower charmed us into many a wildwood ramble. How gloriously the sympathetic genius of a Burns, or a Moore, would have sung of that lovely scene!

At noon we had reached the broad plateau above "Hill City," from which we had a superb view of Harney's peak. The "city" was like "Sweet Auburn," a deserted village, tenanted by one solitary mortal, who kept a ghostly looking "ranch" for the "benefit" of travelers. We asked this stouthearted hermit why the place had been abandoned, and he answered sententiously, "Indian scare and no gold dust." We continued our ride to Custer City. I have seen more sublime, but never more charming, scenery. The hand of nature never shaped anything more beautiful than the groves and parks that then ornamented every foot of that enchanting road. The soil was not rich, but the queen of beauty might have fixed her throne securely there—at least while summer lasted.

The sun was dipping into the western cloud banks, on the evening of September 18th, when we entered Custer City, and received a warm greeting from the inhabitants. Captain "Teddy" Egan, of the 2d Cavalry, a renowned Indian fighter, was there with his troop of gallant grays—the same which led the charge on the village of Crazy Horse on St. Patrick's Day in the Morning, 1876.

The hotel experience at Custer could hardly be called pleasant. The partitions were thin, and a sick infant made the veterans, who had slept with the war yells of the Indians ringing in their ears, lie awake most of the night. After having slept for several months in the open air, it is very difficult to come back to the ways of civilization, especially such as was then furnished on the frontier. Couriers from General Sheridan to General Crook arrived, during the night, with despatches which requested the latter officer to meet the former at Fort Laramie within forty-eight hours.

Captain Egan, at General Crook's request, furnished horses from his splendid troop to the commanding officer, Colonel Chambers, Colonel Stanton, Surgeon Hartsuff, Major Powell, Major Burt, Lieutenants Clark, Bourke, Schuyler, four correspondents, including myself, and an orderly. The General determined to leave his escort and pack train behind, with orders to follow by easy marches, under Major Randall and Lieutenant Sibley. The officers and others selected to accompany the General sprang upon the backs of Egan's superb grays early on the morning of September 19th, and set out on a forced ride of 106 miles—the distance between Custer City and Camp Robinson. How soul stirring it is to ride at full speed on a swift, strong horse, after lumbering along for weeks on some jaded sorry hack! It is like changing from a stage coach to a lightning express. We made first-class time until the General got tired of the road, and resolved to strike out a short-cut trail to the South Cheyenne river. Tin's led us into a handsome, but rugged, country which retarded our progress to a great extent. Custer City "civilization" had told on a few of the party, and Surgeon Hartsuffs hands were full in attending to the wants of the disabled. But there was no time for extra halts, and those whose stomachs were not in good repair had to take their horseback punishment without growling.

About 2 o'clock in the afternoon we reached the banks of a charming, sparkling mountain stream. The General, with his usual luck as a hunter, ran across and shot a fine, fat deer, and we all enjoyed a hunters' dinner. That being over, we again saddled up and followed our experienced leader through the ever winding defiles of the wooded hills. The sun was low in the west when we emerged from the southern rim of the Black Hills group, and we found great difficulty in getting our horses safely across the marshy bottom lands running along the handsome stream, whose course we had followed to the great plains. As we cleared the last of the foot-hills, we saw, not more than a quarter of a mile in our front, the waters of the South Cheyenne river, and felt recompensed for the toil of our journey.

After fording the famous stream, we found ourselves on an unbroken prairie, and soon struck the main wagon road, leading from Buffalo gap to Red Cloud agency. We increased our pace to a round trot, and then broke into a gallop, which we kept up for a number of miles. In all my equestrian experiences in the great West, I never enjoyed anything more heartily than that wild ride, in the evening shadows, across the plains of the South Cheyenne. I wished for a horse that could gallop without ever tiring, and the others with, perhaps, the exception of the unimpassioned Crook, felt all the mad ardor of the chase or the charge. Egan's grays did credit to the old 2d Dragoons, and covered the ground with a swinging stride that showed good blood and good grooming.

We continued our ride until 10 o'clock that night, when we reached a branch of War Bonnet creek, where we halted to water the horses. It was decided to keep on, as there was no time to be lost, and we did not halt again until 2 o'clock on the morning of the 20th. 'We picketed the horses, lay down on the frosty ground, put the half blankets we had along over us, and, tired out as we were, slept soundly until about 4 o'clock. The General called us at that hour, and away we went again. At daylight, General Crook pointed out to me a box-shaped formation on a ridge of bluffs some twenty miles away, and said that beneath it lay Red Cloud agency and Camp Robinson.

The rest of the road lay through a rough and barren strip of country, not far removed from the condition of "bad lands," and we were so covered with dust that it was next to impossible to tell whether we were young or old, soldiers or citizens, miners or robbers. We were about as hard a looking set of customers as ever rode through that country.

As we rode into the agency, a large body of soldiers from the neighboring post were standing around the saw mill. One of them shouted to the General, "Hello, where the d — hare you fellows been?"

One of the staff answered sharply, and instantly, "In Hades of course! "and the soldier, recognizing, under all that dust and dirt, a shoulder strap, disappeared in double quick time. The poor fellow was not to blame, if he mistook us for a squad of highwaymen.

Thousands of Indians flocked to see us—tall, powerful savages with lowering visages—all anxious to have a good look at "the Gray Fox," as they called General Crook. The latter remained only a short time, and set out for Fort Laramie attended by a small escort. Our horses were used up, so we had to wait the arrival of Randall and Sibley before proceeding further. They arrived during the afternoon of the 21st, and I, meanwhile, was the guest of Captain Hamilton and Lieutenant Andrus, of Troop H, 5th Cavalry. I also received much courtesy at the hands of as dashing and handsome a young officer as ever graced the service of the United States—Lieut. John A. McKinney, of the 4th Cavalry, who fell gloriously in battle with the tribe of the Cheyenne chief, Dull Knife, on Clear Fork of the Powder river, the following 24th day of November.

The officers stationed at Fort Robinson gave us all a hospitable reception on the night of September 21st. They crowded the commodious sutler's store, and enjoyed themselves in true military fashion. All formality was dropped for the occasion, and officers of all ranks mingled in the closest good fellowship. It was a most delightful reunion, and no two men were more beloved in that brilliant assemblage than they who are now but ashes and a memory—John A. McKinney and Philo Clark.

Our party, under Major Randall, marched for Fort Laramie on the 22d. We enjoyed the hospitality of General McKenzie, whose fate has been a sad one, at his camp between Red Cloud canon and Rawhide creek on the night of the 23d. He had most of his regiment, the 4th Cavalry, with him, and informed us that he thought there would be a winter campaign. McKenzie was then a noble specimen of the *beau sabreur*—tall, well built and with a frank, handsome face. Some of the fingers of his right hand had been lost in a Virginia battle, and, on that account, the Indians called him "Bad Hand."

I reached the railroad, from Fort Laramie, on September 27th, and reported at the headquarters of the Chicago Times about a week later. Mr. Storey, who was by no means liberal of praise, gave me his best congratulations, and I settled down again, for awhile, to the routine of journalism and city life.

CHAPTER XXIV

DEFEAT OF DULL KNIFE. SURRENDER OF CRAZY HORSE

The prediction of the late Gen. Ranald S. McKenzie— a soldier whose premature death is mourned by the nation as well as by the army—that there would be a winter campaign against the hostiles, turned out to be prophetic. Early in November, 1876, General Crook made up a column consisting of six troops of the 4th; two of the 5th; two of the 3d and one of the 2d Cavalry; four companies of the 4th Artillery, acting as infantry; six companies of the 9th, two of the 14th and three of the 23d Infantry, together with some guides and Indian scouts, to operate chiefly against Dull Knife's band of fierce Cheyennes, who were believed to be somewhere on the Powder river or some of its very numerous branches. The scouts discovered an Indian trail leading up the valley of Crazy Woman's Fork toward the mountains, and Crook immediately detached McKenzie to follow it up. That intrepid soldier carried out his orders to the letter, and struck the hostile village, after a cold, dismal march through deep snow, on the morning of November 24th. He attacked immediately and met with a brilliant success. Dull Knife's band was almost wiped out. Their tepees and other property were burned, their pony herd captured, and the chief himself escaped with great difficulty. He soon afterward surrendered at Red Cloud agency, and appeared upon the war-path no more. The gallant death of Lieutenant McKinney, already mentioned, and of several soldiers, attested the desperation with which the brave Cheyennes, although surprised, had fought. Most of the survivors of the tribe were subsequently sent to the Indian Territory, from which they made their escape by an unparalleled march. They were placed in the guard house at Camp Robinson, broke jail, escaped to the bluffs, killed a number of soldiers, and were finally slaughtered to a man by a few companies of the 3d Cavalry. Very few of Dull Knife's people now remain to menace civilization, but the gallant band has left behind a name of terror, at which the white settlers of the conquered territory still grow pale.

The Sioux hostiles, under Crazy Horse, who carried with him a majority, perhaps, of the warriors, became convinced, after Crook's march through rain and mud, from Tongue river to the Yellowstone, from the latter stream to the Little Missouri, and from Heart river to Slim Buttes and the Black Hills, that their game was up, and concluded to surrender to the General. They did so, during the winter of 1876 and the spring of 1877. The negotiations were mainly conducted by Col. George M. Randall, Col. T. H. Stanton, the late Capt. W. P. Clark and Capt. John G. Bourke. They were elaborate and very successful. Starvation had taught the hostiles a lesson that war of itself could not impart. They were keen enough to recognize that they could no longer depend on game for their subsistence. Peace was thus restored to the Big Horn and Black Hills regions, which were soon afterward thrown open to settlers by the government.

Thus of all the Sioux who, in the pride of numbers, had held their own against Crook and destroyed Custer in the summer campaign of 1876, there remained hostile only those under Sitting Bull and his immediate lieutenants—Black Moon, Rain-in-the-Face, Spotted Eagle, White Eagle and Gall; and even they had retreated for protection beyond the British line. It remained for General Miles to settle with them a few years later, as will be seen.

Crazy Horse did not remain long tranquil at Red Cloud agency. He was a wily, desperate and ambitious savage, the terror of friends and foes alike. He found that he was "a bigger man" on the war-path than at the agencies, and this made him frantic. He formed a conspiracy to murder General Crook and his escort, but a friendly Indian warned the General just in time to prevent a tragedy. All the malcontents were to attend a council that was to have been held, wearing blankets under which the weapons of death would be concealed until Crazy horse gave the signal for their use. He never got the opportunity. The friendly Indians conspired to kill the turbulent chief, and one of them, No Flesh—a noted Sioux of peculiar physical appearance—actually set out to assassinate Crazy Horse. The latter had gone to the Rosebud agency, where the Brule Sioux chief, Spotted Tail, the ablest of Indian leaders, had him arrested by his scouts and sent back to Red Cloud. When confronted with the guard house, Crazy Horse drew his knife and fought desperately. Little Big Man—as great a scoundrel as ever took a scalp—pinned the chief in his arms. Some soldiers also interfered, and, in the melee, a bayonet was thrust into the side of Crazy Horse, who died hurling curses at the pale faces and the Sioux renegades.

Trouble threatened for a time, but the death of the Indian hero—the bravest of all the brave hostiles—quelled the spirit of the tribes. They fell into apathy, and in that condition, for the most part, they have remained ever since. It is not likely that they will ever again give much trouble to the government, especially as the reservation question has been settled, in a measure, satisfactorily.

Although our regular army suffered cruelly during the war of 1876, it inflicted, perhaps, equal punishment on the enemy, and that, too, under circumstances the most adverse. Had the force sent against the hostiles under Crook, Terry, Gibbon and Custer, in May of that year, been of the strength attained by the army when the two department commanders united their forces on the Rosebud in August, or had either been as strong, individually, as he became in the latter month, the campaign would have resulted more brilliantly for our troops, and might have accomplished the total destruction of the hostiles in the field. As matters terminated, however, America cannot too highly respect the officers and soldiers whose combined heroism and endurance settled, in 18T6, the great Sioux difficulty on the main portion of our long-harassed frontier.

PART II.

THE CAMPAIGN ON THE BRITISH LINE

CHAPTER I

BEGINNING OF THE '79 EXPEDITION

Early in the summer of 1879, the settlers along the Upper Missouri river, in Montana, and the Crow Indians on their reservation in the same Territory, complained bitterly of ceaseless horse stealing raids on the part of Sitting Bull's followers, who regularly crossed the frontier, in spite of the best efforts of the efficient Northwestern police, raised by the Dominion government and commanded by the able and fearless Major Walsh. In addition to Indian encroachments, the settlers had to complain of the Canadian half breeds who kept up a constant traffic with the loose element on our frontier, and who "bagged "thousands of heads of game, from buffalo to antelope, for the value of their flesh (dried meat) and hides. The Washington authorities were duly apprized of this condition of affairs, and, in June, Gen. Nelson A. Miles, then colonel of the 5th Infantry (mounted), and commanding what was called the District of the Yellowstone, received orders to take the field against the hostiles, with his own regiment and the battalion of the 2d Cavalry then stationed at the Montana posts.

General Miles had kept almost constantly in the field in pursuit of the hostiles from the fall of 1876 until the winter of the following year. He is an officer of great energy, and of undoubted ability. His spurs were won early in life, and when almost a boy in years he had commanded one of the divisions of the famous Second Corps in the Army of the Potomac. General Miles did not graduate from West Point, but he is, by nature, a military man and has been eminently successful in his career as a soldier. During the year or more in which he campaigned along the Yellowstone and its tributaries, General Miles had had many conflicts with the savages, in all of which he was successful. He struck the enemy with a battalion of the 5th Infantry on a branch of Maynadier creek, on October 21st, 1876, and drove them beyond the Yellowstone, inflicting upon them considerable loss in men and material.

The General fixed the lines of his cantonment at the junction of the Yellowstone and Powder rivers, near the site of the present Miles City, and, from that point, operated against the Indians with consummate perseverance and skill. He literally gave the savages no rest. In January, 1877, he stampeded their main camp in Tongue river canon and drove them in confusion to a spur of the Wolf mountains, where a sharp fight occurred on the 8th of that month. These Indians were mostly Ogallallas and Cheyennes. They became disheartened and many of both tribes surrendered to General Miles in the months of March and April, 1877.

The severity of the winter had told heavily on the stock, as grain and hay ran low, and some of the animals died from cold and exhaustion. In the beginning of May, General Miles formed a column, consisting of five troops of the 2d Cavalry; two companies of the 5th Infantry and five companies of the 22d Infantry—the two latter battalions being mounted on Indian ponies—and moved up Tongue river for the purpose of scattering Lame Deer's band of Minneconjou Sioux, who were reinforced by renegades and stragglers from other tribes that had been defeated during previous campaigns. The General cut loose from his wagons about sixty miles from the cantonment, and, leaving one company of the 22d Infantry as a guard for the train, moved out with the rest of his force and a pack train to beat up the hostiles in their chosen position. He made an amazingly laborious cross march to the Rosebud, which consumed about 48 hours, and early on the morning of May 7, 1877, he struck the hostile camp on a tributary of Rosebud river, known as Muddy creek.

The village was taken with a rush, by a detachment of the mounted infantry, under Lieutenant Casey, of the 5th; and by Troop H of the 2d Cavalry, under Lieutenant Jerome. The Indians, nothing daunted, retreated to the bluffs surrounding their village and made an intrepid defense. The blood of the troops was up, and, animated by their gallant leaders, they speedily drove the savages from their lairs and pursued them hotly for several miles. Fourteen Indian warriors fell in this affair. Their leading chiefs, Lame Deer and Iron Star, together with nearly 500 animals, fifty-one lodges and an immense amount of buffalo robes, blankets and provisions fell into the hands of the victors. General Miles' loss was one officer, Lieut. A. M. Fuller, of the 2d Cavalry, wounded; four soldiers killed and six severely hurt. The captured ponies were used to mount such of the infantry as had lost their animals, and the hardy little beasts were made useful subsequently on many an arduous march against their former masters.

General Miles was reinforced during the summer of that year by nearly all of the 7th Cavalry, under General Sturgis and by a battalion of the 1st Infantry under Maj. H. M. Lazelle. The pounding of the hostiles was vigorously kept up, and they began to feel that, in reality, on this earth, there is no rest for the wicked. Nearly all of them that remained in the field south of the Yellowstone surrendered at the different agencies during the summer and fall of 1877.

Having disposed of the troublesome native gentlemen in the southern part of his military district, General Miles next turned his attention to the malcontents of the north. He organized a body of Crow scouts, which he placed under the command of Lieut. J. C. Doane of the 2d Cavalry, a gentleman of rare acquirements and picturesque appearance, and moved against Sitting Bull with a regular force, consisting of nine troops of the 7th Cavalry and six companies of the 5th Infantry, mounted, on the Fourth of July. He was condemned for rashness by some of the newspapers at the time, but subsequent events proved that he "builded better" than either himself or his critics knew. Rumors of the celebrated movement of the Nez Perces Indians, from the Pacific slope to the north, had reached the General after he moved out, and he thought it not improbable that he might be in a position to check their progress, if not destroy them, before they could succeed in effecting a junction with the Sioux hostiles who were then mustering in force beyond the British frontier. He made the force under General Sturgis a corps of observation, but Chief Joseph maneuvered so ably on Clark's fork that that officer was baffled, and the cunning Nez Perce, although pursued vigorously to Judith pass, succeeded in escaping from the toils of his enemies once more. The half savage chieftain had encountered General John Gibbon and several companies of the 7th Infantry at Big Hole pass, in August, and, although he suffered terrible loss, and was greatly crippled in strength, he succeeded in escaping with a large portion of his force, after having inflicted grievous blows upon his heroic assailant. Among the officers of distinction who perished at Big Hole pass were Captain William Logan and Lieutenant English of the 7th Infantry. Captain Logan was a very noted officer, and was affectionately known to the whole army by the sobriquet of "Sage Brush Bill." Only a few days before the battle of the Big Hole, Captain Rawn, with a detachment of his regiment, had succeeded in barring the route of Lolo creek, in the Bitter Root valley, against Joseph, and compelled that leader to seek another thoroughfare by way of Big Hole pass. The memory of the conflict at the latter place is not among the least of General Gibbon's well-earned honors.

CHAPTER II

MILES' BATTLE WITH CHIEF JOSEPH

General Howard, marching conscientiously in pursuit of Joseph, over a difficult country, formed a junction with General Sturgis about the 10th of September, but it was then too late to intercept the Indian Xenophon. General Miles, at once creditably ambitious and boiling with native courage, saw that a great opportunity had been lost; and that it was still possible to repair the error and pluck new laurels from the brow of war. He rallied his available forces, and, on the morning of September 18th, crossed the Yellowstone, having first made dispositions for the forwarding of supplies, and marched directly toward the Musselshell. By making incredible exertions, the General soon succeeded in collecting a force, consisting of three troops of the 2d Cavalry—those of Tyler, Jerome and McClernand, Captain Tyler commanding the battalion; Hale's, Godfrey's and Moylan's troops of the 7th Cavalry, Capt. Owen Hale commanding the battalion; Snyder's, Bennett's, Carter's and Romeyn's companies of the 5th Infantry mounted, Captain S. Snyder commanding, and a detachment of white and Indian scouts, commanded by Lieut. M. P. Maus, of the 1st Infantry. The General also took along a 12 pound Napoleon gun, which, together with the pack train, was placed under the charge of Capt. D. II. Brotherton, of the 5th Infantry, who commanded Company K and a detachment of Company D of that regiment. A breech-loading

Hotchkiss gun, operated by Sergeant McHugh of the 5th Infantry, also accompanied the column.

Having thus organized his command, Miles at once swung it into a position which commanded the pass, or gap, between the Bear's Paw and Little Rocky mountains, which, he judged, would be naturally selected by Joseph as an available line of retreat. He made three forced marches, and reached the Bear's Paw range on the 29th of September, but was sorely disappointed at having failed to cross the trail of the retreating redskins. He scattered out his scouts in all directions, and, finally, on the evening of the 29th, they reported that the Indian trail entered the Bear's Paw mountains, considerably to the left of the position which he then held. He marched, accordingly, on the morning of September 30th, and very soon after, having made nearly 270 miles since he started from the Yellowstone, came upon the Nez Perces' trail, just where it debouched from the mountain range and struck out toward the north. Suddenly some Indian scouts rode up to the General and reported that the hostile encampment was only a few miles further on.

Dispositions were at once made for the attack. The battalion of the 2d Cavalry was ordered to make a slight detour, in order that the village might be taken in rear, and the pony herd captured. The 7th Cavalry and 5th Infantry battalions were ordered to charge directly upon the village, accompanied by the friendly Sioux and Cheyenne scouts. All the orders were executed with dauntless courage. The battalion of the 2d Cavalry drove in the Nez Perces' herders and captured 800 ponies, while those of the 7th Cavalry and 5th Infantry rode directly on the lodges and, meeting with a desperate resistance, fought, hand to hand, with the gallant and infuriated foe. Capt. Owen Hale, at the head of his three troops of the fated 7th, charged over an exposed place, and, being mounted, he and his men were perfect targets for the enemy. He fell, dead, almost at the first fire, and Lieutenant Biddle, with twenty two enlisted men, also bit the bloody dust. The ground could not be reconnoitered in the haste of the attack, and many military men have held that the sacrifice of life was unnecessary, but Miles, having served in the Army of the Potomac throughout its bloodiest campaigns, and having witnessed the heaviest slaughter at the Death Angle of Spottsylvania, is not a man who cares much about exposing his officers and men to death, if an object is to be attained. He felt, doubtless, that he had to deal with a desperate enemy in Chief Joseph, and that the only way to use him up, was to go in, Second Corps fashion, neck or nothing.

The Nez Perces, although surprised and driven from the first positions of their choice, proved themselves entirely worthy of the reputation they had won on Camas Prairie, at Big Hole pass and elsewhere, and fought with the most admirable steadiness. In vain did Miles' three battalions, dismounted and determined, enfilade the positions of the foe. Even the west end of their village, most gallantly assailed by Captain Carter and Lieutenant Woodruff, commanding a detachment of the 5th Infantry, was so valiantly defended, the ravines were so difficult and the Indian fire, from magazine puns, so close and terrible, that the brave officers named were compelled to come to a standstill, after having lost about 35 percent, of their men. They did not fight in vain, however, because they fought coolly, laid many a stalwart warrior low, and stubbornly held the position, until Miles, seeing that his men were exposed to no purpose, ordered them to withdraw.

Gen. Miles, who sat on his famous black charger nearly behind the center of his line of attack, a mark for the bullets of the enemy, received no wound, although the balls struck close enough to make his horse snort and tremble with excitement. The uproar in the village was, according to eye, and ear, witnesses of the battle, terrible. Never, on any occasion, did the American aborigines display more heroic courage, and never did the American soldiers exhibit more unshaken fortitude.

Miles had failed to capture the village by charging, and began to think that it would be better to worry his enemy into a surrender. He counted the cost of his first experiment, and it amounted to the two officers already mentioned and twenty-two men killed ; and Capt. Geo. W. Baird, A. A. G., Captains Moylan and Godfrey, of the 7th Cavalry, and Lieutenant Romeyn, of the 5th Infantry, together with thirty-eight soldiers, wounded. He had to his credit, as a counterbalance to his loss, the Indian pony herd, captured early in the fight by the battalion of the 2d Cavalry. He knew that the loss of the ponies, and of a large number of warriors, had seriously disabled Joseph so. like Surrey at Flodden Field, he drew back his shattered bands, and placed them in new positions, where they could command the savages from all sides, and starve them into submission. He knew, like Surrey, that when the Indians came to estimate their losses, and their hopeless position, they would be glad to come to terms, unless reinforced from the north by the Sioux under Sitting Bull, which was one of Chief Joseph's great expectations.

General Miles anticipated such a movement on the part of the hostiles beyond the line, and made due preparations to meet the threatened danger. Twenty percent, of the troops engaged in the fight of September 30th had been killed or wounded, and, as the weather, which had been fine, suddenly changed for the worse, the wounded, the command being destitute of tents, suffered greatly. Everything was done to relieve their sufferings, under the able direction of the chief medical officer of the command, Surgeon H. E. Tilton. A cold wind and snow storm set in at night, and all of Miles' energy was taxed to alleviate the agony of the more seriously wounded of his officers and men. He was relieved from absolute want, on October 1st, by the arrival of Captain Brotherton with train, supplies and artillery. This greatly altered the aspect of affairs, and raised the spirits of both officers and men.

As General Miles anticipated, Chief Joseph soon began to realize the helplessness of his position. The General, accordingly, proceeded to open negotiations with the aboriginal leader immediately. On the morning of the 1st, Joseph and several of his men left their intrenchments under a flag of truce, and manifested a willingness to surrender. For sonic reason, the main body held on to their arms, although Joseph and ten other Nez Perces surrendered theirs. Lieutenant Jerome, who was sent by General Miles into the Indian village soon after Joseph came out of it, had an interesting experience, He was arrested by the chiefs in command, and detained as a prisoner, until Joseph returned to his lines on October 2d. He was treated well while in captivity, but, nevertheless, felt vastly more comfortable when he found himself once more safe in the encampment of his comrades.

The siege continued for several days, but was not marked by any very stirring event. Sitting Bull's expected reinforcements from the north failed to appear, and, at last, on October 4th, the Nez Perces formally agreed to surrender. General Howard, who had been previously notified by General Miles, at his headquarters on the Missouri river, came through on the evening of the 4th, with an escort, and saw the surrender of the copper-hued heroes, which was finally accomplished on October fi, 1877, and that remarkable episode in Indian war history was at an end. The government dealt leniently with Joseph, in view of the humanity and valor he had displayed throughout the whole brilliant, but lamentable, affair. The Nez Perces, inclined to be friendly, and Indians capable of progress, had been harshly treated, and much unnecessary misery and bloodshed was the result. General Miles' name is inseparably, and gloriously, associated with the surrender of Joseph and his band—all but a few who managed to slip through the lines and subsequently joined Sitting Bull—at Bear's Paw mountains. He says, in his report of the battle and siege, to his department commander:

"As these people have been hitherto loyal to the government, and friends of the white race, from the time their country was first explored, and in their skillful campaign have spared hundreds of lives and thousands of dollars' worth of property, that they might have destroyed, and as they have been, in my opinion, grossly wronged in years past; have lost most of their ponies, property and everything except a small amount of clothing, I have the honor to recommend that ample provision be made for their civilization, and to enable them to become self-sustaining. They are sufficiently intelligent to appreciate the consideration which, in my opinion, is due them from the government. The Nez Perces are the boldest men, and the best marksmen, of any Indians I have ever encountered, and Chief Joseph is a man of more sagacity and intelligence than any Indian I have ever met. He counseled against the war, and against the usual atrocities practiced by Indians, and is far more humane than such leaders as Crazy Horse and Sitting bull. The campaign of the Nez Perces is a good illustration of what would be the result of bad faith or ill treatment toward the large tribes of mountain Indians that occupy most of the Rocky mountain range."

Since General Miles wrote the foregoing, most of the Indians have been drawn in toward the Missouri river agencies, or sent down to the Indian Territory. Those settled along the Missouri have been peaceful for many years, but, as the General well remarks, injustice or ill treatment might kindle them into "a living blaze" at any time. White greed is not by any means satisfied, even though the fairest portion of the Sioux reservations have been given up to settlement. The cry is still for "more."

The blood of Oliver Twist must be plentiful in this free land, if we are to judge by our dealings with the unfortunate aboriginal race. Patience in the red man has narrower limits than the same quality in the white mortal, and we of the Caucasian race must confess, however reluctantly, that even the red Indian has some rights on the soil which bore him that the whites are bound to respect. The Indians have their vicious qualities, many of them borrowed, it is sad to be obliged to admit, from their invaders; but they have fought bravely, in every generation, for their families and their hunting grounds, from the Connecticut to the Missouri, and from the Missouri to the Columbia. Their misfortunes have been many, their crimes innumerable, but the honor of the American nation demands that the remnant of this mysterious, indomitable and interesting people should be protected against those of the white race who would not, if they could, leave an Indian a single rod of his native land, except for the purpose of sepulture.

CHAPTER III

ENCAMPED ON THE BIG MUDDY

I had just completed a tour of the Indian Territory, and was engaged, with Professor Paige, formerly of Council Bluffs, Iowa, and now of Chicago, in exploring the great bad lands lying along the Cheyenne river in Dakota, when, returning for a brief rest to Fort Sheridan, then commanded by Capt. Emmet Crawford, of the 3d Cavalry, I received an order from Mr. Storey to join General Miles' expedition, somewhere near old Fort Peck, on the Upper Missouri.

I reached St. Paul without loss of time, and there fell in with Lieutenants Quinton and Fredericks of the 7th Infantry, who were in command of one hundred recruits, sent from the Eastern depots to reinforce General Miles' regiment. We had a tedious journey up the Missouri, after we reached Bismarck, and embarked on the steamer Josephine. The recruits were noisy, but Lieutenant Quinton soon brought them to order, by appointing half a dozen provisional sergeants, from those who had served before, to keep them under strict discipline.

The boat, a small one, was greatly crowded, which added to the discomfort. One day, when about half way from Bismarck to Fort Peck, she got on fire, and then we learned that she had 2.200 kegs of powder on board for the use of the miners around Butte and Helena. Had that powder ever caught, everybody and thing on board would have been blown into atoms. We kept the ugly knowledge from the few ladies on the boat, and Captain Wolfgang, our pilot, spread tarpaulins all across the bows for greater safety, as occasionally the shifting wind blew clouds of smoke and millions of sparks down on the forward deck, beneath which lay the dangerous freight.

We reached a point on the river, near old Fort Peck, at an early hour on July 2d, and went into camp at once. As General Miles had not yet come up, the commanding officer, pursuant to orders, directed the construction of a breastwork of logs and clay, the better to resist any attack of the hostiles upon us. Our position was in a bottom-land, on the north bank of the Missouri river, the only available place of defense in the neighborhood, as the ruins of the old fort are commanded by high bluffs which would have rendered the building untenable. The worst feature about the post was a growth of underbrush, which ran close up on one side, allowing some chance for surprise; but then, there is hardly anything in this world that would not admit of improvement. The country around presented the average appearance. There was nothing in the least striking about it.

The river was about as muddy as ever, but had perceptibly narrowed, since we left behind us the deep volume of the Yellowstone at Fort Buford. As regards adaptability for grazing and agricultural purposes, I think it was averagely good—much better than a large section of the region further east. With the Indians extirpated, I thought it might soon realize the enthusiastic picture of the poet:

There's a land where manly toil
Surely reaps the crops it sows— Glorious woods and teeming soil,
Where the broad Missouri flows.

At that time there was a great tendency toward "farwest" immigration, Fort Benton and Helena being the main objective points. That part of Montana would have settled up rapidly enough, even at that period, if the ominous shadow of Sitting Bull in the north did not present visions of death and horror to the necessarily widely-scattered ranchmen. And yet, nothing better illustrated the dauntless spirit of the Caucasian race, than to see, here and there, along the hostile side of the river, a log cabin inhabited by some daring whites, who were prepared to risk all their worldly interests against the wild Sioux, at the muzzles of their long and deadly rifles.

As usual, the air was full of rumors, not unmixed with facts. Some said that all of Sitting Bull's outfit was encamped on Frenchman's creek, not very far from our redoubt. Others said he was on Milk river, and yet others thought that only a strong war party was on our side of the frontier, the main body being still guests of the British. 'We had information that the Assiniboines, from Poplar Creek and Wolf Point agencies, were out on a hunt, and that the hostiles were not very far beyond their line of operations.

Lieutenant Fredericks had left us, with a party of recruits for Fort Keogh, at the mouth of the Yellowstone, so that our small social circle at the stockade consisted of our alert and experienced commander. Lieutenant Quinton; Assistant

Surgeon Shue, a young Kentuckian, exceedingly fond of hunting, which, in the bottom lands of the Missouri, led him into ludicrous difficulties; Lucius Q. C. Lamar, Jr., of Mississippi, son of the Southern statesman of that name, and myself. Lamar was determined to follow Miles' expedition, although Quinton warned him that he would find Sitting Bull a sullen entertainer. The lieutenant had no doubt, however, but that General Miles, who was himself of adventurous disposition, would gladly grant Lamar the permission desired.

Our warlike preparations gave a color of romance to our situation. Our center was an old log cabin, which the former occupiers had quit in great haste, judging by the household apparatus left behind. The "make-up" of our fort reminded me of the descriptions of the famous redoubt on Bunker Hill —the great difference being that we were on a dead flat, covered with sage brush, undergrowth and weeds. As we had no horses, that did not materially distress us. The recruits hauling the dead trees to build the walls of our citadel were, like all greenhorns in the military art, boisterous to an almost deafening degree. Nevertheless, knowing that their safety depended on the solidity of their defenses, and, having a valuable knowledge of how it fared with commands that trusted too completely to luck, they worked excellently well, and we were soon fairly fortified. We experienced one bad disappointment. Two Hotchkiss howitzers, that might have been very valuable to us, were shipped from the ordnance department headquarters destitute of friction primers for the explosion of the cartridges. That was a stupid omission.

Just before supper, while the sun was a couple of hours high, a soldier looking at the bluff above old Fort Peck, the crest of which was clearly defined against the sky, had his attention arrested by the appearance of a large, dark object. "There goes a horseman," he exclaimed. Everybody looked, and then there were three horsemen. "Indians," cried the few veterans among our one hundred. "Cavalry," cried the recruits. Soon the crest was dark with horsemen scattered well out. There could be no further mistake. They were Indians, sure enough, and more appeared every moment from behind the ridge. The late afternoon is a favorite time for an Indian surprise party. Therefore, we thought we were in for a skirmish. Three of the men were out a short distance hunting and saw the Indians on the heights. They came running in at a pretty lively pace, which was small blame to them under the circumstances. Half a dozen mounted Indians dashed down the bluffs and rode at full gallop toward our camp. We thought, at first, they were a reconnoitering party, as the main body kept on the ridge. "To your places, men," commanded the lieutenant. "Reserve your fire until I give the order!"

The recruits showed a good deal of steadiness. Our three hunters soon appeared very near us, making first-class pedestrian time. The boys all laughed, although each man felt in his heart, that he, too, would have accelerated his footsteps if similarly placed. Such is human nature. Presently the leading squad of Indians appeared within two hundred yards, and, at their head, Ingram, a white man associated with the Assiniboine tribe. They were, then, agency Indians out on a hunt. If they had not been accompanied by Ingram, who was personally well known to him, Lieutenant Quinton would have halted the party within hailing distance. The savages on the hill, seeing their comrades amicably received, came riding in also. They numbered about sixty, doubtless not half their available strength. As usual, they had something to beg for. Their chief, Red Stone, made an appeal for tobacco, which could not be given him. We were told the hostiles were only forty-five miles away. After boring us for an hour or so, and eating up all our loose hard tack, the aborigines took their departure. Ingram promised to keep us informed relative to the movements of the hostiles, and said, also, that he would send in some fresh buffalo meat within a few days. He was as good as his word, and his supplies, which also included antelope, enabled us to celebrate July 4, 1879, in good form. A steamer, going down river, put on shore Lieut. H. K. Bailey, of General Miles' staff, who was a most agreeable addition to our little social circle.

The recruits enjoyed themselves greatly, and one of their refrains still rings in my memory:

Perhaps she's dead, perhaps she's not;
Perhaps she's on the sea,
Perhaps she's gone with Brigham Young,
A Mormon wife to be.

The evening exercises concluded with the singing of "The Star-Spangled Banner." It was certainly an unique Fourth-of-July celebration. Before it became entirely dark, the lieutenant made observations in the vicinity of the stockade and posted a few pickets in advantageous spots to guard against surprise. With Sitting Bull only forty miles away, every precaution was justifiable. Some of the recruits had never stood guard before—at least not picket guard—and their natural steadiness was attested by the fact that although frequently half scared by seemingly moving objects during the night, not a man of them fired off his musket.

CHAPTER IV

MILES ARRIVES AT FORT PECK

Capt. Sam. T. Hamilton, of the 2d Cavalry, arrived on the steamer Benton from Fort Buford on the morning of July 8th, and assumed command of the recruits and stockade, thus relieving Lieutenant Quinton, who was overjoyed at his release from that pestilential swamp, where heat and insects made life really not worth the living. The Benton, and, later in the day, the Rosebud brought supplies for General Miles' command, and two companies of the 6th Infantry, under Lieutenants Crafts, Thompson and Byrne, who were on duty at the supply camp. They also landed a number of ponies for the "conscripts" of the 5th Infantry. The latter looked at the "Cayuses" with anything but assured eyes, as among their many accomplishments horsemanship was not included. Even for a trained rider the average broncho is no joke to mount. His capacity for "bucking" leaves the active mule nowhere.

Meanwhile the mosquitoes had become so thick that, like the darts of the Persians at Thermopylae, they darkened the sun. We were obliged to "smudge" them out with damp sage brush and weeds, which raised a tremendous pungent smoke, and worked wonders with the intolerable pests. The recruits, mostly unused to great personal discomfort and driven half crazy from the combined effects of mosquito bites and the poison of the "itch weed," which grew all around the camp, ceased to sing and began to swear like Marlborough's troops in Flanders. They wanted to move northward, to go anywhere, in fact, so long as it led them away from the yellow waters of the Missouri. Many of those recruits were excellent mechanics and workmen, but preferred enlistment, with the certainty of small pay, to civil life, with the precariousness of wages. At that time, too, and I believe conditions have not much changed since, the United States enlisted man, was, to all intents and purposes a sort of day laborer. He was forever on fatigue duty to the manifest injury of his technical efficiency. This cannot be helped in the absence of a military labor corps, independent of the rank and file, which would allow the blue coats to become proficient in what has been called "the soldier's glorious trade." How absurd it sounds to have a batch of recruits sent into the field before they have acquired even the manual of arms, and while yet their ideas of "facings" are confused and necessarily awkward!

Per contra, it must be acknowledged that, although technically, the American recruit could not hope to be as efficient as the European soldier in the ornamental part of his profession, he had, up to 1879, the advantage of practical experience in the field from the start. Guard duty, picket duty, knowledge of Indian tactics, all came to him in his daily rounds, and, after a comparatively short period, he became veteranized to a wonderful extent, considering the irregularity of his training. Naturally "smart," the American "Johnny Raw" got seasoned in less time than, perhaps, any soldier of the civilized world.

At 11 o'clock, on July 9th, about two dozen horsemen appeared on the plateau beyond the "Big Muddy." We could tell by their "jibs" that they were mostly Indians. "They are Miles' scouts," said Lieutenant Bailey. Observations made through a field-glass confirmed his opinion. The party, consisting of friendly Sioux, Cheyennes and Bannocks, and a few white scouts, all commanded by Lieutenant Long of the 5th Infantry, rode down to the river bank and "hailed" us. The lieutenant was ferried across, and told us that General Miles and the main body were only a little distance behind. They had marched from the Yellowstone on July 3d, and had seen nothing on their line of march—about one hundred and fifty miles from Fort Keogh—except half a dozen straggling Sioux who were out after buffalo. The troops from Fort Custer, he said, had not yet joined the column.

The main expedition appeared on the south bank at noon, and General Miles began to cross his command on the steamers Sherman and Rosebud without delay. The infantry and wagon train were first moved over to the high plateau above the site of old Fort Peck. All the soldiers were mounted and many led extra horses. The pack train, for use in case of rapid marches, was admirably organized, and comprised remarkably fine animals of the mule persuasion, kept in order by a band of packers who were used to the business.

The Fort Keogh battalion of the 2d Cavalry, which was a portion of General Crook's column in 1876, remained on the south side of the river for the night. I found comparatively few of the old officers with the command. Some had died, and many had been retired from active service. It was pleasant, however, to renew acquaintance with Capt. Tom Dewees, Lieut. 'W. P. Clark, and Lieutenant Kingsbury, all of whom, in spite of continuous hard service, looked as well as they did three years before. Three years! The period is hardly a drop in the ocean of eternity, but what a gap it can create in human lives and in human fortune!

I met General Miles on board the Sherman. I had not seen him previously since August 10, 1876, when he was sent back from Rosebud valley to the Yellowstone to escort, with his regiment, Gen. Terry's wagon train to "the landing," with orders to forward supplies by steamer to Glendive, in order to provision Crook's column. The supply boat missed connection, with the result narrated in Part I of this book. Miles was beginning to show the effect of his arduous campaigns, in the deeper lines of his manly face and the occasional sprinkle of gray in his closely cut hair. Otherwise he looked in as fine physical condition as when I met him on the occasion already stated. I asked him what he thought of the prospects of a fight. He said it was hard to say, but added:

"If Sitting Bull wants a battle he certainly shall have plenty of opportunity from me."

"Won't he take advantage of the British line to elude you, General, if he finds himself too weak?" I asked.

"That's one of the troubles of this business," the General answered. "It is becoming so serious that our government must soon do something toward coming to a definite understanding with that of the Dominion."

"The Indians have been supplied with arms and ammunition within British territory, have they not, General?"

"The inference is plain," he answered. "When the Sioux were driven across the line, they were virtually helpless, they had lost almost everything. Now they have fine arms and plenty of powder and lead. They could only have procured such supplies in the British possessions."

"Supposing you have an engagement with Sitting Bull and whip him, will you respect the boundary line in case he should retreat across it?"

"That must be an after consideration," said General Miles. "I can hardly give a specific answer at this stage of the proceedings."

Subsequently I met Captain Baldwin, A. A. G.; Dr. Girard, surgeon of the expedition; Major Rice, chief of ordnance; Lieutenant Bowen, field quartermaster, and other officers, all of whom were glad to get away from the monotony of garrison duty during the hot months. I don't think any of the gentlemen anticipated much excitement, but in Indian warfare that always comes when least expected.

I camped with Captain Dewees and Lieutenant Clark on the night of the 9th, on the southern bluffs. The day had been fiercely hot, indicating that a storm was brewing somewhere.

My meeting with the hospitable officers mentioned was productive of many reminiscences of the campaign of 1876. Dewees was an excellent story teller, and was gifted with an open, generous nature, which made him a universal favorite in the army. He was a man of large physique, and his laugh was of that hearty, contagious quality which always sets a table in a roar. He remembered all the "characters" in the Big Horn and Yellowstone expedition, and delighted in recounting some of their peculiarities. After enjoying the primitive soldier supper, which made up in quantity what it lacked in quality, Dewees, Clark and I sat outside the tents smoking and chatting, after the manner of men who have campaigned together, and who have been separated for some time.

"You remember Major of the — Cavalry in '76?"

Dewees asked of me. I replied in the affirmative.

"Well, do you know," said he, "that Major was one of the queerest men I ever met in the army? He was brave as a lion, but slow and generally peculiar. He was more fitted to be a professor in a college than a major in command of rough soldiers. He never associated with his brother officers.

In fact, he seemed to shrink from their society. He devoted himself mostly to books, and was well read on almost every subject under the sun."

I remembered the indicated officer's peculiarities distinctly, and was obliged to confess that the Captain had drawn a perfect pen picture of him.

"Well," continued Dewees, "you also remember Colonel of the same regiment?"

"Yes, very distinctly," was my reply.

"They never could get along together, he and Major ,"

continued Dewees, "and many a time I enjoyed a hearty laugh at the verbal shots exchanged between them, whenever duty brought them in contact. The hearty old colonel delighted in treading on the corns of his irritable subordinate, and the latter never failed to get in a suitable word of retaliation. They kept spatting at each other all summer. Finally, after that wearisome cross march, Crook's men reached the junction of the Yellowstone and Powder rivers. It was, as both you and Clark know, most infernal weather.

Major , who had been wounded in the leg, was slightly lame, and Colonel , desirous of annoying him, affected to believe that the major was suffering from rheumatism.

"' I regret to see that the campaign is having a bad effect upon you, Major ,' said Colonel , in the blandest accents he could muster.

"' Thank you very much, Colonel ,' replied the testy major, 'but men of your years take comfort in making yourselves out stronger than your juniors. I am not ill, I assure you. I am only suffering from that old wound. You were never wounded, colonel, were you?'

"Now," said Dewees," Major could not have touched the brave old colonel on a sorer point than that. The latter had several scars on his head and body, all made by the sabre, and this the major knew as well as anybody in the whole outfit. Colonel flushed hotly for a moment, but, instead of making an angry reply, he merely said: 'I see, Major , that Colonel has been promoted to the rank of general. I should think that a man of your infirmities, who does not wish to be retired, would find the position of assistant very comfortable and enjoyable.

"'Thank you very much, colonel, for your kind consideration,' replied Major , with his most courtly manner, but I happen to know Colonel whom you mention. A little of him goes a very long way with me, colonel. He is entirely too much like you Colonel, entirely too much. Good-day Colonel , good-day.'

"The major marched off with flying colors, and for once, the sharp old colonel acknowledged himself beaten."

"That is a good story, Dewees," remarked Lieutenant Clark, "and, what is better, it is entirely true. But you recollect Captain G of the cavalry? He was not in that campaign, but he is a character, too, in his way. He is very absent-minded, and, having seen much hard service, is now rather used up. Ho uses many peculiar expressions in a thoughtless manner, and the habit often occasions him great embarrassment. Well, one day he was traveling in a Pullman car, between Sidney and Fort Steele, and was in undress uniform. After a little time, he settled down to read a newspaper. A lady sitting on the opposite side of the car, a hard-faced, practical looking dowager, approached the captain and said, 'You are Captain of the Cavalry?'

"'Yes madam, I have that honor,' replied Captain G with all the suavity of which he was capable.

"' Well,' said she, 'I am Mrs. , wife of your brother officer, Captain , stationed at Fort Steele.'

"' Well, well, who'd have thought it ?' said Captain G in his usually absent manner. The dowager collapsed, and Captain G was allowed to read his paper in peace during the rest of that journey."

Clark's story, told in his inimitable way, made both of his auditors laugh heartily, and thus passed the evening of our pleasant reunion.

We were all tired, and went to bed early. I was sound asleep, when, suddenly, a tremendous peal of thunder disturbed my dreams. Scarcely had I opened my eyes when a tornado burst upon the camp. Our tents were lifted like so much paper, and swept away. The rain fell in blinding torrents, and, in less time than it takes me to write this, we were all drenched to the bone. So dense was the shower that I had to cover my face with a blanket until the worst was over. The lightning that accompanied the storm was vivid beyond description, and the continuous roll of the thunder, heard above the fierce howling of the wind, was sublime in all its crashing continuity. In spite of the wet, when the wind subsided, I slept soundly until the sun was well up. Nearly everybody in camp did the same. When a man goes into the Indian expedition business, he must never make himself unhappy about trifles. Whatever may occur to him, he should always be thankful that it is no worse. And yet there are hundreds of strong men in civilization who would be killed by sleeping in wet clothes for one night. Rheumatism and pneumonia ever follow the storm cloud.

General Thomas, paymaster of the department, paid the Indian scouts next day. Most of those fellows were hostile in the days of Custer, but since they came into the government service, they were wondrously "loyal"—for Indians. People who imagine that the aborigines possess none of the finer feelings of humanity, will, perhaps, be enlightened by the following list of remittances sent to their families by our allied Sioux and Cheyenne warriors:

Spotted Bear, $20; White Horse, $20; Spotted 'Wolf, $20; Brown 'Wolf, $15; Two Moons, $15 ; Hump, $10; Tall Bull, $10; Yellow Dog, $10; Little Bull, $10; Poor Elk, $10; Bobtail Horse, $10 ; Point, $10; Bull Head, $10; Spotted Wolf, $10; Little Horse, $10 ; Old Two Moons, $10.

Some of these provident savages sent the cash to their wives and children, some to their fathers and mothers, and not a few to collateral relatives and impecunious friends.

As Old Two Moons is mentioned, it is worthy of remark that he, as a Cheyenne chief, took a leading part in the battle of the Little Big Horn. Later in our campaign, when Long Dog, Sitting Bull's friend, who came with Major Walsh to visit General Miles, reproached him with having gone back on the Sioux, the stout old warrior scornfully replied: "No, the Sioux went back on my people. When we fought you ran away." Long Dog, who was a politic old rascal, did not find it necessary to continue the conversation. He, at least, changed the subject.

The Fort Custer battalion of the 2d Cavalry, commanded by Maj. David S. Gordon, as good a soldier as ever set squadron in array, arrived on the south bank of the river on the evening of the 11th, and crossed to the north side early on the morning of the 12th. This operation united the whole command, and we knew that a forward movement would be ordered immediately.

It was not a large body of troops, but it was well put together and ably commanded. Miles was then, and is now, a splendid field soldier, prompt, bold and magnetic. He was always in high spirits, which is a good thing in a commanding officer.

As the General, from reports made to him, entertained grave doubts as to the loyalty of the Assiniboines—a branch of the Sioux tribe—toward the government, he sent for their chiefs immediately on his arrival, and they came in, headed by our old acquaintance, Eed Stone, to talk peace and friendship.

The chiefs complained that they were unjustly treated and crushed, as it were, between two mill-stones. On the one side were the soldiers, ready to fly at them on the first pretext as friends of the Sioux, while, on the other hand, the hostiles insulted and menaced them as being friends of the whites.

"Well," said the General, imperturbably, "you will have to choose right away between Sitting Bull and the army."

The chiefs then promised twenty good warriors for the expedition as an earnest of their great loyalty to the Great Father.

The head soldier, Old Necklace, said to the General: "1 hope you'll have a good time north. The Sioux up there are like the grass."

"And like the grass, we shall burn them up," was the General's retort.

The training of the recruits to back their ponies properly, recalled the scene on Goose creek, in 1876, when General Crook mounted his infantry on mules preparatory to marching on the Rosebud.

The ponies were pretty wild, and the city boys, utterly unused to equestrianism, were tossed around like so many footballs. Some of the "conscripts," when their animals got started, would clutch fiercely at the cantle or at the pommel, just as drowning men are said to catch at a weed in deep water. Others rode so loosely that a quick step, or a sharp turn of their steeds, sent them flying like spread eagles through the air, to the great amusement of their more seasoned comrades.

One fellow, who mounted a cayuse bare-backed, forgot to remove his spurs, and when the pony began to jump, he attempted to hold on with his rowels. The animal did not appreciate that style of riding, and soon gave a buck-jump that sent poor "Johnny "a good way nearer heaven than he had ever anticipated. A few men were severely bruised in falling.

Major Rice had been experimenting with his guns, and was delighted with their efficiency. The new Hotchkiss revolver is a most remarkable piece of ordnance. It has five barrels of small diameter, and is fed by a kind of "hopper" at the left side of the breech. It can fling shell or shot with remarkable accuracy, to a great distance, and against "Lo" proved a very efficient agent of panic, if not of destruction. Our Indians regarded the weapon with awe, and did not care to be too close when it was fired with rapidity. With all extra trappings, this excellent cannon does not weigh more than 3,500 pounds, and, like the single-barreled Hotchkiss, can be hauled along and handled without any particular embarrassment. Its range is 2,500 yards, and its effect among a body of green troops, or savages unused to artillery, could not fail to be demoralizing in the extreme. Had Custer had this arm at the Little Big Horn, the issue of that disastrous day might have been reversed. Artillery has been somewhat improved even within the short space of the last decade, but I much doubt whether a better arm, for light field service in a difficult country, than the Hotchkiss gun could be devised.

CHAPTER V

SITTING BULL'S LAST FIGHT

General Miles began his march from Fort Peck, along the right bank of the Milk river, on the morning of the 15th. We halted that day on Box Elder creek, where we went into camp. The rain came on at night, as usual, rendering the old Red River wagon road a perfect slough. Next morning we were off again, Lieut. Philo Clark and his Indians in advance, because some Cheyennes had seen pony tracks, which indicated the neighborhood of a hostile hunting party. General Miles placed a signal station on Tiger Butte, some dozen miles from Fort Peck, and kept up communication by means of the heliostat, the same kind of apparatus used by the English in Afghanistan and Zululand. It is an idea borrowed from the Indians of both hemispheres, and is simply a method of telegraphing information by reflections of the sun in small mirrors. The flashes, bright as lightning, can be seen at an immense distance on a clear day, but when the sky is cloudy the heliostat is powerless to operate. Some genius might fill the gap by means of electric-light signals. The system is very efficient, if careful men are employed, but a steady hand and quick eye are needed to send or receive messages correctly.

Milk river is a considerable stream, with deep water and a quicksand bottom through most of its course. The banks are high and abrupt, and the watering of stock is attended with danger in all places, and, at most points, is impracticable. The fords are few and treacherous, and, like those of the Rio Grande, shift their channels every few hours. I suppose it is hardly necessary to say that Milk river takes its name from the color of its water, which bears some slight resemblance to lacteal fluid. As it is very alkaline, the similarity ends with the color.

We observed some herds of buffalo on our left during the forenoon, and some of our Indians amused themselves by chasing them in the whirlwind style peculiar to the native American. The day, toward noon, became distressingly sultry, so much so that nearly all the horses in the column were covered with foam and sweat. As we neared the old crossing of Milk river, near Campbell's houses, the site of an old trading station, the Cheyennes saw a couple of horsemen on the other side and immediately pursued them. In this work they were joined by the Crow allies. The aborigines stripped off their clothing, and swam their ponies over the fordless river, themselves hanging on to the head gear of their animals. They were soon "whooping up "the fugitives on the left bank, going forward in groups, as is the invariable custom of scouting Indians. We encamped on the river, just in time to baffle a fierce storm, to await developments. To go into any description of a camping scene—something painted and pictured oftener, perhaps, than any other on earth—would be stupidly tedious. Enough to say that, on an Indian scout, General Miles, like all experienced soldiers, always picketed his horses in the center of his battalions, so that there must have been a fight before the Indians could stampede any portion of the herd.

The country through which we moved from the Missouri was rich and pastoral in appearance. It is not unlike some of the better portions of Minnesota, and was then one of the best buffalo ranges in North America. This, no doubt, accounts for Sitting Bull's interest in keeping so fine a country for himself and his people. It is true that the wily savage was, to all intents and purposes, a British subject, but his influence crossed the line, and no settlers would venture on Milk river until the implacable savage was thoroughly whipped and humbled. I don't care what anyone says about Sitting Bull not having been a warrior. If he had not the sword, he had, at least, the magic sway of a Mohammed over the rude war-tribes that engirdled him. Everybody talks of Sitting Bull, and, whether he be a figure-head or an idea, or an incomprehensible mystery, his old-time influence was undoubted. His very name was potent. He was the Rhoderick Dhu of his wild and warlike race, and, when he fell the Sioux confederation fell with him, even as drooped the pine of Clan Alpine when its hero sank before the sword of the Knight of Snowdoun.

A delegation of the Yanktonnais, headed by Black Catfish, came into camp on the 16th, and had a talk with General Miles. They made the customary complaints about insufficient supplies at the agency, and requested a change of agents, professing to have no confidence in the incumbent. They also complained that no ammunition was furnished them and that they had to hunt with bows and arrows.

The General said he would report what they said to the Great Father. Personally he had nothing to do with the agent. As regarded the ammunition, none would be allowed them while any hostiles remained south of the line and while their young men showed a hostile spirit. If they proved loyal and peaceful, all the wrongs they complained of would be righted. They all uttered "Ugh!" drew their blankets around their manly forms, and, mounting their ponies, rode back to Fort Peck, vowing friendship. This was nearly always the result of an Indian council, but, in the long run, very little came of their good resolutions, for the Indian department pigeon-holed reports adverse to its pet appointees, except in extraordinary cases, and, "Lo," very justly, thought that no white man's promise could be relied upon. If the just complaints of the agency savages had been attended to in Washington, Sitting Bull's recruits would have been much less numerous than they were. But, then, is not the capital the seat of all wisdom, and why should any person on the far frontier, who saw how the thing worked, find fault?

About sundown our Indians came into camp, howling like fiends. They swam back across the river with a halfbreed prisoner tied to his horse. The poor devil looked half scared to death, which was hardly to be wondered at. The Cheyennes caught him after a chase of twenty miles, and subsequently captured his camp, people and seven wagons. Only for the strict orders given by General Miles and Lieutenant Clark, the whole party would undoubtedly have been killed and scalped. They brought the prisoner in as a hostage.

There was an engagement between Lieut. Philo Clark, with two companies of soldiers, and the Indian scouts, and a hunting party of hostiles, some distance up Beaver creek on the 17th. The Sioux made a running fight, falling back on their main body. Clark pursued, but immediately notified General Miles, who moved with all his available men to the assistance of the lieutenant. It was a regular forced march for twenty miles or so—the cavalry and mounted infantry trotting or galloping most of the way. The Crows and most of the Cheyennes stood faithfully by Clark, but the Assiniboines and the Bannocks came streaming back disconcerted. They had hardly bargained for hostiles so soon. The head of the supporting column came up just as Clark drove the Sioux over Milk river. Major Rice, by making great efforts, brought up two Hotchkiss guns and shelled the stubborn hostiles with such good effect, that they broke and ran like hares. They hate the sound of cannon and dread its long range power. One Sioux, when Miles and his staff ascended the bluff overlooking the creek, deliberately led his pony several hundred yards down the opposite eminence and fired at the group, without any effect. Then he mounted and rode off to join his retreating companions.

The manner in which the troops were brought into action —if the Sioux had wished for a general fight—was admirable. The artillery, in advance, fired over Lieutenant Clark's command in the creek ravine. The cavalry formed the front skirmish line and the mounted infantry the second. General Miles and all the officers of his staff were with the forward skirmish-line. The hostiles did not covet any further encounter after the cannon came in play, and, having thrown away tons of buffalo meat, pack saddles, lariats, and other articles of Indian wealth, made fine time toward the north. Our Cheyenne and Crow allies picked up several abandoned ponies and followed up the Sioux retreat until night came.

Five scalps, taken on the field, were the trophies of our side, but, without doubt, the enemy carried off some of their dead and badly wounded. Lieutenant Clark's loss amounted to two Indians killed, and two Indians and two soldiers of the 2d Cavalry wounded.

The sun was near the western horizon when the affair ended. Our train was several miles behind, because the roads were too miry to permit of fast driving. The clouds and the atmosphere denoted the approach of a furious storm and we were ordered to counter-march so as to go into camp with our train. I think every one who participated in that night march will agree with me in pronouncing it one of the most disagreeable ever experienced. The rain came down in blinding, bewildering splashes. The wind blew a hurricane. The thunder absolutely shook the ground. The night was pitch-dark, except when the fierce and fitful flashes of forked lightning revealed the fast-moving ranks for a second, and then left them wrapped in impenetrable blackness, except for a peculiar phosphorescent glow on the horses' ears. We had to keep close up on the heels of each other's animals, in order to make it possible for us to move at all. Under the dense pall of night we forded Beaver creek, which, in its swollen condition, was no easy matter. The stream was full of boulders, and the horses slipped and stumbled every instant. It was nearly eleven o'clock when the shrill braying of the mules announced the presence of the train. We had no chance of seeing where to go, and several officers and men lost their respective companies for a time. In the midst of the storm we tumbled in where we could, glad of an opportunity to get dismounted. It is not wonderful that Indian campaigners become prematurely old. All of us were heated by the long gallop of the afternoon. A few hours later we were drenched to the skin, and in that condition most of us slept until morning. The lightning at times seemed to be showered down as in sparks. Taken altogether, the situation was, if uncomfortable beyond measure, interesting in the extreme. But such is military life on the frontier—a compound of mud and romance.

Mr. Booth, a New York capitalist, went out there for a summer's amusement. He got the full benefit of the entertainment, but bore it pluckily. When we were nearing the Sioux in the afternoon, the New Yorker discovered that he was unarmed. He borrowed a pistol from a soldier, and, with the weapon naked in his hand, rode forward to glory. "Our mess" insisted that it was Booth's naked pistol, as much as Clark's rifles and Rice's cannon, that made the Sioux warriors take to their heels.

When the violence of the storm had in a measure abated, Major Gordon, of the 2d Cavalry, called my attention to a conical tent, which was pitched at some distance from us, and which was revealed by a candle light within it. After unsaddling our horses, we made for that tent, because we knew it to be headquarters. When we got there, we found General Miles and some of his staff listening to a gigantic, almost naked, Crow Indian, who was boasting of his deeds during Clark's affair with the Sioux, and who, occasionally, flourished a scalp that he had taken during the engagement. The General, having listened to the boastful savage, good-humoredly gave him a present and sent him on his way rejoicing.

Major Gordon, with the combined thrift and hospitality of his Scottish blood, produced a flask of excellent usquebaugh, which warmed the hearts of those who were as wet and miserable as it was possible for men to be. General Miles managed to procure us a slight lunch before we lay down to rest on some tent flies and blankets that were almost as moist as ourselves.

CHAPTER VI

ON JOHN BULL'S FRONTIER

The storm fiend never quitted us for a day after we marched from Fort Peck. The country was soaked through and through, the rainfall being almost without precedent. All the streams were flooded above their banks, which retarded our progress northward materially. We crossed Milk river on the morning of the 21st, with the water up to the bodies of the wagons. The infantry recruits, mounted on spirited but short ponies, found the fording rather a big job. Some got "bucked off" in the stream and some were run away with after the other bank was reached. Many of the situations were laughable in the extreme. The imprecations hurled at the animals by the New York contingent could not be matched anywhere on earth. Our Indians swam across like water-dogs—even the pappooses disdaining assistance. They are a wonderful race.

Our march to Frenchman's creek, on the 22d. was uneventful, beyond that we were drenched, as usual. The stream was so full at the Red River Half-Breed ford that we were unable to cross that afternoon. The country is a beautiful rolling prairie—a magnificent cattle range in summer, but a polar district after the middle of November. The gigantic mosquitoes nearly ate us alive that night. They and the rains make life very uncomfortable in northern Montana.

Early on the morning of the 22d, Lieutenant Long, our engineer officer, was ordered to try the ford. He swam his horse across, returned and reported progress. General Miles said: "That water -will run out in two hours. It will take us about that time to get ready." The clouds were lead colored, the wind was cold, and matters generally were provocative of the blue devils. Nevertheless we packed up and marched for the ford. The creek was a mill-race, and was positively dangerous. The General ordered in a wagon as an experiment. What won't an American mule driver accomplish? Despite the current, the "M. D." whacked his animals over. Their feet just touched bottom. "Let the cavalry cross," said the General. The cavalry half waded and half swam across. It was evident that the river was falling slightly. The wagons were forced over one by one.

After them came the infantry on their ponies. There was a constant shout from the officers of "Keep your horses' heads well up stream!" Most of the men obeyed. One fellow, a recruit, became terrified at the swiftly rushing flood, He turned down stream, pulling madly on his animal's bit. The pony reared up and the rider fell, catching his foot in the stirrup. He went under water immediately. His foot somehow got loose, and while the pony swam ashore, he tumbled down the current, evidently drowning. In a second, a little Irish soldier, Private Dowd, of Company A, 5th Infantry, spurred his horse into the current and clutched the submerged recruit, who grasped his arm with the grip of despair. For a moment it seemed as if both must go under. Dowd, with rare presence of mind, left the pony to himself, and the brave little beast swam safely to shore, bearing the men along with him. Dowd's gallant deed was heartily applauded by officers and men. Such a heroic act deserved public recognition, and General Miles appointed Dowd on his headquarters' staff at once.

The command came near losing Lieutenant-Colonel Whistler, whose horse became restive and nearly drowned the veteran officer. His escape was very narrow, but he spurred out of the danger manfully. Other accidents occurred, but nothing of a fatal nature. The Cheyennes and Crows were grinning on the banks at the awkwardness of the "Johnny Raws." The mules did nobly, and so did the artillery horses. We did not lose an animal at this difficult crossing. The movement was superintended by General Miles in person, assisted by Lieutenant Bowen and Trainmaster Curly. The latter is the man who, a few years before, was stuck full of arrows—seventeen having been cut out of his person—by Indians. Where he had room for all of them, is a mystery. They must have been as thick in him as porcupine quills.

That night we slept on Rocky creek, on the upper part of which there is no wood. The cooks utilized buffalo "chips," despite their dampness, and sage brush. The long billed insects made it exceedingly hellish for us. A very swift wind swept down nearly all the tents, and the untiring rain wet our clothing and bedding most vexatiously. And yet, a general wrote a pamphlet, or something of the sort, to prove that it hardly ever rained in that belt of country! I have had the experience of two campaigns to prove the very reverse. The mud of Montana can find no rival this side of Bulgaria.

The morning of the 23d broke gloomily. It was, we all knew, only one march to "the line." We were on the trail of the Indians defeated by Lieutenant Clark's party on the 17th. The air fairly stank with heaps of green buffalo meat, flung away in the hurry of the flight. A bow and arrows, with the scalps of two Crow Indians attached, were picked up by some of our men. The Crows were very much rejoiced at this "find," and preserved the trophies for the widows of the killed. The howling for the Cheyenne and Crow dead was hideous, but, as the Sioux had a man butchered later than they, the savages were in some measure comforted. The Cheyennes are as proud as Lucifer, and rarely beg. They fight like lions, and arc, taken altogether Indians of the dime-novel type. Some of them are amazingly intelligent, and, strange as it may seem to my readers, are of gentlemanly deportment. Brave Wolf was as graceful as a courtier, and had a face of remarkable refinement.

The Crows are the handsomest of all the Indians. Some of ours were better looking than the whites. Their eyes were very large and brilliant, with long lashes. They were mercurial fellows. One day they would fight like demons, and the next night take to their heels like dastards. They are not over honest, and their women have a reputation for lack of chastity. They say they never killed a pale face, but this is questionable, as they are very savage in their dispositions, and are much more treacherous than either the Sioux or Cheyennes, although not accounted nearly as fearless as either. Their hatred of the Sioux amounts to a monomania. This is the chief reason why they are such faithful allies of the whites. It was the Crows who killed "young Sitting Bull" and five other Sioux, who came in under a flag of truce to Fort Keogh during the winter of 1876-77. This brutal act necessitated a renewal of the war. General Miles ordered the murderers to be hanged, but, during a great snow storm that followed the massacre, they escaped across the Yellowstone. Many got frozen to death during the flight. The savages subsequently explained that they did not know the meaning of the flag of truce, but that of course, was false. They said "How!" to the Sioux, indicating friendship, then hold their hands while others shot them from behind. This occurred within two hundred yards of the post. The Sioux say they will never rest until they get even with the Crows for that infamous slaughter. I don't blame them, for, fierce as they are, Sitting Bull's men would never be guilty of such dastardly work as that. But the exigencies of Indian warfare compel military leaders on the frontier to overlook a great many acts against which every instinct of humanity rises in revolt. This explains why the Crows still marched with the troops.

We had along about a dozen friendly Sioux, under the leadership of the famous warrior "Hump"—who had a nose like a bill-hook—with the column. Hump was a favorite lieutenant of Sitting Bull and Crazy Horse, but, being a man of sense as well as of courage, he saw the end had come after the buffalo began to grow scarce, and surrendered. He did his best to get the Uncapapas and other malcontents into an agency, and on their refusal swore he would take the field against them. He kept his word, and did some very excellent service.

Little Wolf, the Cheyenne chief, was regarded with respect by all the officers, on account of his honesty and fearlessness. He and Brave Wolf were accounted the two best Indians in the command. After these came "Old Smoke," a brave but ferocious Crow, who had killed twenty Sioux with his own hand. The Assiniboines and the Bannocks did not appear to have much fight left in them— especially the former, who were comparatively harmless Indians. The poor fellows had been whipped too often to have much stomach for leaden pellets. The whites had hammered them on one side, and the wild Indians on the other.

We had a fine hunt on the 21st, for "the British line." The Indians insisted we were then ten miles from it. We saw Woody Mountains, the hostile headquarters, quite near us in front, and knew we could not be far from "Europe," as the soldiers called the Dominion. We saw no material difference in the color of the grass, or of the sky as we neared the British dominions where Sitting Bull hobnobbed comfortably with his cousin John. After a prolonged search we came upon a rude heap of stones, with a small trench dug around it, which we knew marked the frontier, because three other structures of similar appearance were visible, a couple of miles apart, on a direct line east and west. Our scouts could see the hostile Indians viewing us from afar. General Miles went into camp immediately south of the boundary, and awaited developments. They came that evening in the person of Major Walsh and escort, who were received by Captain Whelan and Company G of the 2d Cavalry. The interview was short and formal, the major agreeing to visit camp next day. He had six Sioux Indians with him, and did not like to trust them with our gentle Crows. I think his head was decidedly level. The temptation to kill the Sioux would have been too strong for even Crow caution. Miles would have hanged the Crows afterward, if he could have caught them, but *cui bono*?

Lieutenant Tillson, of the 5th Infantry, who had been on a secret mission in the Dominion, came in during the afternoon. Our red allies saw him from afar, and thought he was old Bull himself. They were in their war paint, and one hundred of them immediately rode out of camp like so many wild beasts. They were awfully disgusted when they recognized Tillson, and came back, saying gruffly: "Ugh! White chief—tepee Keogh!" They wound up with the alleged indelicate remark of Cambronne at Waterloo.

That country is full of square pitfalls, some two feet deep, and covered by grass. Nobody knows their origin. They may be the work of the Indians or of animals, probably badgers. In any case, they caused numerous falls, and reminded me of the traps set by Robert Bruce for King Edward's cavalry when they charged the Scottish front at Bannockburn.

Major Walsh came into camp, according to promise, and we had a good time in the General's tent. He was a right pleasant man, with a strong love for Sitting Bull and his tribe. The Major did not inflict a red coat upon us, but was dressed in a very handsome buckskin suit. His orderly wore a scarlet arrangement, which looked like a drayman's undershirt, sweaty under the arm pits.

General Miles, after the usual courtesies, told the representative of the Empress of India that he had orders to drive all hostile Indians over the line; they had no business raiding into American reservations.

The Major said he had orders to notify our government of any hostile proceedings on the part of the Sioux. He did not know whether going to hunt the buffalo could be called a hostile act or not. The people were hungry.

General Miles said he had to obey orders. Our own Indians needed the buffalo. The hostile hunters did not confine themselves to game. They also, he was informed and believed, killed settlers and stole horses. He had knowledge that some stolen horses were then in the Woody Mountains camp. Major Walsh said he would assist in every way that lay in his power to have identified property returned to the rightful owners.

General Miles remarked that there were some Indians who had committed murders on the Yellowstone in the Sioux village. He wanted them. There was an United States marshal (Beidle) along to take them into custody.

Major Walsh said that would be a question of thorough investigation. It would be necessary to communicate with the Dominion government on the subject.

The General further notified Major Walsh that the property, horses, wagons and cargoes of all Canadian or other half-breeds found trading ammunition with the Indians, would be seized and confiscated, if found on American soil.

To this the Major replied that the post-traders in Canada sold ammunition to Indians for hunting purposes only. He had no instructions with regard to the half-breed traffic.

The conversation then became general, Major Walsh painting the Sioux character in such glowing colors that, were it not for his pleasant Irish accent, he might be suspected of consanguinity with the aborigines. He said they could outfight their own number of any white troops brought against them.

General Miles thought there were some American troops not far off who would not be afraid to try issue with the hostiles one to two, or even more.

Major Walsh smiled at this, and remarked that he had seen the best regiments of England, and did not think them equal to the Sioux as horsemen or shots.

A wrathful American citizen present remarked: "That may all be so, because the English have hardly recovered the panic following Braddock's defeat yet."

The Major laughed good-naturedly, and changed the subject with military dexterity.

He fully confirmed the strength of the hostiles, but said that the artillery had had a very demoralizing effect on them in the recent engagement, in which Sitting Bull himself had participated.

"The fact is," said the Major, "I tell you honestly, General Miles, the Sioux don't want to fight the white people any more." Old Spotted Eagle said to me, "Tell the white chief I don't want to fight with him, but let him give my young men a chance at those Crows and Cheyennes!"

The Major pantomimed the Indian chief very expressively. The rest of the afternoon was spent in "spinning yarns" and in having a general good time. Finally, Major Walsh took his departure, accompanied by his orderly. He waved a friendly adieu to all of us, and said that, on his return, he would invite me to visit the Teton camp in person.

The weather grew so cold, as evening came on, that we were obliged to don our overcoats. Even then we shivered, as there was only enough wood to cook coffee and fry bacon. I don't think Americans need lament that the "54—40 or fight "business fell through. We have quite enough of that country at 49, without a fight.

Major Baiter, with four companies of the 2d Cavalry, was ordered to march upon Milk river and capture such half- breeds as he might find there, on the 22d. This greatly reduced our force, but the General had about made up his mind that there would be no further fighting. Most of the officers grew tired of the inaction of camp, and, in the spirit of Fitz Eustace, said:

Unworthy office here to stay.

No hope of gilded spurs to-day.

There was some slight skirmishing between our Indians and an outlying party of hostiles on July 23d, in which a Cheyenne chief called Shadow-Comes-Out, was killed, and a Sioux fell also. Several were wounded on both sides, but it became evident, daily, that Sitting Hull's men were not nearly as dashing and reckless as in 1870, when the buffalo could still be counted by millions.

Starvation will tame the boldest, as has been proven a thousand times in civilized, as well as in savage, warfare. One reason why our Indian scouts remain so loyal when on a campaign, is that they are generally sure of being well fed. This appeals to the animal instinct of the savages. They are not much troubled with sentiment. As nomads, they never cultivated strong love for localities, except such as served them for depots of food supply. Mountain and plain are very much alike to the Indian, so long as he can feed himself.

CHAPTER VII

FACE TO FACE WITH SITTING BULL

I was a visitor at Sitting Bull's camp, on Mushroom creek, Woody Mountains, Northwest Territory, on July 30, 1879. The temptation to visit the village of the historic savage, known as Sitting Bull to the people of civilized lands, was too great to be resisted when the invitation was extended by Major Walsh, of the mounted police, who again visited General Miles' camp on Rocky creek, a few days after his first appearance there. I had a not unnatural desire to represent the American press before the Teton chiefs in their war paint, especially as the famous red marauders were making themselves quite at home, and supposedly comfortable, on British soil. I felt then, and I still feel, under great obligations to Major Walsh, for having given me an opportunity that otherwise might never have fallen to my lot, or that could only be attained by the sacrifice of my hair, and a scalp once taken, like a neck once broken, is beyond all human aid. So much by way of preface.

General Miles, whose spirit of adventure is very strong within him, laughed when I told him I was going, and, in his bass voice, he sang gayly:

We're marching off for Sitting Bull! And this is the way we go—

Forty miles a day, on beans and hay, With the regular army, I thought, as I heard the words and the familiar air, how much better pleased the dashing soldier would be if he were allowed to advance on the Sioux camp with a force capable of pounding the copper-colored enemy into subjection. My memory of American policy toward England forbade the entertaining of such an idea, because our policy on the northern frontier is essentially different from that in vogue on the line of the Rio Grande. Were Sitting Bull, at that time, protected by Senor Diaz' government, instead of by that of Queen Victoria's son-in-law, McKenzie would have been allowed to "whoop him up." McKenzie was managed with a "snaffle," while Miles was held in hand by a curb bit. Such is the difference between our affection for England and for Mexico.

We set out—Major Walsh, four scarlet-coated policemen, Long Dog, another Sioux Indian, and myself—from Rocky creek, over twenty miles from the British line, at noon on July 29th, and made forty-three miles that day, halting at Medicine Lodge creek, in Woody Mountains, just as the sun was sinking. The day was one of the warmest in my experience. The ruthless mosquitoes, which are a positive plague in that region during the summer months, swarmed by millions, their venomous bites covering our hands, necks and faces with blotches, resembling smallpox pustules. We went at a gallop most of the time, but even the breeze created by rapid motion, did not free us from the winged tyrants. T don't think that even in grass-favored Montana I ever saw finer ranges of pasture land than exist in that portion of British Columbia. The Woody Mountains, so called, are, for the most part, gentle bluffs, the crests of which form broad plateaus, where the herbage is knee deep. They are full of small ravines, or "coulies," many of which are watered by clear, spring streams, cool and sparkling as the dews of morning. Some timber grows verdantly on the banks of the water courses, and, frequently, on the sheltered sides of the slopes, and from this the "mountains" take their title. Medicine Lodge creek, where we bivouacked, was the favorite camping place of the Tetons, when they held their sun dances and other fanatical celebrations. Their "medicine poles" were still standing there, and the immense ring formed by their trampling horses and whooping warriors, told the story of how well the barbaric ceremonies had been attended. A strip of country bearing a close resemblance to bad-lands, skirts Medicine Lodge creek, and makes the position formidable, because of the comparatively rugged nature of the ground. It was at this point the Tetons were assembled, when the news of Miles' advance reached them.

Major Walsh, fearing a collision, persuaded them to retire to Mushroom creek, which is more than twenty miles northwest from the medicine grounds.

In order to obtain some sleep—the insects being viciously troublesome—we were compelled to swathe ourselves in blankets, at the risk of suffocation. Singularly enough the pair of Sioux suffered most from the little tormentors. Long Dog kept running around nearly all night, slapping his face and neck with great energy, and exclaiming "G "and "What you say ?"—nearly all the English he had picked up —every few minutes. The old chief, who had over a dozen bullet wounds on his person—some received from the Americans and some from the Crows—could not get the Hotchkiss revolving gun, which General Miles ordered fired off for his especial benefit, out of his head. We could hear him say, when he imagined no one was listening: "Bang! Bang! Bang! Bang!" and then, in imitation of the explosion of the shells, a few minutes later: "Pop! Pop! Pop! Pop! Pop! of a "The old savage, having so delivered himself, would lie back and laugh like a demon. Yet, old Long Dog was not so very bad a fellow for an Indian. He had a most remarkable face—well cut and with a lively expression. He was full of dry jokes, and, altogether, may be set down as an Indian original. If Long Dog were Sitting Bull, some romancist would have depicted him as a disguised white lord, because his hair is very light, although there is no reason to believe that his blood is crossed with that of "the pale face."

We were glad when morning came, and, having breakfasted with the frugality of frontier life, started for the village which so many American generals had looked for in vain, and which lured one of the bravest to his sad and sudden doom. I left the American side of the line prepared to believe that the numbers of the Indians had been considerably exaggerated, and said as much to Major Walsh. "Very well," he replied, "you shall soon see for yourself." A rapid ride of twenty miles brought the Major and myself, accompanied by two orderlies, to the last" divide" that separated us from the Sioux. The rest of the party, with Long Dog, were allowed to take things more slowly, as they were encumbered with a wagon team. I confess to having felt a queer sensation when, on mounting a high point, looking nearly northward, I saw, five miles away, a large village of white tepees covering the valley. It was the camp of Sitting

Bull, but I then saw only a small part of it. Hardly had we descended the hill, when the rude wooden buildings, which were once a half-breed trading post, and were then occupied by the police and a Canadian trader, stood before us, and a squad of mounted Sioux made a wild rush to meet us. They shook hands with the Major, but looked at me with an expression of evident displeasure and hostility. I wore a blue shirt and broad-brimmed white hat, such as our army people use on the plains, and they mistook me for a soldier. They spoke rapidly and excitedly to Major Walsh, pointing toward Rocky creek at the same time. He said a few words to them and they rode sullenly toward the camp.

"Those," said he, "are Long Dog's family." Some half-breed scoundrel has come in and told them that the old chief, the other Sioux, and myself were murdered in Miles' camp. That is why they are so excited." As we approached the village, the sound of a "tom-tom, "a buffalo-hide drum, and the fierce chanting of many voices announced that some kind of a savage dance was in progress. A broad circle of warriors, mounted and dismounted, was formed on the hill in front of the trader's store. We inquired what was up, and were informed that the Ogallalla war-chief, Broad Trail, better known as Big Road, and his band were having a scalp-dance. We dismounted at Major Walsh's quarters, and, having put away our traps, went up to see the wild exhibition. Elbowing our way through the dense throng of "young bucks," all painted, befeathered and insolent in demeanor, and all armed, too, with the best improved weapons of the day, we soon reached the dancing ring, which was occupied by about fifty men, mostly chiefs, sub-chiefs, and "head soldiers" of the Ogallallas, who were three-fourths naked, and painted in streaks and patches about as hideously as savage genius could possibly devise. They executed the most grotesque "steps" and figures, while the old men beat the "torn torn "and the shrill voices of the thronging squaws added wildness to the satanic uproar. A dozen magnificently mounted chiefs—their war bonnets all trimmed with eagle feathers and ornamented with quills, beads and spangles after the most approved Indian style— kept order while the "scalping tuft "of some unfortunate Cheyenne, quite fresh and ghastly, was displayed in triumph.

Seated on a Red River cart, beside a fierce looking, flashy Indian I noticed a very pretty young lady, with soft, brown eyes and cheeks of exquisite bloom. "Who is she?" I inquired of Major Walsh, for I was astonished at seeing so sweet a female blossom amid such horrible surroundings. "Oh, that is Mrs. Allen, wife of the post trader, "replied Major Walsh. "She is very much scared, as you can see, and looks on simply to please the Indians. She will go home to Canada at the first opportunity."

"Who is that Indian with the improved Winchester and gorgeous vest, sitting near her?"

"Oh! that is Big Necklace, a Minneconjou scout, and one of the biggest villains in the Teton camp," he answered.

At this moment the young savage fixed his eyes on us, and the Major, to distract his attention, introduced me to Mrs. Allen. This seemed to make a good impression on Big Necklace, for he at once reached out his hand and, grinning fiercely, said "How!" He was the first of the Tetons who took any notice of me in words.

The dancing and singing grew fiercer as the day advanced, and the circle of warriors grew larger every moment. At length some of the older chiefs came up to the Major and said something in the Sioux tongue. He turned to me and said: "You are in luck. They are going to meet in council, and all the chiefs will be present. They will meet outside my quarters when the scalp dance is over.

"So," thought I, "I am going to see the elephant. I have followed Sitting Bull around long enough, and now I shall behold, 'the lion in his den,' in earnest." Presently the tramping and shouting of the scalp-dance ceased, and the chiefs, their many colored blankets folded around them, after the fashion of the ancient toga, came filing down to the council, seating themselves according to their tribes in a big semicircle.

Major Walsh had chairs placed for himself and me under the shade of his garden fence. The chiefs seated themselves on the ground, after the Turkish fashion. Behind them, rank after rank, were the mounted warriors, and still further back, the squaws and children. The chiefs were all assembled, and I inquired which was Sitting Bull. "He is not among them," said Major Walsh. "He will not speak in council where Americans are present, because he stubbornly declares he will have nothing to do with them. You will see him, however, before very long."

Soon afterward, an Indian mounted on a cream-colored pony, and holding in his hand an eagle's wing, which did duty for a fan, spurred in back of the chiefs and stared stolidly, for a minute or so, at me. His hair, parted in the ordinary Sioux fashion, was without a plume. His broad face, with a prominent hooked nose and wide jaws, was destitute of paint. His fierce, half bloodshot eyes gleamed from under brows which displayed large perceptive organs, and, as he sat there on his horse, regarding me with a look which seemed blended of curiosity and insolence, I did not need to be told that he was Sitting Bull.

"That is old Bull himself, "said the major. "He will hear everything, but will say nothing until he feels called upon to agitate something with the tribe."

After a little, the noted savage dismounted, and led his horse partly into the shade. I noticed he was an inch or two over the medium height, broadly built, rather bow-legged, I thought, and he limped slightly, as though from an old wound. He sat upon the ground, and was soon engirdled by a crowd of young warriors with whom he was an especial favorite, as representing the unquenchable hostility of the aboriginal savage to the hated "pale faces."

Among the other Indians present, I particularly noticed of the Uncapapas, No Neck, a fierce-looking savage, who was said to be one of the most potent men in the hostile camp; Lone Bull, "Old Sit's" nephew, a tall, handsome, dashing warrior, quite young, but even then already high on the roll of martial fame; he was a savage of the romantic order, and will, no doubt, be heard from again, should the Tetons make another war against the whites; Bad Soup, Sitting Bull's brother-in-law, lean and hungry looking, like Cassius; he wore his hair somewhat as Lawrence Barrett docs when playing the part of the great Roman conspirator; Little Assiniboine, Sitting Bull's adopted brother, shot through the thigh on the 17th, at Beaver creek, and riding around since the day before I arrived, as if nothing had happened; White Guts, tall, thin, and gaudily dressed; he was young, but hard looking, and had the reputation of being a good fighter; Long Dog, who has been already described ; Pretty Bear, brother of the foregoing, much younger, more wily, and altogether an undesirable acquaintance; The Crow, Sitting Bull's orator, plainly dressed, middle aged, and dark featured ; Gall, a restless vagabond, who looked like a horsestealing gypsy, and was by repute a double-dealing, skulking rascal.

Sitting Bull told him plainly that he must choose between the Teton camp and the American agencies; since then he had remained comparatively quiet. Bear Cap was a chief verging on age, but still vigorous. He had been a noted fighter in his day, and was still quite capable of lifting hair if called upon to do so. Little Knife, old and sick, was once a gallant chieftain, and even then a man for whom high regard was felt by white and red men alike, because he was truthful, honorable, and, for a savage, humane even to his enemies. Clouded Horn was middle aged and plain looking, but said to be a wise chief in council, and a spirited one in battle. Rain-in-the-Face looked dark and fierce, but was lame from an accidental wound. This famous warrior bore the reputation of having killed General Custer, but the Indians refused all information on the subject, and Rain-in-the-Face himself was not an inviting person to ask many questions of, although his form and features were comely enough. Nobody, I firmly believe, knows who gave Custer his death wound, but there is little doubt that the remains of Col. Tom Custer were mutilated by Rain-in-the-Face, who bore a personal grudge against that brave soldier.

Of the Ogallallas there was Broad Trail, in the prime of manhood, finely built, small handed, and gifted with a fine, manly face. He came forward in his war paint before all the chiefs and shook hands with me. This was about the first attention paid me by any of the noted characters of the camp. The Hero, Broad Trail's brother, was a great orator, and a thorough Indian in every feature. Bear Killer, who like Henry Flood, had a "broken beak," was marvelously subtle and eloquent. Stone Dog was then young but already famous. Fierce in war, he was gentle in peace, and deserved a better fate than to be born an Indian. Low Dog was brave and sullen. He had little to say, but was a man of considerable action when it came to blows.

The Sans Arcs were represented by Spotted Eagle, who, like the wolf hound of yore, was

Gentle, when stroked; Fierce, when provoked,

This Eagle was a fine specimen of the North American native—tall, rather slender and very graceful. He was about forty-five years old. While his features were very dark his eyes were rather light—a contrast very remarkable. He has no white blood in him, however. The Spotted Eagle was one of the foremost warriors of the wild Sioux, but never carried his martial hostility into camp with him. He knew how to fight and shake hands. Sitting Bull and he are said to be about the same age. Bull's reputation was more of the agitator than of the warrior—a kind of Sioux Daniel O'Connell, with much more venom in him than "poor old Dan," because the latter never advocated bloodshed, whereas Sitting Bull did, and practiced it until very recently.

The Spotted Eagle was eloquent as well as valorous, but was not a mischief breeder. Some minor chiefs of the Sans Arcs were also present, but they require no particular notice. The hostile lodges of the Yanktonnais were represented by Pretty Hawk and Strike the Ree—the former then regarded as "the coming man" of the tribe. Little Mountain represented the hostile faction of the Assiniboines, and Iron Horn and Big Necklace the turbulent element of the Sans Arcs and Minneconjous. White Eagle, a famous Uncapapa leader, and Red Hand, chief of the San tees, were reported coming in from a hunt with over three hundred lodges.

Major Walsh, when all was made quiet, motioned the interpreter, Larrabee, to approach, and opened the council as follows: "I have come from the camp of the white chief. Bear's Coat (General Miles). He says none of you must go south of the line which has been shown to you and which will be your protection so long as you behave yourselves. ["How! how!" "Ugh!" and other expressions of attention.] The 'White Mother cannot protect you if you violate her laws. Your hunting parties must not cross the boundary in search of buffalo and other game. Wait until they come here. They are heading this way now. I saw droves of them near the line as I came in. ["How! how! how! kolah!"] Your young men can chase them after they come into the White Mother's country. I know your meat is nearly gone, and if the buffalo do not cross the line, then I don't know what can be done for your relief. One thing is certain— you cannot be permitted to violate the laws. I am willing to do all I can to aid you, within the law."

At this point a mounted Indian moved into the circle and communicated something to the Uncapapas. The interpreter inquired what it was, and was informed that two young warriors, who had crossed to Timber Buttes, on the American side, for the purpose of "rounding up" a buffalo herd, had been attacked by General Miles' Cheyenne scouts, one, Pretty Face, being killed and another wounded. Major Walsh continued: "Your young men will not hear what I say, therefore they must suffer the consequences. If they had kept here, as I asked them, nothing fatal would have occurred to them. So long as you remain deaf to my counsel, so long will there be death at your doors and mourning in your tepees." ["Ugh!"]

Bad Soup (through the interpreter): "Who is that man sitting beside you?"

"This man," responded Major Walsh, "is a friend of mine. He writes for the white men's newspapers, and will tell the straight truth about you."

Bad Soup asked, "Is lie not a head soldier?"

Major Walsh replied, "He is not. It is enough that he is a friend of mine. He has no bad heart against the Sioux."

The Hero (Ogallalla) then sprang forward, shaking hands with the Major and myself. He made a sweep with his arm southward and said, in his own language, fiercely: "When my young men go hunting over there, they are met with fire. My women are killed and my children starve. ["Ugh! ugh !"] My grandmother (the Queen of England) says I must not go to war, and I obey her. I see my people starving, and I go to kill the buffalo. The Great Spirit made no lines. The buffalo tastes the same on both sides of the stone heaps. I can find no change. Why then do the Americans meet us with fire when we only wish to feed ourselves and our women and children? The Great Spirit has given me a stomach— He has given me the buffalo. I see the buffalo near the stone heaps and I must not shoot him, even while my children cry for his meat. The Great Spirit never meant to tempt me with the buffalo so near while my people are hungry. This strange white man hears me. Will he put my words straight before the people of his natron?"

I nodded, and the Hero proceeded thus: "The chiefs would like to hear the stranger talk. My brother, who is chief of the tribe, would speak himself, but he is in his paint. I have spoken for him and the Ogallallas. The Americans ask us to smoke to-day and shoot us to-morrow." ["How! How!"]

It is not every day that even a newspaper correspondent has an opportunity of addressing an assemblage of Teton chiefs, with the renowned Sitting Hull himself for an auditor.

However, I considered brevity the soul of wit for the occasion, as will be seen. Through the medium of Larrabee I delivered myself of these words:

"I cannot rival the eloquence of your chiefs. The Sioux are renowned in oratory as well as in war—["How! how! how ! "] but I will speak with an honest heart. My business is to write what my people may read. I have not come to fight you or to spy upon you, but to see how you live and to talk with your wise men. ["How! how! how!"] All white men have not bad hearts for the Indian. Were I your enemy I could not sleep in the tepee of the White Sioux (Major Walsh); he would cast me out. ["How! how! how!"] I need not tell my brother why the white man meets him with fire beyond the stone heaps. I am not an agent of the American government, nor am I a soldier in its pay. I can do no more than a simple citizen of the United States—hear what you say and put it before my people. There is no need for me to say more than that Americans do not desire to starve your families or yourselves if you cease to make war upon them. Like yourselves, the Americans do not always hear the truth. There is no more for me to say." ["How! how! how!"]

Major Walsh further explained that my mission was to visit different nations and write about them. My father and his came from the same country.

Bad Soup then came forward and made a speech, in which he said that few Americans spoke the truth. He hoped I would prove an exception. "The Americans," said he, "have taught the Sioux how to break their promises. They took our land, piece by piece, until everything was gone, and we had to take refuge in the country of our White Grandmother. Are they a people that the Sioux can love? They send Bear's Coat and his soldiers to shoot us down. They arm the Crows and Cheyennes, the Bannocks and the Assiniboines, to murder our young men. Are the Americans afraid to fight themselves, that they hide in a cloud of Indian renegades?" [Fierce cries of "How! how! how!" while Sitting Bull's face was lighted up by a savage smile.] To Major Walsh: "How long will the Bear's Coat remain on Milk river?"

Major Walsh said, sharply, "It is none of your business, Bad Soup. He may remain there all summer, if your young men keep crossing the line. What need you care how long he remains there, so long as you obey the laws of the White Mother? I have heard that your young men threatened to cut the tents of the half-breeds if they went to chase the buffalo. The White Mother's laws must not be tampered with in that way. The young men who spoke of such a thing must have badness in their hearts."

Bear Killer came forward and said the young men did not mean what they said. He had also a pile of grievances to charge the Americans with. Chiefs could not always restrain the young men, but he thought it hard to have them shot down simply because they went across the line to round up the buffalo.

Major Walsh asked, "How often have I told them they must not cross the line on any pretext?" To this there was no answer. Spotted Eagle said that a hunting party would start out in the morning to look for buffalo near the mud houses, on the British side of the line. The Major said: "Very well, and, Spotted Eagle, you see that my instructions are obeyed." "How!" said Spotted Eagle.

Sitting Bull shook his blanket, mounted his horse, and rode off. The young warriors followed him. The other chiefs suggested a smoke, and I ordered the tobacco. After filling their pipes, they all came forward, Bad Soup, who aped Sitting Bull, excepted, and shook hands with me. The Spotted Eagle said he would have come up before, but he took me for Bear's Coat, whom he had seen at a distance once. He shook hands with him on another occasion, he said, but his features were hidden by a slouch hat, and he could not remember him well. I was somewhat flattered at being mistaken for so noted an Indian fighter as General Miles, but felt much more comfortable when the Indians were convinced that my scalp was not quite so valuable after all. The Spotted Eagle, who is a chivalric foe, would have treated the General well, but some young buck, thirsting for fame, might have murdered him just for the notoriety of the act, even though himself were killed immediately afterward.

Major Walsh and I then retired, and the council, which was, perhaps, the most singular experience of my life, was ended. During the evening Sitting Bull's wife, nephew and other members of his family called upon the major. Lone Bull and Little Assiniboine, also called Painted Face, treated me quite civilly. "Old Sit" amused himself in front of the quarters breaking in young horses. He was an excellent rider and a thorough paced Indian in every characteristic. He had, however, one grand virtue, which all must acknowledge —Sitting Bull never begged. He may have been acting a part, but it was, at least, a dignified and consistent one. The agitator denied that he ran away in a panic from the fight on Beaver Creek. He commanded the rear guard until the women and children got over Milk river, when Little Assiniboine took his place, as some one had to superintend the retreat, and Sitting Bull, being the elder of the two, was induced to retire. This shows that the great Sioux was not entirely insensible to the good opinion of the hated Americans.

To counterbalance the killing of Pretty Face at Timber Buttes, Grass Woman, Black Moon's daughter, reported killed at Beaver Creek, reached the Teton camp after a journey of twelve days and nights on foot, her only refreshment having been water. She was a middle-aged, hard featured woman, and her escape was one of the most remarkable on record. When the fighting commenced, she hid in the sage brush and remained there until night, although the Crows and Cheyennes nearly rode over her several times. She was nearly drowned while fording Milk river in the dark, and was obliged to keep a northwestern course, in order to avoid the Indians of Miles' command. This made her journey much over one hundred and twenty miles. The poor wretch was nearly dead when she reached her father's tepee. Her two brothers were counted the most dangerous men in the hostile camp.

What inventions of the romancist can equal in startling events the actual experiences of Indian warfare?

I retired to rest, pretty well tired out, "lulled "to sleep by the wild death wails of the Sioux whose relatives fell in the then recent conflict along Milk river.

CHAPTER VIII

HOBNOBBING WITH THE HOSTILES

I amused myself on July 31st by accompanying Major Walsh to a bluff immediately overlooking the Sioux camp, and from which a complete view of the numbers and surroundings of that great horde of savages could be obtained. On the level only a portion of their village could be seen at a time, but from that commanding elevation nearly every tepee of the tribes already mustered there, under the name of Tetons, was visible. Expecting, as I did, to see a great gathering of the Indian clans, I had no idea they were so formidable at that time in men and horses. As I was not in imminent danger, something that is claimed to multiply the numbers of Indians remarkably, I thought there were, at the lowest calculation, from 1,000 to 1,100 lodges in that encampment. There must have been 2,500 fighting men, at the least, in the confederated tribes. Arms and ammunition were plentiful, but food of any kind was scarce. The Indians did not seem to trouble themselves about concealing their strength; on the contrary they seemed to glory in it. and the young warriors wore an air of haughty hostility whenever I came near them. Their leaders, however, treated me respectfully. Sitting Bull only stared at me occasionally, but was not rude, as was often his habit when brought in contact with people he supposed to be Americans, whom he hated with inconceivable rancor. He said, to Larrabee, the interpreter: "That man (meaning me) is from the other side. I want nothing to do with the Americans. They have my country now. Let them keep it. I never seek anybody. Least of all do I seek any Americans."

This rather nettled me, for I had made not the slightest attempt to speak to Mr. Bull, and, in fact, did not care much to interview him, as he had been long ago pumped dry about his hatred to our people, and that was about his chief stock in trade, although I am not going to deny that he had some great, mysterious power over the Sioux, and especially over my own tribe of Uncapapas. He was in fact their *beau ideal* of implacable hostility to the pale face, and, like Walker from the well defended walls of Derry, he shouted at the United States, from the safe recesses of the Queen's dominions, "No surrender."

"Tell Sitting Bull," I said to Larrabee, "that if he does not seek me, neither do I him. I am not going to beg him to speak to me."'

The interpreter laughed and said: "It is just as well not to take any notice. He may be in better humor bye and bye." But this takes me away from the subject of the Teton camp. It was placed in a lovely valley, through which wound the crystal stream known as Mushroom creek, and was shaped somewhat like the figure 8, the upper and larger side containing the Uncapapas, Ogallallas, and Sans Arcs, while the lower held the Yanktonnais, Santees and Nez Perces, not to mention the ferocious Minneconjous and the broken remnants of different tribes assembled there for protection. There were, undeniably, among the Sioux some well-meaning men, for savages—men who believed they had been cheated, cajoled and robbed—but there were also among them some of the greatest cut-throats on the plains, demons whose names are written in the shame and blood of the helpless and the innocent, and who deserved to die a thousand deaths for their nameless crimes against decency and humanity.

Many of the high-minded and most of the vicious men among the Indian nations of the Northwest found their leader in Sitting Bull, who, although often unpopular with his fellow-chiefs, was always potent for evil with the wild and restless spirits who believed that war against the whites was, or ought to be, the chief object of their existence. This was about the true status of the Indian agitator in those days. He had strong personal magnetism. His judgment was said to be superior to his courage, and his cunning superior to both. He had not, like Crazy Horse, the reputation of being recklessly brave, but neither was he reputed a dastard. Sitting Bull was simply prudent, and would not throw away his life, so long as he had any chance of doing injury to the Americans. The agitator was then verging on fifty, but hardly looked it.

Mrs. Allen said he was the nicest Indian around the trading-post, always treating her with the most marked consideration, and never intruding upon the privacy of the household by hanging around at meal time, as some of the others did. In the hostile camp I had had several opportunities of studying his face, and I can say, honestly, that "Old Sit" has a fine aboriginal countenance, and, once seen, he can never be forgotten. I heard his voice many times—deep guttural, but, at the same time, melodious. He called my friend, Walsh "Meejure," his nearest approach to the pronunciation of "major." In manner he was dignified, but not stiff, and when in good humor, which occurred pretty often, he laughed with the ease of a school-boy. The traditional idea of white people, that Indians never laugh, is but a time honored absurdity. Among themselves they are often gayly boisterous, and I know of no people who can enjoy what they consider a good joke better.

But I have been again digressing. I ought to have said something about the enormous pony herd, which constituted, with the tepees and some household apparatus, the wealth of the Sioux. No matter in what direction we looked, there were the ponies and "war horses" grazing on the thick buffalo grass, or capering around, kicking up their heels in the full enjoyment of savage liberty. There could not have been less than fifteen thousand animals—enough to mount Murat's cavalry when he rode down the Russian center on the bloody snows at Preuss-Eylau. Perhaps some of them were rather undersized for a bold dragoon.

My eyes were fascinated by this spectacle—wild horses and wilder men, constituting the lingering chivalry of the barbaric nations, against whom, from the days of Columbus to our own, the hand of advancing civilization has been steadily uplifted. It was strange that, after centuries of relentless war, so large a body flushed with the memory of more than one gallant victory, should still exist and with all my confidence in General Miles as a soldier, and my high opinion of the men of his command, I declare frankly, although I was willing to take whatever chances might have come, I am glad it did not become a part of his duty to charge that nest of human hornets with the five hundred available men of his command. Like "Bonnie Dundee" at Both well brig, I knew Miles would not shirk the responsibility, but quite enough American bones had found nameless graves in frontier clay already. Custer's defeat should warn American generals not to follow too rashly the headlong creed of Claverhouse:

Though the grave before him lay.

Still, "Forward" would that soldier say; And his shout with latest breath Would be, "Victory or death!"

I don't think I'll write any more than has been written on the Custer massacre. No matter how interesting the subject, people soon tire of a single theme, and the Custer business has been written, so to speak, to satiety, each version of the catastrophe being, if possible, more melancholy than the preceding one. I will say this much only about it: The Indians said that one of Custer's companies dismounted and fought fiercely, killing nearly all the warriors they lest. The horses of the others stampeded and all became confusion. No one recognized George A. Custer, and no one knew how he fell, or at what period of the battle. The Cheyennes, who were then with General Miles, thought he was mortally wounded early in the fight and then carried where he subsequently died. How he received a small bullet wound in the head, is only a matter of conjecture, as. indeed, is all connected with the last moments of the ill-starred hero. I also learned that a certain high-flown interview, alleged to have been held with Sitting Bull, in which Custer is made to figure as the Long Hair—his hair, as already stated, was short at the time of his death—owed a great deal to the eccentrically brilliant imagination of the gentleman who wrote it.

White Eagle, of the Uncapapas, who bore quite a resemblance to Spotted Tail, and who was a fine type of his race, called upon me, in company with Red Hand, of the Santees, and other chieftains. We had a very sociable talk, and those warriors said they did not desire war, unless forced to it by sheer starvation ; then they might have to fight rather than starve.

Major Walsh stated to them the ultimatum of the American

government in regard to receiving such as desired to return to the agencies, on condition of surrendering their horses and arms.

This announcement did not please them at all. The chiefs said they had always been horsemen and warriors, and did not desire to be reduced to the level of slaves and beggars. It was no use, they said, to make treaties with the Americans. They never kept any with the Indians.

Even while we were talking, a wild wail rent the air in our immediate neighborhood. It grew louder and louder. An old Indian, with his face disfigured by grief, rushed in and said that his son, mortally wounded by our Cheyennes two days before at Timber Buttes, was just being taken home. The major did his best to soothe him, but the old man looked at me with a most revengeful expression, and, I have no doubt, had I not been with the officer, would have felt called upon to sacrifice me in retaliation for the loss of his hopeful offspring.

White Eagle remarked that the warrior was of his band, He had been hunting with Pretty Face, who got killed, and they did not know there was an order against crossing the line. The young man was shot through a very important and altogether indispensable portion of his anatomy— this is a very delicate translation of the Sioux chiefs version— and could not possibly recover. "Even if he did get well," said White Eagle, "he'd have to be dressed like a squaw forever more." Hardly had he done speaking when three or four women came in to announce the death of the warrior. He breathed his last as he entered the village. In spite of the terrible nature of his wound, the tenacious savage brought his two ponies to Medicine Buttes, where his friends picked him up, carrying him the rest of the way on a travoi. He saved his scalp which was accounted a great triumph by his relatives.

After the chiefs had left, I strolled out through the suburbs of the village. When near the trader's store, I stopped to observe some boys racing their ponies. As I did so, a middle-sized, well built young Indian came in front of me, and dropped the butt of his Winchester on the ground with a bang. I looked at him, and he looked fixedly at me. It was one of the Indian prisoners made by General Crook at Slim Buttes, in September, 1876! I wore a beard and was much thinner at that time, so he failed to identify me to his perfect satisfaction, but I remembered him well. He had served faithfully as a scout and then rejoined the hostiles. Had he recognized me thoroughly, the chances would have been very much against my safe return to General Miles' camp. He would certainly have taken me for an emissary from the American army, and that would have been quite enough to destroy my reputation with his savage comrades. Indians have little or no idea of what a non-combatant means, and all people who associate with their enemies are held to be hostile, unless vouched for by those in whom they have full confidence, as was the case with Major Walsh. When I told the latter of my adventure with the young warrior, he looked thoughtful, and said it was best that I should not notice the incident further.

White Eagle, for whom I formed quite an attachment, because he was a thorough soldier and disdained to be a beggar, called in the evening and smoked a pipe with old Larrabee and myself. He warned me, through the interpreter, not to remain too long, as the Indians were greatly excited over the death of Pretty Face and his comrade, and had sworn vengeance on the Americans.

CHAPTER IX

THE FRENCH HALF-BREEDS.BALAKLAVA'S CHARGE

The Indians appeared to be pretty short on meat supply during my stay in their camp, but the poor creatures had no more idea of the imminence of the famine which subsequently compelled their surrender, than so many children. The faithful squaws went out on the wooded bluffs and gathered all kinds of berries to make up for the lack of animal food. Yet it was the intense humanity of Major Walsh that absolutely kept the wretched people from eating their horses. I knew then that the reign of Sitting Bull would not belong in the land.

The question has often been asked, "Are there any really pretty squaws?" I will answer it here: There are not very many, but there are some. Many of the girls have quite attractive features, but, when they marry, hard work speedily disfigures them. In point of virtue these women, married or single, are like most of those belonging to the Northern tribes that have not come too much in contact with white men—as nearly perfect as human nature, civilized or savage, can be. This, I think, is one of the reasons why the Sioux nature is so vigorous, warlike and unsubdued. With all this virtuousness, in a physical sense, the Sioux women are not over-elegant in their phraseology. They can talk vulgarly enough, but when it comes to practice they are not false and frail, unless in rare cases. Such as do fall are looked upon as degraded beings, and are sometimes subjected to nameless outrages in order to scare them from the tribe. Notwithstanding the efforts of the French Jesuits for ages among them, comparatively few of the Indians of the full blood are Catholic, or even Christian. Many wear large gilt or plated crosses on their breasts, but they regard them, for the most part, as ornaments, and wear them as they would medals or other "gew gaws."

I failed to observe among the Tetons any of that overwhelming filth which is so often ascribed to the Indian. It has been my fortune to meet most of the great tribes of this country, and neither among the Sioux, nor the Cheyennes, nor the Crows, nor the Shoshones, have I been able to discover half so much slovenliness of person as I have witnessed in many Caucasian communities of the poorer order. They are very far ahead of the Mexicans of the lower classes in point of bodily cleanliness.

The cruel disposition of the Indians is as much a part of their traditional education as of their fierce natures. It may be impossible to change, at this late day, their undeniable tendency to bloodshed and human torture.

From infancy they are trained to endure suffering themselves and to inflict it upon others. Generations of this kind of thing can plant a vice so deeply in the human heart that generations of milder teachings can hardly efface it. When next, if ever, the savages shout their battle cry, civilization must meet them with a stern front and crush them relentlessly.

The half-breeds are chiefly of French and Scottish descent, the result of long-continued marital relations between the old French settlers, the employes of the Hudson Bay Company, and the females of the native tribes scattered all through that vast, wild region. Those people are, mostly, vehement Roman Catholics, blending the Indian and Caucasian characteristics most singularly. Their carts, nearly always drawn by single horses, are the most primitive affairs imaginable—old in style as the days of the House of Valois —with wheels bound in wood, and, in most cases, octagonal in shape. How they contrive, with such conveyances, to ship the amount of merchandise they do, is most astonishing to the uninitiated. Their harness is entirely destitute of iron. Their saddles are mere pads, easy on a horse's back, and, very frequently, elaborately worked with

Indian finery. They inherit the appearance of natives, slightly diluted with the paler blood of the Gaul and Scot. Ireland, too, has a representation among them, and both America and England can see their maps printed on not a few of the physiognomies that beam upon the traveler. Prejudice against color may, in some countries, retard the march of equality, but never will obstruct the increase of population. Woman, white, black or red, yellow or cream-colored, ever wears the crown. There being no white beauties in British Columbia, a hundred or two hundred years ago, the adventurous white men, who found themselves unmated, forgot the color of their skins and took unto themselves Indian wives, carrying out Tom Moore's free and easy philosophy, as expressed in the words:

Tis sweet to think that wherever you rove, You are sure to meet something blissful and dear.

And when you are far from the lips you love, Be thankful for kisses from those that are near.

I am afraid that same Tom Moore, the sublime and sycophantic and still matchless Tom Moore, was not a success as a teacher of morals.

The half-breeds occasionally live in log houses, but, as a rule, prefer the conical tepee, covered with the hides of beasts, so that often in camp they are mistaken for the aborigines themselves. They are very polite, and only in rare cases, however tricky and dishonest, do they approach barbarism. Not even the Indian cavaliers excel them in horsemanship. They distrust the Sioux, and hardly felt safe with the explosive savages so close to their primitive abodes.

In the evening I bade good-bye to the chiefs, intending to make an early morning start for the camp of Miles, which was down on Milk river by that time.

At daybreak on the morning of August 2d, while a fierce storm was just beginning to subside, I left the home of Sitting Bull, accompanied by four mounted policemen, and a half-breed. Major Walsh was kind enough to insist on sending this escort with me to Medicine Butte, for fear of accidents, I suppose. We reached there and breakfasted. Then Sergeant-Major Francis and one man returned to the post, leaving Corporal Burns and Private Bliss, who were carrying despatches to General Miles, to see me through the Sioux country. This was eminently necessary, as my horse was badly foundered and I was compelled to ride homeward some of the way in the major's private "gig." The redcoats, quite intelligent and respectable men, treated me well. I confess I felt a little odd at being escorted by them, because, for certain political reasons, I thought there was only one kind of place to which men in scarlet uniforms could possibly escort me, namely, the historical "British Dungeon." I could not get rid of this idea for some time, and imagined I was being conveyed through some of the green vales of Ireland on my way to Clonmel jail or Mountjoy prison. Truly, a traveling correspondent sees queer sights in the course of six months. In February of that year I was *en route* from Vera Cruz to the Mexican capital, escorted by the soldiers of Diaz. In August I was *en route* from Sitting Bull to the American camp, escorted by Queen Victoria's red-coats! I hope that, on the latter account, none of my "green, immortal friends" in Chicago or elsewhere will imagine that I had all of a sudden become "trooly loil" to the British crown. Truth compels me to admit, however, that said crown occasionally has for defenders men whom I should feel sorry to have to shoot at. After all. as I am but an indifferent marksman, I think they could stand the ordeal without much risk. If ever I am correspondent for the Irish or American army, which may lay siege to London some of these days, and this small part of the British Lion's forces should fall into our hands, I'll do my best to have them well treated.

In looking at the sergeant-major's uniform before he left us, I observed the Crimean and Turkish medals on his breast. He rode with the seat of the old British dragoon, when it was deemed necessary that every soldier should "bump the saddle"—the top of his big toe alone in the stirrup—at the risk of rupture.

"What," said I, "a Crimean veteran?"

"Yes," he answered.

I read on the clasps, "Alma." "Balaklava," "Inkermann," "Sebastopol."

"You have been a hussar?" I inquired.

"Precisely," responded the gallant veteran, whose hair and mustache were then almost snowy in their whiteness. "One of the 13th Light Dragoons, now 13th Hussars."

"What," I exclaimed, "one of the regiment that charged with the six hundred?"

"Right into the Valley of Death," said the old man, kindling up.

"Into the mouth of hell," I followed on.

"By gad, you know it all!" cried he. "I was a young fellow then—enlisted in '52—an English lad, wild as the devil. We were all wild in the noble 13th! How we longed for a war! We got enough of it afterward!"

"I wish you'd tell me all about it—I mean that glorious charge," said I.

"Then I will, although I have told it a thousand times to the young fellows," said he, proudly.

"Go ahead—you are about the first genuine Six-Hundred man I have met since I was a boy."

"Can I ever forget it?" he said. "Can I ever forget Balaklava? Its rush and clash and thunder are still in my ears, as that bracing 25th of October, 1854, comes swiftly back in the tide of memory! We had been skirmishing all the morning—my regiment, the 8th Royal Irish, the 4th Light Dragoons, and the rest—when all at once I found myself riding right behind the Earl of Cardigan. Captain Nolan dashed down, and, as near as I can remember, and as I heard afterward, which may have fixed it in my mind, in a ringing voice cried out, 'My Lord, the Light Brigade goes forward! Yonder are the Russian guns, and you are to take them!'"

"What did you think then?" I asked.

"I didn't think at all. There were the Russian guns extending clear across the valley far in our front and flanking us on both sides from the hills, so that when we rode on a short distance we were exposed to a crossfire. After a few seconds we recovered from the shock of the order— the humblest soldier could see something was wrong. Tennyson struck it about right when he said 'someone had plundered.' But what could we do? Cardigan wheeled his horse, his drawn sabre flashed for a moment, and he gave the word. Closing up, our men, stirred by the splendid peril of the situation, uttered a shrill cheer. Our walk became a trot—our trot a canter—our canter a gallop—at last a mad race right on the Russian cannon! The astonished enemy did not seem to understand for a little time. At last they did understand, and, with an appalling peal, their batteries opened full upon us. I saw, even in the excitement of that moment, Nolan reel from his saddle and fall to the ground. Everything swam around me, for Nolan was a favorite with the cavalry. I felt a mad impulse to kill, and could see nothing but the smoke of the Russian batteries and through the smoke dimly the tall figure of gallant Cardigan at the head of his thinned brigade. Right and left my comrades, horse and man, went down, but I had little time to note such things, for suddenly it seemed we were among the Russian artillery, cutting them down from helmet to collar. They fought furiously but died all the same. We had nothing with which to spike the captured cannon. Their cavalry came on like a storm-cloud, but we cut through them as if they had been mist, rode around and reformed again. Above all the noise we could hear the orders of Cardigan, which were repeated by his officers.

"The Russian infantry, massed behind the batteries, were afraid to fire, because we were mingled with their horsemen. Three or four times we broke through the cavalry, forming and reforming. At last it seemed as if the whole Russian army was coming down upon us. Then Cardigan, seeing further slaughter useless, gave the order to retire, himself being the last. Not one of us would have found his way back but for the courage of the French *Chasseurs d'Afrique*, who silenced one of the Russian flanking batteries. The whole thing was a dream to me. The world knows how few of us returned. As one of the 8th Royal Irish said in the hearing of most of us when we got in: 'Faith, I'm more astonished at escaping than if I had been killed!'"

The sergeant-major laughed at this bit of Celtic lightness amid the superb tragedy of Balaklava. "That," he said, "is my remembrance of the charge of the Light Brigade. Scores have told it before me, and every man has his own version. In material facts we all agree. After nearly twenty-five years, it is pretty difficult to be entirely cor. rect."

The story of the old dragoon interested me greatly, and, as I wrung his hand at parting, I felt that his uniform covered a man who deserved better of his country than to be arresting Indian blackguards among the wilds of British Columbia. It is not unlikely that this Balaklava hero may have had his head mashed by the stone hatchet of some blanketed savage. I know that he disliked "Lo" intensely, and resentment always begets a return in good time.

Our little party, reduced to four, made quick time to the "stone heaps," where we dined. The road, up to that point, had been excellent, but soon became a little rugged. A big prairie fire in our front told either of carelessness in the camp or of some Indian deviltry — more probably the latter. It appeared to be on the site of the camp where I had left Miles' column. We all suffered from the heat, but, nevertheless, kept steadily on. Toward sundown, having made about sixty miles, we topped a bluff that commanded a view of the old camp on the main stream of Rocky creek. No tents were there, and I knew we could not join the command that night. Accordingly we went into bivouac near where the headquarters had been, kindled a huge fire to bother the mosquitoes — the grass around the camp was nearly all burned down before — cooked and ate supper and went to sleep under the dews and the full, magnificent light of the August moon.

A pack of wolves serenaded us most vociferously. There was a heavy, white frost, which quieted the winged pests, and I never enjoyed a night beneath the "blue canopy" more thoroughly. At dawn I aroused the corporal, and, before an hour, we were again on the road, following Miles' trail. When within a few miles of his camp, we observed a procession, which we took to be an army corps at first, coming over the prairie from the west. Four dark groups in front indicated companies of soldiers on the march. I then concluded it was Baker's battalion, of the 2d Cavalry, having in tow nearly five hundred half-breed teams, with the families who owned them, captured up Milk river, and this subsequently proved to be the fact.

Just as we recovered from the surprise of seeing the host advancing in the dim distance from the west, the half-breed, who carried an old pair of field glasses, made a gesture of fear and uttered the word "Lacota!"which meant Sioux.

"If they're Sioux," said Private Bliss, "they'll respect our uniform, but if they're any of Miles' Crows or Cheyennes, we'd better look out."

We observed horsemen in motion on a bluff in our front, a mile or two away, and that they were Indians, became apparent very soon. The red-coats did not like the situation, and neither did I. If they were Sioux, the soldiers were all right—but was I? If they were Crows or Cheyennes, I might be all right—but would they ? These questions revolved themselves in my mind as the savage horsemen, now galloping their ponies like mad, came toward us in gallant, if terrible, array. The soldiers and half-breed got ready for action, but I told them to keep cool and await developments. But, for all that, I felt uncomfortable. If they were Miles' Indians, how could I tell what they might do with the soldiers, even though they left me alone?

Soon they reached near enough to make us out, and, according to their custom, they fired several shots in the air, and uttered their shrill, unearthly yells. Their leader was dressed in a light-colored garb, and I had the satisfaction of recognizing in him the famous Cheyenne chief, Little Wolf. who had surrendered to Lieut. Philo Clark, after a gallant fight, the previous year.

Little Wolf looked black at the soldiers and half-breed who had their rifles at full cock, ready for business, but, reining in, reached his hand to me and said," How!" Then he motioned to his followers, and they all swept off toward the north like a tornado.

"May I never!" said Burns, addressing me. "If you had not been along, those fellows would have scalped us, sure."

I don't think they would, because they feared General Miles' wrath and discipline, but, after all, I think it was much better for the soldiers that I happened to be with them.

We had some difficulty in following Miles' trail, but we subsequently found him very neatly encamped in the valley of Milk river, near the mouth of Frenchman's creek. Both he and his officers gave me a very kind reception, and they were much interested in what I had to tell them respecting my experiences in the Teton encampment.

CHAPTER X

IN THE LAST DITCH

The General informed me, after I had rested and refreshed myself, that the campaign was at an end. He had received orders from Washington to confine himself to patroling the Missouri river! This turn of affairs was rather annoying. The soldiers sent by Major Walsh brought despatches from that officer which hinted at a peaceful settlement of the difficulty. Miles telegraphed Washington to know what disposition he should make of the multitude of half-breeds captured by Baker's command. He resolved, however, to keep them near him until he received final orders.

Those picturesque people pitched their camp in a mighty circle a mile or two away from ours. The weather had grown delightful, and the moon was at its best. Accordingly, in the evening, the General, his staff, some other officers and myself mounted our horses and rode down to the half-breed camp. The light-hearted creatures had had supper, and, to the inspiring sound of dozens of violins and other musical instruments, were dancing on the green, under the gracious beams of the ever-beautiful orb of night, as calmly as if they were beyond the line, and not under the thumb of a very resolute American general,

The sight was an exceedingly pretty one, and several of the soldiers were granted the privilege of dancing a round or two with dusky, but, for all that, graceful and lovely partners. We enjoyed this interesting spectacle for an hour or so, and when we left the fun had not yet ended.

Next day we broke camp and moved nearer the Missouri river, the half breeds, under escort, following our trail. We crossed Milk river, near Campbell's houses, and there left most of the 2d Cavalry, under Col. Baker, who was ordered to look after the half-breed outfit until Washington could be heard from. The rust of the military were sent to their respective posts by different routes, with the exception of a detachment of the 5th Infantry retained by General Miles.

On our last march in, we met Captain M , of the ordnance department, and Mr. S , of the Winchester Arms Company, of New England, *en route* to join us. They had been out one night. S had never been on the plains, or, in fact, on horseback, before. He was full of the Indian business and saw a great many savages in his dreams. The captain, although an excellent officer, had not had much experience of the wilderness either. S agreed to stand watch alternately with the captain during the night. Through the uncertain moonlight he saw some wicky-ups that had been used and abandoned by our Indian allies on the march northward. He called Captain M , who inspected the structures sharply. Presently there was heard on the midnight air a loud and prolonged howl, followed by sharp, savage yells.

"That is an Indian war whoop, sure," said Mr. S .

"It sounds very like it," concurred the captain, "but I cannot make out the tribe. They may be Sioux, or they may be our own Indians."

"Either would be bad enough," remarked Mr. S .

"We had better keep still until we find out," suggested the military man.

Both warriors grasped their repeating rifles, flung themselves on the ground among the sage brush, and kept watch and ward until morning.

At daylight another howl and yelp arose. Captain M , who could now see clearly, sprang to his feet and shouted, "By Jove! that is a war party of coyotes!"

As he spoke the wolves scampered off.

The story was too good to keep and all of us enjoyed it hugely, but the General more particularly. Each of the gentlemen who figured in the adventure accused the other of being the party who could not make out the Indian dialect. Poor S has long since passed away, but during his life he never heard the last of the coyotes.

We reached the Missouri on the 7th, and some days afterward I took passage at Fort Peck on a steamer bound for Bismarck. At that place I learned that the government had ordered the release of the half-breeds, on condition that they would refrain from hunting on our side of the border. I don't know whether the released captives respected the conditions, but it made little difference, as nearly all the game had disappeared from that region a couple of years afterward. General Miles and staff, from a high bluff above Milk river, saw the last grand muster of the great northern herd of buffalo, once counted by the million, on the evening of August 4, 1879. The only specimens of the noble game now existing are to be found near, the staked plains of Texas, in the Yellowstone National Park, and in some of our zoological parks or gardens. The hide hunters, by exterminating the buffalo, did not a little toward permanently driving the Indians to their reservations.

The Indian difficulty, with the disappearance of the bison, soon settled itself. Canada could do little or nothing toward feeding and clothing the Tetons, so, gradually, their stubborn natures yielded, and, after negotiating with our government through that of the Dominion, they began to come into our agencies. Sitting Bull was among the last to surrender, but, with his surrender, when it came, "the war of centuries was at a close," and the final conquest of the Sioux was consummated.

ADDENDA.

CHAPTER I

"DESSERTERS AND DOG ROBBERS"

The subject of army desertion is occupying, at the present time, the attention of the War Department and of the country. It may not come amiss to say something about it in this volume. A dozen different reasons are given for its prevalence. Some suggest that it is ill treatment; others that the cause is laborious or menial employment. There may be something in these theories, as far as they apply to individual cases, but it is impossible that there can be enough tyranny in the army to cause over 3,000 men to forsake their colors in a single year. During the active periods of which I write, desertion was comparatively rare. The man who deserted at the beginning of an Indian campaign was indelibly branded as a coward. I have seen whole companies, difficult to manage in garrison and when near alcoholic supplies, throw up their hats with enthusiasm when the order to march against the hostiles was given.

There is hardly any monotony equal to that of American garrison life on the once "frontier" during these peaceful days. Officers and men assigned to small posts, feel very much as if confined on board a ship. All the acerbities and smallnesses of human nature naturally come to the surface. and a man, whether officer or private, must be much superior to ordinary human nature to stand the intolerable mental strain. The latter is much heavier on the enlisted men than upon their officers. The officers have, at least, the distraction of responsibility and their official duties keep them fairly well employed. Besides, they are men of education, and many of them have literary or scientific tastes, which serve to vary the dullness of professional routine. They are mostly married, and their wives, sisters or daughters make a charming social circle, which no amount of frontier isolation can break up. The ladies of the army officers, accustomed to the most courtly gallantry at the hands of their liege lords, brothers or friends, are, in the main, women of gracious dignity of manner, capable of subduing into refinement even those of the commissioned defenders of their country not endowed by nature, or by advantages, with patience or with polish. Occasionally, indeed, the ladies have small fights among themselves about matters of precedence, or something of the sort, but such little things cut no figure in the light of the high moral tone given by their presence and their example to the army posts of the wild West.

The enlisted men, on the other hand, have no such attractions to keep them in the path of duty. It is true that libraries and reading rooms have been established in all, or nearly all, of our garrisons, but men cannot read forever. Gambling is generally frowned upon by commanding officers, and drinking only leads to excesses and the guard house. Drills or other duties do not take up all the soldier's time. He is up with the lark, and he must be in bed when "taps" are sounded at 9 o'clock. It is an unfortunate fact that the American enlisted soldier is socially ostracised, except by laundresses and camp followers. This seems a hard thing to write, but the disagreeable fact remains. There may be a few—a very few—exceptions to the rule, since promotion from the ranks has been opened to our soldiers by act of Congress, but it is undeniable that the overwhelming mass of American civilians looks upon the poor United States private with suspicion, if not contempt. Thus it happens that nearly every soldier is glad of an opportunity to "shed" his uniform, when he goes on furlough or leave of absence. This, surely, is not as it should be, but where is the remedy? We must have an army. It is impossible to get along without it, although it is but a skeleton and ridiculously small in numbers for a great nation. As a rule, native born Americans refuse to enlist, first, because the pay—although the most liberal in the world—is comparatively small, and, second, because the average American, unless prompted by patriotic or ambitious motives, hates to be under the orders of anybody. He dislikes to surrender his individuality.

Therefore, the country is obliged to rely mainly upon recent immigrants, or the children of recent immigrants, who have not been fortunate in life, for the rank and file of its army. No rank and file on all the earth are better or braver than ours; but having, almost from the beginning, aped the English system, we have divided our army into two extreme classes. Its officers are by precedent, tradition, custom and conditions, aristocrats, if such a term may be properly applied to the chiefs of a republican army; while its enlisted men, wearing an honorable uniform, rendered heroic and illustrious by a thousand victories, are regarded, although not generally treated, as serfs. About the only parallel to ours is the English army, which is also an enlisted body. The conscripted armies of Europe, especially the French and Belgian, present no such unfortunate condition. But the evil is accomplished here, and can hardly be remedied in our day.

It is not the discipline within the army, but the disdain outside of it, that oppresses the American enlisted soldier. The more work he has to do, within the line of his duty, the better for him. He grows musty blue molded, when left inactive. Summer marches and cantonments, instructions in the higher branches of the military art, such as grand maneuvers, the construction of redoubts and field defenses in general—all these serve to occupy the soldier's mind and to give him a higher idea of his profession. The farther he is removed from garrisons where liquor is accessible the better, although a majority of our soldiers are sober men. But one drunkard or spasmodic "spreer "in a troop or company is sometimes sufficient to demoralize it. In the case of an officer addicted to drink the effect on the morale of his men is disastrous. A drunken officer is the greatest curse that any troop, company or regiment can be afflicted with.

As regards the, at present, vexed question of enlisted men doing menial work for their officers, there is reason in all things. Some of the very best soldiers I have known never refused their officers any reasonable request. Many of them, at a sacrifice of their feelings and their peace of mind among their comrades, became "strikers" simply because their officers could not procure civilian servants, and they could not bear to see them reduced to the necessity of waiting upon themselves. In times of peace, it may frequently be possible for an officer to procure civilian servants, but in war times it is generally simply impossible. Civilians, for example, do not care to take the chances of being killed or maimed, if duty should carry them under fire with their employers. They are apt to think of their families, or of their own position—in the event of death, or severe injury. They know very well that there is no provision in the pension law to cover their cases.

I know that many soldiers employ the offensive name "dog robbers" to comrades who do what is called menial work for their officers. They never think of applying the term to the company cooks, whose labors are not, to say the least, particularly aristocratic. The government provides rations for the soldier upon the campaign, but the officer has to look after his own supplies. I have seen, more than once, on Indian campaigns, officers without coffee, and, to their eternal honor be it recorded, I have seen the enlisted men, in the most delicate manner, supply the temporary deficiency. They were willing to share their last crust, if necessary, with the men who led them under fire; and, when under fire, I have seen the abused "dog robbers" do their duty quite as bravely as those of their comrades who put on unnecessary airs, and used uncalled-for language.

While messing, on one occasion, with an energetic officer who had an Irish "striker" named F , I remember the latter coming to his chief and complaining that one of the soldiers, a new recruit from New York City, had called him "a dog robber." "Well," said the captain, "You have my permission to knock him down the next time he insults you." F soon had the opportunity and exercised it. The captain called both the belligerents before him.

"How many battles have you been in ?" he asked of the offensive recruit. "None, sir," was the answer. "How many have you been in F ?" he inquired of the "striker." "I can't count them, without thinking, captain," replied F , modestly, "but I guess close on to a hundred!"

"You see," remarked the captain to the recruit, "that bravo men and veterans are always modest and accommodating. I shall order the first man of my troop who uses the term 'dog robber,' to a comrade, under close arrest. Go to your quarters."

The recruit did as ordered, and there was no more heard about "dog robbers" in that troop during the remainder of the campaign.

In the half dozen campaigns and scouts which I accompanied with the regular army, I was waited upon, as a general thing, by veteran soldiers. I always respected their feelings, and told them not to fall out of their ranks, to take my horse, until we got into camp. Notwithstanding, they usually did. During the Ute campaign in Colorado, October and November, 1879, I was waited upon, as far as attending to my horse was concerned, by a fine looking veteran of the 3d Cavalry, named McIntyre. He was a little wild in garrison, but, in the field, was a model soldier. He frequently insisted on paying me the attentions usually reserved for officers, such as riding behind me in orderly fashion.

I said to him once, "McIntyre I'd rather you'd remain in your place in the troop until the column halts."

"Oh, sure," was his reply, "our boys of the 3d Cavalry make no difference with you. You've been under fire with the regiment!"

There is a whole volume in the simple words of McIntyre. In the soldier's code of obligingness everything depends upon how you stand with his corps. When I told Col. Guy V. Henry, who commanded the troop, what McIntyre had said, he laughed most heartily and called me "Finerty of Ours."

Thus there are, as usual, a couple of sides, at least, to every question.

Nobody detests an official bully more than I do. I have met a few of that character in the army, but they did not remain there very long. Bullies are chiefly drinking officers, and sometimes they carry their offensiveness to extremes. Their brother officers, so far from shielding them, take the very earliest opportunity of having them court-martialed. In most cases they are dismissed from the service, and then they devote most of their lives to an effort to get back. Occasionally, in cases where reformation is thorough and sincere, they are restored, but this happens very rarely. An unjust officer is looked upon with contempt by those above him, as well as by those under his command.

The enlisted man of the American army is not always without faults. He frequently comes from the slums of great cities, and needs to be tamed a little before he becomes a good soldier. Once fairly broken of insubordination and wild habits, the American city-born soldier has no superior as regards intelligence, courage and loyalty. His country born comrade has fewer faults and vices, but I doubt very much whether he can equal the city-reared man in the matter of endurance, although he may be, at least, equal in all other respects.

The recruits enlisted from Ireland, Germany, Scandinavia and other European countries are, generally, more tractable than those, of any race, born here. The Irish are sometimes restive in garrison, because of their mercurial temperament, but, in the field, their cheerfulness, alacrity and elan make them the pride of their officers. An Irish soldier, even if he should sometimes happen to drink, rarely ever stands up against any order of his commander. He may kick and growl a little, but, in the end, he remembers that the first duty of a soldier is obedience.

The German recruit is, generally, docile, cool and well "set up," owing to his military experience in the fatherland. He is less restive in garrison than his Irish comrade, and, in the field, often lacks the Celtic dash, but he can stand fire as long as any soldier in the world, and, in case of panic, is as easily rallied as an American or an Irishman.

The Scandinavians have been famous for centuries as soldiers, and. in the American ranks, they have not degenerated. In fact our cosmopolitan army, made up of all the races of Europe, and also including Americans of African descent, possesses all the military qualities which have made the nationalities already named, as well as the French, the Poles and other warlike peoples, famous in martial annals.

The colored troops in our service are not without their shortcomings, but they are, as a body, faithful and obedient, and, in Indian warfare as well as during the Rebellion, have proved that they are good fighters, if only ably and courageously led, as in the case of Captain Dodge, of the 9th Cavalry, when he made that memorable ride to the rescue of Thornburgh's command, cut off and surrounded by the Utes in Colorado, in October, 1879.

In concluding this chapter, I can conscientiously declare that desertion from the American army is not, in the vast majority of cases, due to the tyranny of officers, to fatigue duty, to alleged menial employment, but to that invisible foe to the contentment of all armies, after "wild war's deadly blast has blown," and gentle peace rules the land— ennui. If the government can find some means of routing that ethereal enemy, our ranks will retain their full complement of men, and the American army will no longer have to blush for the base crime of desertion.

CHAPTER II

"SANDY" FORSYTH'S FAMOUS FIGHT

Often at the evening camp-fires of Miles' command, the officers used to relate their experiences of flood and field, and recall many a stirring incident or heroic deed, which deserves to be immortal in American history. Thus the Fort Phil. Kearney massacre, the Custer disaster, the Sibley Scout and other remarkable events would come up for discussion.

Colonel Baker, of the 2d Cavalry, a famous Indian fighter, was full of reminiscence and anecdote. One evening, while we were fighting-Indian battles over again, in front of his tent on Beaver creek, he said." I recall an incident that occurred about the time Fetterman was killed, at the Crazy Woman crossing. A small party of officers and their ladies, with a sergeant's guard for escort, together with some civilians, drivers and so forth, went into camp in that dangerous locality. A chaplain, the Rev. Mr. , was of the company. He was an eminently pious man, quiet and dignified, and, in fact, the last person in the world you would select for any dangerous undertaking. Everything remained quiet in the little camp until early morning, when the Indians, according to their custom, made a sudden attack and came near surprising the party. The vigilance of the sergeant, who was an old Indian campaigner, alone prevented a catastrophe. The Indians, baffled in their first attempt, fell back to cover, and kept up an almost continuous fire upon the white people.

Fortunately, the precaution had been taken, on the previous evening, to construct earthworks and dug-outs, as the Indians in that region had been troublesome for some time. As the day advanced, other Indians came up and joined in the attack. Several of the soldiers got hit, and, I think, a few were killed. The ladies and some of the civilians began to pray rather loudly. The chaplain, who used to be about as pious as a monk, while in the post, suddenly seized a musket, and said: "Ladies and gentlemen, there is a time for praying, and there is also, as we may gather from Holy Writ, a time for fighting. This is the time for fighting! God aids those who are willing to aid themselves. Now, stop praying and turn in to make some 'good Indians!'

"The effect of the address was electrical. Even the women were stirred by it to heroism, and loaded the guns for the men to fire, when the situation became hot. The fight lasted all through the day, and, when night came, that brave parson managed to get through the Indian lines, reached the nearest post, Fort Reno, and brought a strong party to the rescue of the beseiged. The Indians, immediately on the arrival of the troops, took to the woods. I greatly regret that I cannot recall the chaplain's name, but I can vouch for the truth of the story."

Another officer, in talking over Indian adventures, said that nothing in the annals of border warfare equaled in cool heroism and stubborn defense, the fight between General George A. ("Sandy") Forsyth and the Indians, on an island in the Republican river, in the fall of 1868. Forsyth had been one of Sheridan's "boy generals," in "the Valley" and around Richmond, and had gathered an armful of laurels with his sword while still in the greenness of youth. At the period mentioned, the brave and enterprising Southern Cheyennes, allied with the Arapahoes, Kiowas and other warlike tribes, were making it exceedingly warm for white settlers, stage coaches and, in fact, everything civilized in the Kansas valleys, traversed by the Republican, Smoky Hill and Solomon rivers. They had killed hundreds of men, captured and outraged women by the score, and stolen property to a vast amount.

Troops were rather scarce in Kansas at the time, so the 'War Department granted permission to the military to employ frontiersmen on short terms of service, for the purpose of punishing the Indian marauders. George A. Forsyth, who was then inspector-general of the Department of the

Missouri, was about the first of the regular officers to take advantage of the permission granted by the government. He organized a force of fifty picked frontiersmen at Fort Harker and Fort Hays, and selected to command under him Lieut. F. H. Beecher, of the 3d Infantry, a nephew of the late Rev. Henry Ward Beecher, of Brooklyn, and a young man of the most intrepid spirit. Dr. J. S. Movers, of Hays City, Kansas, accompanied the outfit as surgeon. The choice for chief scout and guide fell upon a daring borderer named Sharpe Grover, who, in that day, was almost as well-known as Kit Carson himself. The first sergeant of the expedition was nothing less than an ex-brigadier-general of New York Volunteers, W. II. H. McCall, a man who had distinguished himself most heroically in repelling the assault made by the rebels on the Union lines, in front of Petersburg, in the spring of 1865.

Nearly all the men who made up the company were inured to Indian warfare, and, looking through the sights of their rifles, feared no enemy, white, yellow, red or black, on the face of God's green earth. All were well mounted, excellently armed and supplied with ammunition enough to "stand any racket" the Indians might have in store for them. Moreover, incensed beyond measure by the frightful atrocities committed on the white race by the Cheyennes and Kiowas in particular, they were a thirst for vengeance, and, at Forsyth's word of command, moved out on the war-path with the alacrity of bridegrooms on the wedding day.

They scouted the country for several days without finding any Indians, and had to go in to Fort Wallace for fresh supplies. The Indians killed some teamsters, and ran off a few oxen near the town of Sheridan on the 10th of September, and this outrage filled Forsyth and his band with ungovernable rage. They reached what is known as the Arickaree Fork of the Republican river on the evening of September 16th, and went into camp, after taking the usual military precautions of plainsmen. All night long everything in and around the camp remained quiet, but, at early dawn, the sentinels discovered a party of Indians in a bold attempt to stampede a portion of the stock which was farthest removed from the guard. They succeeded in getting a few animals, but were easily driven from the field.

General Forsyth and the scout, Grover, came to the conclusion that there was a large force of savages in the vicinity and that the party would be immediately attacked. He gave his orders with the coolness for which he is famous, and the remaining animals were immediately saddled up. Scarcely was this accomplished, when the Indians, uttering their most terrible war cries, and all splendidly mounted, came riding over the "divides" by the hundred, from all directions. Even the veteran scout, Grover, was astonished at their numbers, and could not conceal his surprise, although he remained perfectly cool throughout the fierce ordeal.

Forsyth, who saw at once that he was not alone overpowered, but was also in a rather defenseless position, determined to retreat cautiously to some point where he could make a strong defense, and, at least, sell his life, and the lives of his men, at the highest possible price to the Indians. He immediately retreated to a small island in the river, which lay but a short distance from him, covering the movement by the fire of a few of his best sharp-shooters, posted under the river bank. He placed his men inside the circle formed by his animals, so as to give them some shelter. The horses were tied to the bushes that grew upon the island, and every man flung himself flat on the earth to avoid being too much exposed to the Indian fire, which immediately opened upon them.

Grover recognized, in the attacking Indians, Sioux and Cheyennes, as well as Kiowas, Comanches and Arapahoes. Their numbers were estimated at about 900 warriors, under the chief command of Roman Nose, a Cheyenne, and the most reckless Indian leader on the plains. Owing to the loose quality of the sand on the island, Forsyth's men had no difficulty in throwing up small breastworks, by digging into the gravel with their large hunting knives. But the Indian fire was so close and galling that, within a few minutes after the first attack, Forsyth himself had been struck by a rifle ball in the thigh, which caused a most painful wound, and several of his men were killed or injured. The gallant leader, soon afterward, received a second wound, which broke the bone of his left leg, between the knee and the ankle. His surgeon, Dr. Movers, was shot through the head about the same time, and, although he lingered for some days, never regained consciousness, or the power of articulation.

The Indians had all the advantage of position, and made the most of it. Their fire was simply terrible, and very soon they had killed all the horses of the command. The carcasses of the poor beasts served as ramparts for their surviving riders, who were cautioned by their wounded, but ever heroic, chief to remain cool and waste no lead by blind firing.

This kind of fight was kept up until late in the forenoon, when Grover, who remained unhurt, perceived that the Indians were preparing for an offensive movement at close quarters. They had stripped themselves to breech clout and feathers, and had mounted their best war horses, preparatory to charging home Forsyth's anything but strong position. The rifles of the killed and wounded of the party were taken and loaded by the survivors in readiness for the emergency, which they saw was rapidly approaching.

The mounted force, mustered by Roman Nose for the direct assault, numbered fully three hundred picked warriors, and he employed the remainder of his men to silence by their fire the rifles of Forsyth's party, while the attack was being made.

General Custer, in his "Life on the Plains," describing the Indian assault on this occasion, says, in his peculiarly vivid style: "Seeing that the little garrison was stunned by the heavy fire of the dismounted Indians, and rightly judging that now, if ever, was the proper time to charge them, Roman Nose and his band of mounted warriors, with a wild, ringing war-whoop, echoed by the women and children on the hills, started forward. On they came, presenting even to the brave men awaiting their charge, a most superb sight. Brandishing their guns, echoing back the cries of encouragement from their women and children on the surrounding heights, and confident of victory, they rode bravely and recklessly to the assault. Soon they were within range of the rifles of their friends, and of course, the dismounted Indians had to slacken their fire for fear of hitting their own warriors. This was an opportunity for the scouts, and they were not slow to seize it. 'Now !' shouted Forsyth. 'Now!' echoed Beecher, McCall and Grover, and the scouts, springing on their knees, and casting their eyes coolly along the barrels of their rifles, opened on the advancing savages as deadly a fire as the same number of men ever yet sent forth from the same number of guns.

"Unchecked, undaunted, on dashed the warriors steadily rang the clear, sharp reports of the rifles of the frontiersmen. Roman Nose, the chief, is seen to fall dead from his horse, then Medicine Man is killed, and, for an instant, the column of braves, now within ten feet of the scouts, hesitates—falters! A ringing cheer from the scouts, who perceive the effect of their well-directed fire, and the Indians begin to break and scatter in every direction, unwilling to rush to a hand-to-band struggle with men who, although outnumbered, yet knew how to make such effective use of their rifles.

"A few more shots from the frontiersmen, and the Indians are forced back beyond range, and their first attack ends in defeat. Forsyth turns to Grover, anxiously, and inquires, 'Can they do better than that, Grover?' 'I have been on the plains, General, since a boy, and never saw such a charge as that,' was the reply. All right,' responds 'Sandy,' 'then we are good for them.'"

Several of the Indian dead lay only a few feet away from the position of the scouts, and the ground was thickly strewn with the corpses of the brave savages. The loss of Forsyth's party was also very heavy. Lieutenant Beecher, an officer of great promise, received a mortal wound, and died at the close of that eventful day. The Indians kept up a hot fire on the position, while daylight lasted; and when Forsyth, wounded and in great pain, looked over the situation, he did not feel (mite so confident of ultimate escape, notwithstanding his splendid repulse of the attack of Roman Nose. In addition to Lieutenant Beecher and Surgeon Movers, two of the scouts had been killed outright, four mortally, four severely, and ten slightly wounded—making three and twenty killed and wounded, out of a total of fifty-one men. Provisions, too, were running low, and, owing to the great heat of the day, the horses killed early in the engagement had already begun to decompose.

As the wounded were deprived of the surgeon's care, their sufferings became almost unendurable. The distance to the nearest post was fully 110 miles, and the country was simply filled with warlike and vigilant savages. Nevertheless, what will not Caucasian perseverence and courage accomplish 2 Forsyth determined to try and open communications with Fort Wallace, and called for volunteers to make the perilous trip. Two scouts, named Trudeau and Stillwell, immediately responded, and left camp for Fort Wallace on the night of the battle. They were furnished by General Forsyth with a map and compass.

The Indians, having suffered great loss in the fight of the 17th, remained generally quiet on the succeeding day, only firing once in a while in a desultory manner, but they kept strict watch from the hills on the movements of the beleagured party. Forsyth attempted to send out two more scouts on the night of the 18th, but, after they had proceeded only a little way, the watchful enemy detected them, and they were driven back to the island. But the savages had had enough of Forsyth and his party at close quarters. They merely observed him during the few days following the 18th. On the night of the 19th, the General sent out two more scouts, named Donovan and Pyley, with an urgent letter to' Colonel Bankhead, commanding at Fort Wallace, in which he strongly represented his very critical situation and the miserable condition of his wounded.

All the provisions carried with the command were exhausted on the 19th, and thereafter the party were obliged to subsist on horse and mule meat, partially decomposed. Part of the stuff was buried in the sand, in the vain hope of keeping it fresh. The stench of the decaying carcasses became frightful, and maggots appeared in the wounds of the injured men. To add to the general misery, most of the mortally wounded men died, and some of those severely hurt became delirious from want of proper care.

Forsyth, by his moral, as well as his physical, courage, sustained the spirits of his men, and never ceased to hope for succor. At last, after having been eight days on the island, it came, on the morning of September 25th, in the shape of a squadron of cavalry from Fort Wallace, commanded by Colonel Carpenter. The scouts first sent out, Trudeau and Stillwell, after escaping many perils, had succeeded in reaching Fort Wallace. The chief scout, Grover, first detected objects moving in the distance in the direction of the fort. Presently, he made them out to be a body of cavalry, and then all the scouts, even the poor wounded men, set up cries of joy for their deliverance.

Six of Forsyth's party had died on the island, and, of the wounded, eight were crippled permanently, while twelve, if they still survive, bear honorable scars upon their persons. The wounded were made comfortable as soon as possible, and were escorted to Fort Wallace by Colonel Carpenter and his cavalry.

The battle of Beecher's Island was, perhaps, the most thrilling ever fought in Kansas, or, in fact, anywhere in the West, and reflects immortal honor on the brave defenders, but more particularly on gallant George Forsyth, who still, in good health, survives to enjoy the laurels he so bravely won on that bloody spot.

CHAPTER III

GENERAL CROOK'S CAREER

The connecting link formed by the campaign of General Nelson A. Miles, in 1877, against Lame Deer, Chief Joseph and other hostile Indians, has been dwelt upon in the second part of this book. That General did admirable service throughout the year mentioned, and his name will be indissolubly associated with the arduous campaigns, and remarkable victories, of that period. It is true that Gen. John Gibbon, at the head of the 7th Infantry, crippled the power of Chief Joseph at the bloody battle of Big Hole pass, Montana, in August, 1877, and it is equally true that the wonderful march of Gen. O. O. Howard, from the Pacific slope to northern Montana had much to do with bringing the heroic savage to terms; but it cannot be denied that General Miles' military foresight divined the probable route of Chief Joseph after he had succeeded in eluding the column of Colonel Sturgis, and his subsequent battle of Bear's Paw Mountains, which resulted in the surrender of the valorous Nez Perces, was one of the most brilliant feats of arms in the history of our Indian wars.

But while yielding to General Miles, and other able officers, the credit that is justly theirs, it must not be forgotten, when everything is weighed in the balance, that to the late Major-General Crook, whose lamentable death occurred while these pages were being written, is due the honor of having been the real victor in the great, and practically decisive, Sioux campaign of 1876. His dogged determination and perseverance wore out even Indian endurance and fortitude, and the brave old "Gray Fox" must ever hold first place in the greatest, and most tragical, of all our Indian wars. Crook may have lacked, in some measure, the dash and brilliancy of some of the officers mentioned in this volume, but in honesty of purpose, noble conscientiousness and a courage and fidelity that no disaster could shake, the sturdy old General had no superior in the military service. His whole life was a sacrifice to principle and to duty, and the country he loved so well will long and fondly cherish the memory of as true a soldier and as courtly a gentlemen as ever wore her uniform.

The terrible, and at the same time fascinating, surroundings of General Custer's heroic death have focused the eyes of the American nation, ever romantic and sympathetic, on the glorious victim of the battle of the Little Big Horn, and yet Crook, in his quiet, steady way, did more to settle the Indian difficulty than Custer and all the other dashing cavaliers of the American army put together. He always camped upon the hostile trail, and never let go his hold until the mission he was bent upon had been accomplished.

The room-mate and class-mate of the late General Sheridan, when both were at West Point, it would be impossible to find two characters more diametrically different than were those of these two soldiers. Sheridan was, in everything but birth, a thorough Irishman. Tie was quick, bold and passionate by nature, but military training and a natural talent for war led him eventually to control much of his native impetuosity, and when the hour of trial came, America found in him one of the greatest generals of modern times.

George Crook, on the other hand, was quiet, self-contained, retiring, but, at the same time, unsurpassedly brave. He never betrayed excitement, and, like Key and Nelson, had never made the acquaintance of fear. Both men loved each other with comrade devotion to the last, and the heartwrung tears of manhood's friendship fell upon the bier of Sheridan when George Crook stood above it on the day of sepulture. His own grave, in the soil of Maryland, is now watered by the tears of a nation.

George Crook was born near Dayton, Ohio, in 1829, and entered West Point academy through the appointment of the Hon. (since general)

Robert Schenck, representative in Congress from that district, in his nineteenth year. He graduated with honor in 1852, and was at once assigned to duty with the 4th Infantry, as second lieutenant. His regiment was soon afterward sent to the Pacific coast, and young Crook had an early opportunity of campaigning against the Indians in California and Oregon. He was engaged in the Rogue river campaign and in the Pitt river expedition, and was commissioned first lieutenant March 11, 1856. In a skirmish with Indian raiders, on June 10, 1857, Crook was severely wounded by an arrow, which pierced his side, and the head of which remained in his person—all efforts of the surgeons failing to extract it—up to the day of his death.

He distinguished himself again, on his recovery, by thrashing the hostiles in engagements fought on July 2 and 26, 1857. He was engaged during 1858 in the Yakima expedition, and the celebrated march to Vancouver. He was subsequently stationed at Fort Ter-waw, Washington Ter., until the breaking out of the War of the Rebellion.

He became captain in his own regiment, May 14, 1861, and in the following October was offered, and accepted, the colonelcy of the 36th Ohio Volunteers. He was employed in West Virginia from October 16, 1861, until August, 1862, when he was appointed commander of the 3d Provisional Brigade. He was breveted major in the regular army for gallant and meritorious services at the battle of Lewisburg, Va., where he was badly wounded, in the fall of 1862. He was soon afterward raised to the rank of brigadier-general of volunteers for conspicuous bravery in the field. He was engaged in important operations in West Virginia and Tennessee until July, 1863.

General Crook took command of the 2d Cavalry Division, July 1, of that year and took part in the battle of Chickamauga, September 19 and 20, 1863, and in the subsequent pursuit of General Wheeler, which ended October 10th. He was present at the actions of McMinnville and Farmington. Tenn., and took an active part in the operations against guerrillas from Shelby ville to Rome, Ga., during the month of November. General Crook took command of the Kanawha district from February to June, 1864, and engaged in a raid on the Virginia & Tennessee Railroad in May of that year. He took part in the battles of Cloyd's Mountain and

New River bridge, and in the continuous skirmishing from Lewisburg to Lynchburg, culminating in a battle at the latter place, June 17th.

General Crook was made a brevet major-general of volunteers, July 18, 1864, for gallant conduct in West Virginia. He had a part in the battle of Snicker's Ferry and Kernstown, July 19th and 24th, and in the skirmish around Hall Town in August. He joined Sheridan in the Shenandoah Valley in August, 1864, and was an active participant in the battles at Berryville, Opequan, Fisher's Hill, Strasburg and Cedar creek. From March 26 to April 9, 1865, he commanded the cavalry branch of the Army of the Potomac.

His brevet brigadier-general's rank in the regular forces dates from March 13, 1865, and was given in recognition of his gallant conduct in West Virginia during the campaign of 1864. The General took part in the battle of Dinwiddie Court House, toward the close of the war, and commanded a brigade in the pursuit of the rebel forces during the first week in April, 1865. His last battles in the Civil War were at Jetersville, Sailor Creek and Farmville, and he was in at the death of the Confederacy at Appomattox, April 9, 1865.

General Crook commanded the district of Wilmington, N. C, immediately after the close of the war, and held that command until 1866, when he was mustered out of the volunteer service. He afterward served on a board to examine a code of rifle tactics at Washington, and, that duty concluded, awaited orders.

He was appointed to the command of the Boise, Idaho, district in 1867, and immediately took the field against the hostile Shoshone (Snake) Indians. He was then lieutenant-colonel of the 23d United States Infantry, and succeeded in forcing the savages into submission, after a brief, but arduous, campaign. He was soon afterward appointed to the command of the Department of the Columbia, and speedily subdued a determined revolt of the Umatilla Indians, and chastised the Nez Perces, who were threatening the white settlements.

He assumed, by order of the secretary of war, command of the department of Arizona, on June 4, 1871, and proceeded against the hostile Apaches, who were the terror of that blood-stained Territory, so vigorously that he broke up their principal tribes. In performing this work, he used one Indian tribe against another, and thus established the Indian scout service, which has proved so effectual in all our more recent Indian campaigns. Crook's brilliant success in Arizona led General Grant, who especially admired him, to raise him to the rank of brigadier-general, in October, 1873, although several other distinguished officers ranked him. He assumed command of the Department of the Platte, April 27,1875, and his career in that important position has been already narrated in this volume. (See Part I.)

Relieved of the command of the Department of the Platte, in 1882, General Crook once more went into Arizona where the Apaches were on the war-path. The Chiricahua tribe were located in Old Mexico, whence they made frequent incursions into Arizona and New Mexico, running off stock, firing ranches and murdering settlers. General Crook determined to carry the war into the enemy's country, and May 1, 1883, he crossed the line with forty-two white soldiers and 193 Indian scouts and led the way into the mountain fastnesses of Mexico. His command suffered great hardships, but in forty-one days they recrossed the line into the United States, bringing with them over 600 prisoners— the whole Chiricahua tribe.

After this triumph, General Crook was relieved of the command in Arizona and went back to his old post as chief of the Department of the Platte, with headquarters at Omaha, where he was stationed until his appointment as major general in 1888, when he came to Chicago as the head of the Military Division of the Missouri.

General Crook fell dead, from an attack of heart failure, in his rooms at the Grand Pacific Hotel, Chicago, on the morning of Friday, March 21, 1890, in the 61st year of his age. His wife, who was with him at the time, received his latest breath. He was buried, with great civic and military honors, at Oakland, Md., on March 24th.

Major Roberts, of his staff, thus sums up the dead General's noble character:

"General Crook had been my friend—more than a friend—for the last twenty-six years, and I don't believe that in all that time he did a mean tiling or a wrong act, knowingly. His whole life was duty. He was the tenderest, gentlest, most just, and most unselfish man I ever knew. In all those terrible Indian campaigns of his, it was the welfare of his men that was uppermost in his mind. He was the greatest Indian fighter of the country, but he was never an

Indian hater. He was the Indian's friend. He knew the Indian better than the Indian did. He never promised him anything he didn't mean to give. He never lied to him. The Indians feared him, but they respected him, and his ability to deal with them was recognized in other lines than the military. I remember he was on that commission which went up to Standing Rock to see about opening the Sioux Reservation. He was the only man in the country to deal with Indians. He knew their rights and he knew their wrongs, and he used to study the whole night through, anxiously trying to contrive ways to secure justice for them without injury to the nation."

Chicago, represented by citizens of all parties, and by her citizen soldiery, united with the national army in doing honor to the memory of the modest and heroic veteran, and all who knew the purity of his life, the valor of his heart and the integrity of his motives will unite in praying that the heavenly peace of George Crook may be eternal, as his earthly glory is immortal.

CHAPTER IV

GEN. GEORGE A. CUSTER

Gen. George A. Custer was born at a place called New Rumley, in the State of Ohio, on December 5, 1839. He received a good education in the public schools, and, in 1857, was appointed to a vacant cadetship at the United States Military Academy, West Point, N. Y., by the Hon. John A. Bingham, member of Congress from the district in which young Custer lived. He was gifted with a fine, handsome person, and looked like some Norman knight who had revisited the world after having slept in "cold obstruction" since the long-past age of chivalry. His features were bold and aquiline. He had that remarkable grayblue color of the eyes, which may be described as liquid steel, and, in his earlier military career, he allowed his abundant yellow locks to grow until they fell in profusion around his shoulders. A heavy blonde mustache shaded his mouth, and gave a martial character to his fine countenance. In figure, he was tall—almost six feet—and lithe, but broad-shouldered, athletic and strong as a young Samson. He had a fine, ringing voice, and those who heard his word of command can never forget its inspiring accents. He graduated from West Point in the summer of 1861, and immediately joined the Union army on the banks of the Potomac. His career in that army is a portion of history, and is too well known to need much repetition here. While yet a mere youth, he won honorable distinction, and was looked upon as a peer in battle, where such men as Crook and Merritt led. He was assigned as second lieutenant to the 5th Cavalry, and witnessed the first battle of Bull Run, or Manassas. After having served for a time with his regiment, Gen. George B. McClellan, struck by his chivalrous person and bearing, appointed him an aide-de-camp on his staff. While employed in that capacity, he was instrumental in discovering a ford across the Chickahominy, which enabled his commander to make an important secret movement against Lee's army, in front of Richmond. From that time onward, under every general who had command, from time to time, of the Army of the Potomac, he continued to advance in fame. He served under Sheridan, in the Valley of the Shenandoah, and the Blue Ridge Mountains still ring with the glory of his innumerable feats of arms. He was several times wounded, but never dangerously. At the early age of twenty-three he was a brigadier-general of volunteers, having been promoted to that rank from a captaincy, early in 1864, for brilliant services rendered at Gettysburg and elsewhere. Gen. Sheridan, whose heroic temperament made him admire headlong courage in his youthful captains, soon gathered around him in the Valley most of the brightest and boldest spirits of the army, and, with the penetrating eye of military genius, he at once discovered the particular talent for high command developed by each one. Sheridan always regarded Custer with especial favor, and generally confided to him such movements as needed dashing generalship and rapid execution. During his career as a Union general of cavalry, Custer led sixty successful charges, and captured enough cannon and battle flags to have satisfied the ambitious heart of the "Little Corporal" himself.

A correspondent for an American paper, in describing Sheridan at Five Forks, said: "And, like a gleam of yellow foam upon the 'waves of battle beside him rose and fell the long locks of Custer. There also flashed the potent swords of Merritt, the two Forsyths and the other youthful captains who have outshone in valor and in martial genius the juvenile military prodigies of the Revolutionary armies of France."

Well, Merritt and "the two Forsyths" still survive, but the hot heart's blood of Custer long ago mingled with the "yellow foam" of Five Forks' glorious fray on the bloody bluffs of the Little Big Horn!

In considering the early fate of Custer, the young, the daring, the fascinating and the beloved, the fine lines addressed by Byron to the memory of Murat may, with slight alteration, be applied to the fate of the dashing hero of the American army:

Little didst thou deem when dashing
On thy war horse thro' the ranks,
Like a stream that bursts its banks,
While helmets cleft and sabres clashing
Shone and shivered fast around thee
Of the fate at last which found thee!
Was that haughty plume laid low
By a *Sioux's* dishonest blow?
Once, as the moon sways o'er the tide,
It roll'd in air, the warrior's guide;
Through the smoke-created night
Of the black and sulph'rous fight.
The soldier raised his seeking eye
To catch that crest's ascendency;
And, as it onward rolling rose,
So moved his heart upon our foes!
There, where death's brief pang was quickest,
And the battle's wreck lay thickest
Strewed beneath the advancing banner
Of the eagle's burning crest;
There, with thunder clouds to fan her—
Who could then her wing arrest,
Victory beaming from her breast? —
While the broken line enlarging,
Fell or fled along the plain,
There, be sure, was *Custer* charging;
There he ne'er shall charge again!

Gen. Custer was married in February, 1864, and his gifted widow, Mrs. Elizabeth B. Custer, has painted, in her charming book "Boots and Saddles," a touching picture of the home, garrison and camp life of her own and the nation's hero, during the later years of his gallant and adventurous career. No children blessed the union, but the brilliant deeds and tragical death of George A. Custer will send his name echoing down "the corridors of time" even to the latest generation.

General Custer served in Texas, as major-general of Volunteers, for about a year after the close of the Civil War, and in the fall of 1866 he was assigned to the 7th Cavalry with the rank of lieutenant-colonel. He joined his new regiment in Kansas, which was then overrun by various bands of hostile Indians, and served in that State, and occasionally in the Indian Territory, for five years, During most of that period he was employed in active operations against the Indians, and had several sharp encounters with the savages, in all of which he came out a victor. His greatest Indian battle, excepting that in which he perished, was that fought on the Washita river, near the Antelope Hills, Indian Territory, on November 27th, 1868, against the combined Cheyenne, Arapahoe and Kiowa tribes under Black Kettle, Little Raven and Satanta. These Indians had been troublesome for many years and had filled the southern and western portions of Kansas with horror. Unutterable crimes had been committed. by them in nearly all the exposed settlements. During the summer months it was impossible to bring them to decisive action with any considerable body of troops, but they had lain in wait for, and annihilated, many small parties when their superior numbers gave them assurance of cheap and easy victory. General Sheridan, commanding the Department of the Missouri, resolved to operate against the red marauders while the snows were deep, grass scarce and locomotion difficult. Custer, owing to a disagreement with the Indian Bureau at Washington in regard to his policy toward the savages, was placed in a sort of temporary retirement at Fort Leavenworth, while his regiment proceeded westward to enter upon an active campaign under General Sully. Custer could not stand the enforced idleness at his post, and he obtained leave to go East and enjoy himself among his friends in Michigan and Ohio. He was thus pleasantly engaged when a telegram from General Sheridan summoned him to take command of eleven troops of his own regiment in the neighborhood of Fort Dodge, Kansas. Custer started westward at once, and reached the scene of operations in due time. He at once set about organizing' his troops for a winter campaign and he was heartily sustained by General Sheridan, who knew that he was the right man for such work as was in contemplation.

Everything was in readiness by the 12th of November for the new campaign. It was known that the confederated Indians were concentrated in a large village somewhere in the Indian Territory, but the exact situation could not be determined without closer inspection. The General had provided himself with Osage Indian guides, and he was also accompanied by several white scouts, among them the famous California Joe. The snow fell early and copiously that November, and this circumstance greatly aided General Custer in his designs. As the theatre of the coming struggle was outside the limits of General Sully's command, that officer was relieved from duty with the expedition, and this placed Custer in full control, under Sheridan, who determined to give his gallant subordinate charge of the active operations. The forward movement was begun on the morning of November 22d, and the column proceeded toward the Canadian river under a heavy snow fall. Custer sent out some scouting parties, and, on the 25th, one under Maj. J. H. Elliot came across a fresh Indian trail which indicated a force of about 150 warriors. This discovery convinced the General that the enemy was not far off, and, although the weather became intensely cold, he determined to leave his tents and wagons behind, under guard, and set out to look for the Indians in light marching order. The Osage scouts proved to be invaluable during that expedition, and their keen instincts enabled them to guide Custer and his command unerringly upon the hostile trail. At last, on the night of November 26th, the Osages located the village in the thickly-timbered bottom-lands of the Washita river. They led Custer to a bluff overlooking the valley, where he could plainly hear the barking of the Indian dogs, and the tinkling of the bells on the leaders of the pony herds, He resolved to attack at early dawn, and to do so in his favorite manner, by dividing his command into battalions to operate separately, at first, and then fall unitedly on the encampment of the unsuspecting savages. As the plan of the battle of the Washita was almost a counterpart of that of the battle of the Little Big Horn, it may be well to allow General Custer to explain the movement in his own graphic words:

"Leaving the two Osages to keep a careful lookout, I hastened back until I met the main party of the scouts. They were halted and a message sent back to halt the cavalry. I enjoined complete silence, and directed even' officer to ride to the point we then occupied. The hour was then past midnight. Soon the officers came, and, after dismounting and collecting in a little circle, I informed them of what I had seen and heard; and in order that they might individually learn as much as possible of the character of the ground and the location of the village, I proposed that all should remove their sabres, that their clanking might not be heard, and proceed gently to the crest and there obtain a view of the valley beyond.

"This was done. Not a word was spoken, until we crouched together, and cast our eyes in the direction of the herd and the village. In whispers, I briefly pointed out everything that was to be seen, then motioned all to return to where we had left our sabres, and, standing in a group on the ground, or a crust of snow, the plan of the attack was explained to all, and each was assigned his part. The general plan was to employ the hours between then and daylight to completely surround the village, and at day-break, or as soon as it was barely light enough for the purpose, to attack the Indians from all sides. The command numbered about eight hundred mounted men, and was divided into four nearly equal detachments. Two of these set out at once, as they had each to make a circuitous march of several miles, in order to arrive at the points assigned to them. The third detachment moved to its position about an hour before day, and until that time remained with the fourth, or main, column. This last, whose movements I accompanied, was to make the attack from the point at which we had first discovered the herd and the village.

"Major Elliot commanded the column embracing I, II and M troops, 7th Cavalry, which moved around from our left to a position almost in rear of the village, while Colonel Thompson commanded the one composed of B and F troops, which moved in a corresponding manner from our right to a position which was to connect it with that of Major Elliot. Colonel Myers commanded the third column, composed of E and I troops, which was to take position in the valley and timber, a little less than a mile to my right. By this disposition it was hoped to prevent the escape of every inmate of the village. That portion of the command which I proposed to accompany consisted of A, C, D and K troops, the Osages and scouts, and Col. W. W. Cook with his forty sharp-shooters. Captain Hamilton commanded one of the squadrons, Colonel West the other."

Having thus made his dispositions, Custer and the officers, soldiers and scouts who remained with him proceeded to kill time, as it was too bitterly cold to permit them to sleep, until "the first pale ray of morning "gave the signal for attack. The rising of the morning star was so peculiar that the General and all who were with him took it, at first, for a signal rocket of some kind. It was ever afterward alluded to by him as "the star of the Washita," a companion expression for "the sun of Austerlitz."

General Custer's favorite battle air was "Garryowen," which he used to say always harmonized with the movements and sounds of a body of cavalry charging home the enemy. Accordingly, when the time for action came, "Garryowen," played by the full band, gave the signal, and, simultaneously, the different columns fell upon the slumbering and surprised village. The soldiers poured their fire into the tepees from all directions, but the Indians were of good mettle, and, although taken entirely unawares, stood to their arms manfully and fought with skill and vigor for their lives, their families and their homes. The fight lasted far into the day, and still the stubborn savages held portions of their village, although many had fallen, and among them the renowned chief, Black Kettle. Along in the afternoon, it became quite evident to Custer that he had not one village on his "hands but several. Mounted Indians began to appear on the surrounding bluffs, and commenced, to muster their forces preparatory to attacking the troops, who had by that time silenced the fire of the survivors of Black Kettle's band, He interrogated an intelligent squaw, Black Kettle's sister, whom he had made captive, and she informed him that the Indians he saw were still another band of Cheyennes, together with the Arapahoes, Kiowas, Comanches, and even a portion of the Apaches.

This was anything but cheering information, as the troops had suffered severely in the battle, and a great deal of ammunition had been expended. In fact powder and ball were running discouragingly low, when Major Bell, quartermaster of the 7th Cavalry, arrived with a small pack train and several thousand pounds of carbine ammunition. General Custer saw, however, that it was time to think of retiring, as he did not have sufficient force wherewith to attack successfully the villages situated lower down on the Washita river. Soon after Bell's arrival the Indians renewed the battle with even more determination than before. Capt. Louis McLain Hamilton, a most gallant and promising officer, had been shot dead from his horse at the very beginning of the first fight, and Colonel Barnitz was dangerously shot through the body, soon afterward. Major Elliot and a large party of men were missing. Several of the non-commissioned officers and privates were killed or wounded. Custer caused nearly all the Indian ponies captured—several hundred—to be shot, and destroyed by fire all the property of the savages captured in the village. Then he mounted his prisoners on the ponies he had spared, and, by a daring and brilliant maneuver, succeeded in imposing on the enemy to the extent of being enabled, owing to their state of uncertainty as to his movement's, to extricate his column from its dangerous position, and, after a rapid night march, regained his wagon-train on the succeeding day in safety.

The Indians had lost in the battle nearly one hundred warriors killed, including two of their principal chiefs. Custer's loss was Major Elliot, Captain Hamilton and nineteen enlisted men killed; and Col. Albert Barnitz, Colonel T. W. Custer, Lieut. B. March, and eleven enlisted men wounded. Major Elliot and a portion of his command had been lured into an ambuscade and massacred. Their bodies were found some time afterward, mutilated in a most revolting manner.

The battle of the Washita, although by no means decisive in its results, was by far the most vigorous blow ever struck against the southern hostiles, and had the good effect of taming their pride, and, in a measure, breaking their spirit. They never afterward showed the same warlike disposition. The Washita fight was certainly one of Custer's most brilliant victories, and, very justly, placed him in the foremost rank of Indian fighters. Fortune, that so often befriended him, smiled upon his tactics at the Washita, and frowned upon them at the Little Big Horn.

APPENDIX

ECHOES FROM THE LITTLE BIG HORN

GENERAL SHERIDAN'S ACCOUNT OF THE CUSTER TRAGEDY.
COMPILED FROM THE OFFICIAL DOCUMENTS
AT MILITARY HEADQUARTERS.

The following extracts from the account of the closing scenes of the battle of the Little Big Horn, taken from the official records of the late Gen. Philip H. Sheridan, cannot fail to be of great interest to the readers of this volume:

"The valley of the creek was followed toward the Little Big Horn, Custer on the right of the creek, Reno on the left of it, Benteen off still further to the left, and not in sight. About 11 o'clock Reno's troops crossed the creek to Custer's column, and remained with it until about half past 12 o'clock, when it was reported that the village was only two miles ahead and running away.

"Reno was directed to move forward at as rapid a gait as he thought prudent, and to charge, with the understanding that Custer should support him. The troops under Reno moved at a fast trot for about two miles, when they came to the river, crossed it, halted a few minutes to collect the men, and then deployed. Not seeing anything, however, of the subdivisions under Custer and Benteen, and the Indians swarming upon him from all directions, Reno took position, dismounted in the edge of some timber which afforded shelter for the horses of his command, continuing to fight on foot until it became apparent that he would soon be overcome by superior numbers of Indians. He then remounted his troops, charged through the enemy, recrossed the river and gained the bluffs on the opposite side. In this charge First Lieutenant Donald Macintosh, Second Lieutenant B. H. Hodgson and Acting-Assistant-Surgeon J. M. DeWolf, were killed.

"Reno's force succeeded in reaching the top of the bluff, but with a loss of three officers and twenty-nine enlisted men killed and seven men wounded. Almost at the same time that Reno's men reached the bluffs, Benteen's battalion came up, and a little later the pack-train, with MacDougall's troop escorting it. These three detachments were all united under Reno's command, and numbered about 381 men, in addition to their officers.

"Meanwhile, nothing had been heard from Custer, so the reunited divisions, under Reno, moved down the river, keeping along the bluffs on the opposite side from the village. Firing had been heard from that direction, but, after moving to the highest point without seeing or hearing anything of Custer, Reno sent Captain Weir, with his troop, to try and open communications. Weir soon sent back word that he could go no further; that the Indians were getting around him. At the same time he was keeping up a heavy fire from his skirmish line. Reno then turned everything back to the first position he had taken on the bluff, which seemed to be the best for defense; had the horses and mules driven into a depression; put his men, dismounted, on the crests of the bills, which formed the depression, and bad hardly completed these dispositions when the Indians attacked him furiously. This was about 6 o'clock in the evening, and the ground was held with a further loss of eighteen killed and forty-six wounded, until the attack ceased about 9 o'clock that night.

"By this time the overwhelming numbers of the enemy rendered it improbable that the troops under Custer could undertake to rejoin those with Reno, so the latter began to dig rifle pits, barricaded with dead horses and mules and boxes from the packs, to prepare for any further attack which might be made the next day. All night long the men kept working, while the Indians were holding a scalp dance, within their hearing, in the valley of the Little Big Horn below.

"About half past two o'clock in the morning of June 26th, a most terrific rifle fire was opened upon Reno's position, and, as daylight increased, hordes of Indians were seen taking station upon high points which completely surrounded the troops, so that men were struck on opposite sides of the lines from where the shots were fired. The fire did not slacken until half-past nine o'clock in the morning, when the Indians made a desperate charge on the line held by Troops H and M, coming to such close quarters as to touch with a 'coup-stick' a man lying dead within Reno's lines. This onslaught was repulsed by a charge from the line assaulted, led by Colonel Benteen. The Indians also charged close enough to send their arrows into the line held by Troops D and H, but they were driven back by a countercharge of those troops, led in person by Reno.

"There were now many wounded, and the question of obtaining water was a vital one, for the troops had been without any from 6 o'clock the previous evening, a period of sixteen hours. A skirmish line was formed under command of Colonel Benteen, to protect the descent of volunteers down the hill in front of the position to reach the water. A little was obtained in canteens, but many of the men were struck while obtaining the precious fluid. The fury of the attack was now over, and the Indians were seen going off in parties to the village. * * About two o'clock in the afternoon the grass in the bottom was extensively fired by the Indians, and behind the dense smoke thus created, the hostile village began to move away. Between six and seven o'clock in the evening the village came out from behind this cloud of smoke and dust, the troops obtaining a full view of the cavalcade as it filed away in the direction me of the Big Horn mountains, moving in almost full military order. * * * *

"During the night of June 26th, the troops under Reno changed position, so as to better secure a supply of water, and prepare against another assault, should the warriors return in strong force, but early in the morning of June 27th, while preparing to resist any attack that might be attempted, the dust of a moving column was seen approaching in the distance. Soon it was discovered to be troops who were coming, and, in a little while, a scout arrived with a note from General Terry to Custer, saying that some Crow scouts had come into camp, stating that he had been whipped, but that their story was not believed. About 10:30 o'clock in the morning, General Terry rode into Reno's lines, and the fate of General Custer was ascertained.

"Precisely what was done by Custer's immediate command subsequent to the moment when the rest of the regiment last saw him alive, has remained partly a matter of conjecture, no officer or soldier who rode with him into the valley of the Little Big Horn having survived to tell the tale. The only real evidence of how they came to meet their fate was the testimony of the field where it overtook them. *

"Custer's trail, from the point where Reno crossed the stream, passed along and in rear of the crest of the bluffs on the right bank for nearly or quite three miles. Then it came down to the bank of the river, but at once diverged from it again, as though Custer had unsuccessfully attempted to cross ; then, turning upon itself, and almost completing a circle, the trail ceased. It was marked by the remains of officers and men, and the bodies of horses, some of them dotted along the path, others heaped in ravines and upon knolls, where halts appeared to have been made. There was abundant evidence that a gallant resistance had been offered by Custer's troops, but they were beset on all sides by overpowering numbers.

"Following up the movements of Custer's column from the Yellowstone, starting from Tullock's creek soon after five o'clock on the morning of June 25th, the infantry of Gibbon's command made a march of twenty-two miles over a most difficult country. In order that scouts might be sent into the valley of the Little Big Horn, Gibbon's cavalry [four troops of the 2d] and the battery [three Gatling guns] were pushed on thirteen or fourteen miles further, not camping until midnight. Scouts were sent out at 4:30 o'clock on the morning of June 26th. They soon discovered three Indians, who were at first supposed to be Sioux, but who, when overtaken, proved to be Crows who had been with General Custer. They brought to Terry the first intelligence of the battle. Their story was not credited. [See Curly's statement in Part I.] It was supposed that some fighting—even severe fighting—had taken place, but it was not believed that disaster could have overtaken so large a force as twelve troops of cavalry. The infantry, which had broken camp very early, soon came up, and the whole column entered and moved up the valley of the Little Big Horn.

"During the afternoon efforts were made to send scouts through to what was supposed to be Custer's position, in order to obtain information of the condition of affairs, but those who were sent out were driven back by parties of Indians, who, in increasing numbers, were seen hovering in front of Gibbon's column. At twenty minutes before nine o'clock that night, the infantry had marched between twenty-nine and thirty miles;

the men were weary, and daylight was fading. The column was, therefore, halted for the night at a point about eleven miles, in a straight line, above the month of the stream. On the morning of June 27th the advance was resumed, and, after a march of nine miles, the intrenched position was reached. The withdrawal of the Indians from around Reno's command, and from the valley of the Little Big Horn, was, undoubtedly, caused by the approach of Gibbon's troops. * * *

"On the 28th of June, Captain Ball, of the 2d Cavalry, made a reconnoissance along the trail of the Indians after they left the valley. He reported that they had divided into two parties, one of which kept the valley of Long Fork, making, he thought, for the Big Horn mountains. The other turned more to the eastward. He also discovered, leading into the valley, a very heavy trail, not more than five days old. This was entirely distinct from the one which Custer had followed, and indicated that at least two bands had united just before the battle."

[NOTE.—It would appear from the statements of Major Reno and other officers engaged in the battle on the bluffs, that they were entirely ignorant of the fate of Custer and his five troops until the arrival of Generals Terry and Gibbon. The author was told by some of the soldiers of the 7th Cavalry, after the commands of Terry and Crook came together in the Rosebud valley, August 10, 1876, that the savages had displayed Custer's guidons, and other trophies of ' victory, during the fighting on the 25th and 26th of June. Col. Anson Mills' cavalry detachment recovered, at Slim Buttes, on September 9th of that year, as stated in Part I, one of Custer's guidons, Colonel Keogh's gauntlets and many blouses, etc., which were the property of the slaughtered battalion.

It seems strange that Reno could not comprehend Custer's fate until after the arrival of Generals Terry and Gibbon, when some of the private soldiers did. Where did Major Reno suppose the hostiles procured the uniforms, etc., which they displayed? Lieut. C. C. De Rudio, of the 7th Cavalry, who, with Private O'Neill, of Troop C, was cut off from Reno's command during the retreat from the river to the bluffs on June 25th, says, in a letter to a friend, dated from Camp on the Yellowstone river, opposite the Big Horn, July 5, 1876: "The night (June 25-6), was passed and in the dim light of day I thought I saw some gray horses, mounted by men in military blouses, and some of them in white hats. They were,

I thought, going out of the valley, and those who had already crossed the river were going up a very steep bluff, and others were crossing after them. I saw one man with a buckskin jacket, pantaloons and top boots, and a white hat, and felt quite sure I recognized him as Capt. Tom Custer, which convinced me that the cavalry was of our command. With this conviction I stepped boldly out on the edge of the bank and called to CaptainCuster: 'Tom,don't leave us here!' The distance was only a few yards, and my call was answered by an infernal yell, and a discharge of three or four hundred shots. I then discovered my mistake, and found that the savages were clad in clothes and mounted on horses captured from our men."

Fortunately De Rudio and O'Neill were enabled to escape in the thick undergrowth, and finally succeeded in rejoining the remnant of the command.

A dispatch to the Chicago *Times*, dated Bismarck, Dak., July 31, 1876, says: "One of the wounded of Reno's command, who is in hospital here, says that at one time during the fight they heard the advance sounded on a trumpet from the side of the Indians; that all rose up, thinking it was Custer coming to reinforce them, and cheered lustily, when the Indians sent forth a derisive yell, and made a charge, which was repulsed."

All the dispatches and reports of the period concur in saying that the successful defense of Reno's position was mainly due to the ripe skill and daring bravery of Col. F. W. Benteen.

The united commands buried all the dead of Custer's column they could find—two hundred and four bodies early on the morning of June 28th. Twenty-three bodies were reported missing.

MUTILATION OF CUSTER'S DEAD.
[EXTRACT FROM THE DIARY OF ONE OF
GENERAL GIBBON'S OFFICERS.]

"A survey of the Custer battle field [he wrote on the afternoon of June 27th] is horrible in the extreme. All but Custer were mutilated. [This is disputable.] He was stripped only. Capt. Keogh had left around his neck an Agnus Dei, suspended by a golden chain, and had evidently not been further mutilated after its discovery. It is sickening to look at the bodies stripped. Here a hand gone; there a foot or a head; ghastly gashes cut in all parts of the body; eyes gouged out; noses and ears cut off, and skulls crushed in.

"One sees at a distance a dead horse lying on the plain near the river, and, upon a nearer approach, the gleaming white skin of a dead and naked cavalry soldier, the body cut and mangled beyond description, is brought into view."

According to the statement of this officer, which was published in most of the newspapers in the latter part of July, 1876, Lieutenant Bradley, of the 7th Infantry, killed in the succeeding year at the battle of the Big Hole, was among the first who discovered the remains of Custer and his men, while Lieutenant Jacobs, of the same regiment, was among the first to ascertain the condition of Reno and his command. The operations of the battalion of the 2d Cavalry, which accompanied Gibbon's infantry, were directed by Maj. James S. Brisbin. The fact here stated was unintentionally overlooked in the account of the movements of General Gibbon's column in Part I.

The scout, Charles Reynolds, who generally accompanied Custer, was left behind with Reno, and, on the latter's retreat to the bluffs, was cut off and massacred. He fought heroically to the last, and did not die unavenged. He was to Custer's column what Gruard was to that of Crook.

MISCELLANEOUS
THE SIBLEY SCOUTING PARTY.

The scouting party commanded by Lieut. F. W. Sibley, of Troop E, 2d Cavalry, July 6-9, 1876, was made up of picked men from different troops of the 2d Cavalry, together with a few scouts and volunteers, as follows: Sergeants G.P. Harrington, Oscar R. Cornwell, William R. Cooper, Charles W. Day ; Corporal Thomas C. Warren ; Privates Daniel E. Munger, Hugh J. Green, George Robinson, William P. Egan, Henry Oakey, Martin Mahon, George Rhode, George Watts, Samuel W. Hone, James Dorr, George A. Stone, Joseph Ward, William J. Crolley, William J. Dougherty, Valentine Rufus, Jacob Rheind, Harry G. Collins, Charles L. Edwards, Patrick Hasson, William H. Hills. Volunteers: J. Becker, alias "Trailer Jim," and John F.

Finerty, correspondent for the Chicago *Times*. Guides and Scouts: F. Gruard and Baptiste Pourier.

GENERAL GIBBON'S LOSS AT BIG HOLE BATTLE.

The loss of Gen. John Gibbon at Big Hole fight Aug. 9, 1877, was as follows: Killed—Capt.William Logan, First Lieut. James H. Bradley and twenty-one enlisted men of the 7th Infantry, with six citizen volunteers. Wounded—Gen. John Gibbon, Capt. C. Williams, twice ; First Lieut. C. A. Coolidge, thrice ; First. Lieut. William L. English, twice (one mortal); Second Lieut. C. A. Woodruff, three wounds; thirty-one enlisted men and four citizen volunteers wounded —one soldier mortally. This made a total of sixty-nine killed and wounded out of a force of 191 officers and men. The Nez Perces left eighty-nine dead bodies on the field.

OFFICIAL DOCUMENTS.

The following official and other documents, lists of killed and wounded, etc., will be read with interest:

CROOK S ACCOUNT OF BOSEBUD FIGHT.

General Sheridan forwarded the following dispatch, which contains General Crook's official report of the battle at Rosebud creek, to the War Department on receipt: CHICAGO, June 23, 1876. GEN. E. D. TOWNSEND, Washington, D. C.:

The following dispatch from General Crook is forwarded for the information of the General of the Army:

Camp on the so of tongue river, Wyoming, June 19th, via Fort Fetterman, June 23d. Lieut.-Gen. Sheridan Chicago, Ill.: Returned to camp today, having marched as indicated in my last telegram. When about forty miles from here on Rosebud creek, Montana, on the morning of the 17th inst., the scouts reported Indians in the vicinity, and within a few moments we were attacked in force, the fight lasting several hours. We were near the mouth of a deep canon, through which the creek ran. The sides were very steep, covered with pine and apparently impregnable.

The village was supposed to be at the other end, about eight miles off. They displayed a strong force at all points, occupying so many and such covered places that it is impossible to correctly estimate their numbers. The attack, however, showed that they anticipated that they were strong enough to thoroughly defeat the command.

During the engagement, I tried to throw a strong force through the canon, but I was obliged to use it elsewhere before it had gotten to the supposed location of the village.

The command finally drove the Indians back in great confusion, following them several miles, the scouts killing a good many during the retreat. Our casualties were nine men killed and fifteen wounded of the 3d Cavalry; two wounded of the 2d Cavalry; three men wounded of the 4th Infantry, and Captain Henry, of the 3d Cavalry, severely wounded in the face.* It is impossible to correctly estimate the loss of the Indians, many being killed in the rocks, and others being gotten off before we got possession of that part of the field, thirteen dead bodies being left.

We remained on the field that night, and, having nothing but what each man carried himself, we were obliged to retire to the train to properly care for our wounded, who were transported here on mule-litters. They are now comfortable and all doing well.

I expect to find those Indians in rough places all the time and so have ordered five companies of infantry, and shall not probably make any extended movement until they arrive.

The officers and men behaved with marked gallantry during the engagement.Crook, *Brigadier-General.*

The movement of General Terry, indicated in his dispatch of the 12th inst., leads me to believe that he is at or near the Rosebud about this time. He has formed a junction with Gibbon, and will, undoubtedly, take up the fight which Crook discontinued for want of supplies and to take

* The General omits the friendly Indians killed and wounded and also those of the soldiers whose injuries did not place them *hors de combat* care of his wounded. I communicated to General Crook by courier from Fort Fetterman the position and intentions of General Terry. He must have received it before this date.

P. H. SHERIDAN, *Lieutenant-General.*

CASUALTIES AT ROSEBUD FIGHT, JUNE 17, 1876.

Second Cavalry, Troop D—Sergeant O'Donnell, severely wounded. Troop 1—Sergeant Meagher, seriously injured ; one private, slightly wounded.

Third Cavalry, First Battalion, Troop E—Private Henry Harold, dangerously wounded. Troop I— Killed, Privates William Allen and Eugene Flynn; wounded, Sergeant Grosch, severely ; Corporal Cardy, severely ; Privates Smith, Linskoski, O'Brien, Stewart, and Reilly, severely. Troop M— Wounded, Bugler E. A. Snow, dangerously

Second Battalion —Wounded, Col. Guy V. Henry, commanding battalion, and captain of Troop D, dangerously. Troop B— Wounded, Private Jacob Stiener, severely. Troop L— Killed, Sergt. Nankerchen ; Privates Mitchell, Connor, Minnett and Potts ; wounded, Sergt. Cook, severely ; Private Krazmer, severely ; Private Edwards, seriously. Troop F — Killed, Sergt. Marshall, Private Gilbert Roe ; wounded, Private Town, severely ; Private Fischer, severely; Private Rutlen, slightly.

Fourth Infantry, Company D— Private James A. Devine, Private John H. Terry, Private Richard Flynn, all severely wounded.

Crow Indians — One warrior mortally, and six severely wounded.

Shoshone Indians—One warrior killed and five wounded.

CASUALTIES AT SLIM BUTTES, SEPT. 9, 1876.
[From Author's note book.]
KILLED.

8d Calvalry, Troop A—Private John Wenzel alias Medbury.

5th Cavalry, Troop E—Private Edward Kennedy.

Scouts and guides.—Charley, alias Frank, White, alias "Buffalo Chip." WOUNDED.

2d Cavalry, Troop1—Private J. M. Stevenson, severely; Privates Walsh and Shanahan, slightly.

3d Cavalry Troop E—First Lieut. A. H. Von Leutwitz, shot through right knee joint; the limb amputated on the field.

Troop B—Private Charles Foster, hip joint shattered and amputated.

Troop C— Private William Dubois, severely, and three other soldiers, names not recorded, slightly wounded.

Troop D— Private August Dorn, severely; two men slightly wounded.

Troop E— Sergeant Edward Glass, right arm shattered, disabled for life. Private Edward McKeon severely, and privates Taggert and Kennedy slightly wounded.

Troop . M— Sergt. Kirkwood, severely, and Private Moriarty slightly wounded

5th Cavalry, Troop D— Private Daniel Ford, severely, Private C. Wilson, slightly wounded.

Troop . K— Private Edward Schrisher, severely, three men slightly wounded

There were several of the infantry slightly wounded, but, in the confusion incident on the fight and subsequent march, their names were not ascertained. In fact, slight wounds counted for nothing at that period.

A sergeant of the 2d Cavalry, named Cornwell—one of the two men who failed to ford Big Goose creek during the Sibley Scout— was reported missing. It was supposed at the time that he had strayed from the column in a fit of temporary insanity, and had fallen into the hands of the Indians. A soldier named Miller, who belonged to Major Upham's battalion of the 5th Cavalry, was shot and killed by the Indians, while engaged in hunting, a few days after the Slim Buttes affair.

GENERAL MILES' OPERATIONS IN 1876-7.
[Extract from Gen.Sherman's Report.]
HEADQUARTERS ARMY OF THE UNITED STATES,
CANTONMENT ON TONGUE RIVER, MONTANA, July 17, 1877.

Dear Sir:

I now regard the Sioux Indian problem, as a war question, as solved by the operations of General Miles last winter, and by the establishment of the two rew posts on the Yellowstone now assured this summer.* Boats come and go now, where a year ago none would venture except with strong guards. Wood yards are being established to facilitate navigation, and the great mass of the hostiles have been forced to go to the agencies for food and protection, or have fled across the border into British territory.

With great respect, etc.,
W. T. SHERMAN, General.
HON. GEO. W. MCCRARY,
Secretary of War, Washington, D. C.

*General Sherman was mistaken in the supposition. The Sioux war was not finally ended until after General Miles' campaign of 1879 against Sitting Bull on the British line.—[AUTHOR.]

[Extract from the Report of Lieut.-Gen'l P. H. Sheridan.]
HEADQUARTERS MILITARY DIVISION OF THE
MISSOURI, CHICAGO, Ill., October 25, 1877.

General:

During the months of December and January the hostile Indians were constantly harassed by the troops under Col. N. A. Miles, Fifth Infantry; whose headquarters were at the mouth of Tongue River, and who had two sharp engagements with them, one at Redwater, and the other near Hanging Woman's Fork, inflicting heavy losses in men, supplies and animals.

This constant pounding and sleepless activity upon the part of our troops (Colonel Miles in particular) in midwinter, began to tell, and early in February 1877, information was communicated which led me to believe that the Indians in general were tired of the war, and that the large bodies heretofore in the field were beginning to break up.

On the 25th of that month 229 lodges of Minneconjous and Sans Arcs came in and surrendered to the troops at Cheyenne agency, Dakota. They were completely disarmed, their horses taken from them, and they were put under guard, and this system was carried out with all who afterward came in to surrender within the Departments of Dakota and the Platte. From the 1st of March to the 21st of the same month over 2,200 Indians, in detachments of from 30 to 900, came in and surrendered at Camps Sheridan and Robinson, in the Department of the Platte, and, on the 22d of April, 808 Cheyennes came in and surrendered to Colonel Miles, at the cantonment on Tongue River, in the Department of Dakota, and more were reported on the way in to give themselves up.

Finally, on the 6th of May, Crazy Horse, with 889 of his people and 2,000 ponies, came in to Camp Robinson and surrendered to General Crook in person.

In the meantime, Colonel Miles having had information of the whereabouts of Lame Deer's band of hostile Sioux, surprised his camp, killing fourteen warriors, including Lame Deer and Iron Star, the two principal chiefs, capturing 450 ponies and destroying fifty-one lodges and their contents. I may mention here that this band commenced to surrender, in small squads, from two to twenty, immediately thereafter, until at length, on the 10th of September, the last of the band, numbering 224, constantly followed, and pressed by troops from the command of Colonel Miles, surrendered at Camp Sheridan.

The Sioux war was now over. Sitting Bull went north of the Missouri into British America with his own small band and other hostiles, the number of whom cannot be exactly told, and is now near Woody Mountains. From the Indians who surrendered at the Red Cloud and Spotted Tail agencies, about 1,000 of the Northern Cheyennes elected to go to the Southern Indian Territory, and were sent, under escort from the Fourth Cavalry, to Fort Reno, on the North Canadian. The balance remain as yet at the agencies, and the small band of Cheyennes who surrendered at Tongue River are still there.

> Very respectfully, your obedient servant,
> P. H. SHERIDAN,
> *Lieutenant-General, Commanding.*
> BRIG.-GEN. E. D. TOWNSEND,
> *Adjutant-General of the Army, Washington, D. C.*

ANOTHER INDIAN VERSION OF OUSTER'S BATTLE.

Following is Colonel Poland's interesting account of the first news of the battle of the Little Big Horn, received at Standing Rock agency, on the Missouri river.

> HEADQUARTERS UNITED STATES MILITARY STATION,
> STANDING ROCK, D. T., July 24, 1876.

To the Adjutant General, Department of Dakota, St. Paul, Minn.:

SIR: I respectfully report the following as having been derived from seven Sioux Indians just returned from the hostile camp on July 21st, some of whom were engaged in the battle of June 25th with the 7th Cavalry. Their account is as follows: The hostiles were celebrating their greatest of religious festivals, the sun dance, when runners brought news of the approach of cavalry. The dance was suspended, and a general rush followed, mistaken by Custer, perhaps, for a retreat for horses, equipments and arms.

Reno first attacked the village at the south end and across the Little Big Horn. Their narrative of Reno's operations coincides with the published account. How he was quickly confronted, surrounded; how he mounted, fought in the timber, remounted and cut his way back over the ford and up the bluffs, with considerable loss, and the continuation of the fight for some little time, when runners arrived from the north end of the village or camp with news that the cavalry had attacked the north end, some three or four miles distant. The Indians about Reno had not before this the slightest intimation of fighting at any other point. A force large enough to prevent Reno from assuming the offensive was left, and the surplus available force followed to the other end of the camp, where, finding the Indians there successfully driving Custer before them, instead of uniting with them they separated into two parties and moved around the flanks of his cavalry. They report that Custer crossed the river, but only succeeded in reaching the edge of the Indian camp before he was driven to the bluffs. The fight lasted, perhaps, an hour. The Indians have no hours of the day, and time can only be given approximately. They report that a small number of cavalry broke through the line of Indians in their rear and escaped, but were overtaken within a distance of five or six miles and all killed. I infer from this that this body of retreating cavalry was probably led by the missing officers, and that they tiled to escape only after Custer fell.

The last man dispatched was killed by two sons of a Santee Indian, Red Top, who was a leader in the Minnesota massacres of 1862-63. After the battle the squaws entered the field to plunder and mutilate the dead. General rejoicing was indulged in and a distribution of arms and ammunition hurriedly made ; then the attack on Reno was vigorously renewed. Up to this attack the Indians had lost comparatively few men, but now they say their most serious loss took place. They give no idea of numbers, but say there were a great many killed.

Sitting Bull was neither killed nor personally engaged in the fight. He remained in the council-tent, directing operations. Crazy Horse, with a large band, and Black Moon were the principal leaders on the 25th of June. Killeagle, chief of the Black Feet, at the head of some 20 lodges, was at this agency about the last of May. He was prominently engaged in the battle of June 25th and afterward upbraided Sitting Bull for not taking an active personal part in the engagement. Killeagle has sent me word that he was forced into the fight; that he desires to return to the agency, and that he will return to the agency if he is killed for it. He is reported to be actually on the way back to go to his great father and agent and make confession and receive absolution for his defiant crime against the hand that has gratuitously fed him for three years. He is truly a shrewd chief, who must have discovered that he who fights and runs away may live to fight another day. The Indians were not all engaged at any one time. Heavy reserves were held to repair losses and renew attacks successively. The fight continued until the third day, when runners, kept purposely on the lookout, hurried into camp and reported a great body of troops (General Terry's command) advancing up the river. The Indians, their lodges having been previously prepared for a move, retreated in a southerly direction, tending toward and along Rosebud mountain. They marched about 50 miles, went into camp, held a consultation, when it was determined to send into all the agencies reports of their success, and to call upon their friends to come out and share the glories that were to be expected. In future we may expect an influx of overbearing and impudent Indians to urge, by force, perhaps, an accession to Sitting Bull's demands. There is a general gathering in the hostile camp from each of the agencies on the Missouri river, Red Cloud's and Spotted Tail's, as also northern Cheyennes and Arapahoes. They report, for the special benefit of their relatives, that in the three fights they had with the whites they have captured over 400 stand of arms, carbines and rifles, revolvers not counted, ammunition without end, and some sugar, coffee, bacon, and hard bread. They claim to have captured from the whites this summer over 200 horses and mules. I suppose this includes operations against the soldiers, Crow Indians, and Black Hills miners. The general outline of this Indian report concurs with the published reports. The first attack of Reno's began well on in the day, say the Indians. They report about 800 whites killed, and do not say how many Indians were killed. A report from another source says the Indians obtained from Custer's command 592 carbines and revolvers. I have, since writing the above, heard the following from returned hostiles: They communicated, as a secret, to their particular friends here, information that a large party of Sioux and Cheyennes were to leave Rosebud mountains, a hostile camp, for this agency, to intimidate and compel the Indians here to join Sitting Bull. If these refuse they are ordered to "soldier" them—beat them—and steal their ponies.

Very respectfully, J. S. POLAND,
Capt. 6th Infantry, Brevet Lieut.-Col. Commanding

KILLED UNDER CUSTER, RENO AND BENTEEN, JUNE 25-7, 1876.
[Received by General Sheridan on July 12, 1876.]

FIELD AND STAFF.
Lieut.-Col. Geo. A. Custer, brevet major-general U. S. A.
First Lieut, and Adjut, W. W. Crook, brevet colonel U. S. A.
Asst. Surgeon J. M. DeWolf.
Sergt. Maj. W. W. Sharrow (N. C. Staff).
Chief Trumpeter Henry Ross (N. C. Staff).

TROOP A. [MAJOR RENO.]

COMMISSIONED OFFICERS. 2d Lieut. Benjamin Hodgson.

NON-COMMISSIONED OFFICERS.—Corporals Henry Dalton and Geo. H. King.

PRIVATES. —Jno. C. Armstrong, James Drinans, Wm. Moody, James McDonald, Richard Rawlins, John Sullivan, Thos. P. Switzer, Richard Doran, Geo. Mask.

TROOP C. [GENERAL CUSTER.]

COMMISSIONED OFFICERS. Capt. Thos. W. Custer, brevet lieutenant-colonel U. S. A ; Second Lieut. H. M. Harrington.

NON-COMMISSIONED OFFICERS.—First Sergt. Edwin Baba, Sergt. Finley, Sergt. Finkel, Corporals French, Foley and Ryan.

PRIVATES. Allen, Criddle, King, Bucknall, Eisman, Engle, Brightfield, Farrand, Griffin, Hamel, Hattisoll, Kingsonts, Lewis, Mayer1, Mayer 2, Phillips, Russell, Rice, Rauter, Short, Shea, Shade, Stuart, St. John, Thadius, Van Allen, Warren, Wyndham, Wright.

TROOP D. [MAJOR BENTEEN.]

NON-COMMISSIONED OFFICERS. Farrier, Vincent Charlie.

PRIVATES. —Patrick Golden, Edward Hansen.

TROOP E. [GENERAL CUSTER.]

COMMISSIONED OFFICERS.—First Lieut. A. E. Smith, brevet captain U. S. A.; Second Lieut. J. Sturgis.

NON-COMMISSIONED OFFICERS.—First Sergt. Fred Hohmeyer, Sergeant Egden, Sergeant James ; Corporals Hogan, Mason, Bloom, and Mayer ; Trumpeters McElvey and Mooney.

PRIVATES. Baker, Boyle, Bauth, Connor, Daring, Davis, Farrell, Hiley, Huber, Hime, Henderson 1, Henderson 2, Leddison, O'Connor, Rood, Reese, Smith 1, Smith 2, Smith 3, Stella, Stafford, Achoole, Smallwood, Henry, Kinzie, Walker, Averall, Knicht.

TROOP F. [GENERAL CUSTER.]

COMMISSIONED OFFICERS. Capt. G. W. Yates, brevet colonel; Second Lieut. W. Van W. Reilly.

NON-COMMISSIONED OFFICERS. First Sergeant Kenney; Sergeants Murphy, Vickeryard, Wilkinson; Corporals Coleman, Freman (orderly), Briody, Brandon (farrier), Manning (blacksmith).

PRIVATES. Atchison, Brown 1, Brown 2, Bruce, Brady, Burnham, Cather, Carney, Dorman, Donnelly, Gardiner, Hammon, Kline, Knauth, Luman, Loose, Milton, Madson, Monroe, Rudden, Smeling, Sicfous, Sanders, Warren, Way, Lerock, Kelly.

TROOP G. [MAJOR RENO.]

COMMISSIONED OFFICERS. —First Lieutenant Donald McIntosh.

NON-COMMISSIONED OFFICERS. —Sergts. Edward Botzer and M. Considine; Corporals James Martin and Otto Hageman Benjamin Wells (farrier), Henry Dose (trumpeter), Crawford Selley (saddler).

PRIVATES. —Benjamin F. Rogers, Andrew J. Moore, John J. McGinnis, Edward Stanley, Henry Stafferman and John Rapp.

TROOP H. [MAJOR BENTEEN.]

NON-COMMISSIONED OFFICERS. Corporal George Tell.

PRIVATES. Julian H. Jones, Thos. E. Meader.

TROOP I. [GENERAL CUSTER.]

COMMISSIONED OFFICERS. —Capt. M. W. Keogh, brevet lieutenant-colonel; First Lieut. J, E. Porter (body not found).

NON-COMMISSIONED OFFICERS.— First Sergt. F. E. Varsen, Sergt. J. Bustard; Corporals Jno. Wild, G. C. Morris and S. F. Staples; J. McGucker and J. Patton (trumpeters), H. A. Bailey (blacksmith).

PRIVATES. —J. F. Bradhurst, J. Barry, J. Connors, T. P. Downing, E. C. Driscoll, D. C. Gillette, G. H. Gross, E. P. Holcomb, M. E. Horn Adam Hetismer, P. Kelley, Fred Lehman, Henry Lehman, E. P. Lloyd, A' McChargey, J. Mitchell, J. Noshang, J. O'Bryan, J. Parker, F. J. Pitter, Geo. Post, Jas. Quinn, Wm. Reed, J. W. Rossbury, D. L. Symms, J. E. Troy, Chas. Von Bramer, W. B. Haley.

TROOP K. [MAJOR BENTEEN.]

NON COMMISSIONED OFFICERS.— First Sergt. D. Winney, Sergt. R. Hughes; Corporal J.J. Callahan; Julius Helmer (trumpeter).

PRIVATE. Eli U. T. Clair.

TROOP L. [GENERAL CUSTER.]

COMMISSIONED OFFICERS.—First Lieut. James Calhoun, Second Lieut. J. J. Crittenden (20th Infantry), attached.

NON-COMMISSIONED OFFICERS. First Sergeant Butler, Sergeant Warren; Corporals Harrison, Cilbert and Seeller; Walsh (trumpeter).

PRIVATES. —Adams, Arodelsky, Burke, Cheever, McGue, McCarthy, Dugan, Maxwell, Scott, Babcock, Perkins, Tarbox, Dye, Tessler, Galvin, Graham, Hamilton, Rodgers, Snow, Hughes, Miller, Tweed, Neller, Cashan, Keep, Andrews, Chrisfleld, Harrington, Haugge, Kavanaugh, Lobering, Mahoney, Schmidt, Swan, Semenson, Riebold, O'Connell.

TROOP M. [MAJOR RENO.]

NON-COMMISSIONED OFFICERS. Sergt. Miles F. O'Hara ; Corporals Henry M. Scollin and Fred Stringer.

PRIVATES. Henry Gordon, A. Kertzlwisker. G. Lawrence, W. D. Meyer, G. E. Smith, D. Somer, J. Tanner, H. Finley, H. C. Vogt.

INDIAN SCOUTS. Bloody Knife, Bob-tailed Bull, Stab.

CIVILIANS.

Boston Custer, Arthur Reed, Mark Kellogg, Charles Reynolds, Frank C. Mann.

RECAPITULATION.

Commissioned Officers killed,	14
Acting Assistant Surgeon,	1
Enlisted Men,	247
Civilians,	5
Indian Scouts,	3
Total killed	270

The following died soon after the fight of injuries received:—Private Chas. Bennett (Troop C), Private William George (Troop H).

The foregoing list includes as indicated all of the soldiers killed under Reno and Benteen. Maj. Benteen, Lieut. Varnum, and 51 men were wounded, making a total loss of 328, including Indians and Civilians.

Following is the official list of wounded under Reno and Benteen:

WOUNDED.

Troop A — First Sergeant William Heyn ; Privates Jacob Deal, Samuel Foster, Frederick Homestead, F. M. Reeves, E. T. Strond.

Troop B—Corporal W. F. Smith; Private Charles Cunningham.

Troop C—Privates John Maguire, Peter Thompson, Alfred Whitaker, P. McDonald.

Troop E—Sergeant J. T. Reilly

Troop G—Privates James P. Boyle, Charles Connell, John Mackey, John Morrison.

Troop H— First Sergeant Joseph McCorry; Privates Patrick Connelly, Thomas McLaughlin, John Pahl, P. H. Bisliley, C. H. Bishop, Alex. B. Bishop, John Cooper, William Black, William Farley, Thomas Hughes, John Muller, John Phillips, Samuel Sweres, William C. Williams, Charles Windolph (trumpeter), William Ramel (saddler), Otto Voik.

Troop I—Private Dore Cooney.

Troop K—Privates Patrick Corcoran, Michael Madden (shot while making a gallant attempt to get water for the wounded under the Indian fire) and M. Wilke.

Troop L—Private Thomas Marshall.

Troop M—Sergeant F. Cody; Sergeant Charles White; Privates Daniel Newell (blacksmith), Frank Baum, John H. Meyer, William E. Morris, Roman Bolten, T. P. Norman, James Wilbur and Charles Wiedman.

ORGANIZATION OF THE COLUMNS.
DEPARTMENT OF THE PLATTE.
BIG HORN AND YELLOWSTONE EXPEDITION.
(Summer and Autumn of 1876.)

Brigadier General George Crook, U. S. A., Commanding.Captain Azor H. Nickerson, 23d Infantary, Aidede-Camp.

Second Lieutenant John G. Bourke, 3d Cavalry, Aide-de-Camp. Captain John V. Furey, Assistant Quartermaster.

Major Albert Hartsuff, Surgeon, Medical Officer.

Captain Julius H. Patzki, Assistant Surgeon.

Attached.

Major Alexander Chambers, 4th Infantry.

Captain George M. Randall, 23d Infantry.

First Lieutenant John W. Bubb, 4th Infantry, A. C. S.

A. A. Surgeon Charles R. Stephens, U. S. A.

2d Cavalry, Companies A, B, D, E and I.

3d Cavalry, Headquarters and Campanies A, B, C, D, E, F, H, I, L and M.

4th Infantry, Companies D, F and G.

9th Infantry, Companies C, G and H.

14th Infantry, Companies B, C, F and I. (Joined in August.)

5th Cavalry, Headquarters and Companies A, B, D, E, F, G, I, K and M, and Second Lieutenant Walter S. Schuyler, A. D. C. (Joined in August.)

A. A. Surgeons, R. B. Grimes and Y. T. McGillycuddy, U. S. A.

POWDER RIVER EXPEDITION.
(October and November, 1876.)

Brigadier-General George Crook, U. S. A., Commanding. Lieutenants Bourke and Schuyler, Aides.

Captain Furey, A. Q. M.

Assistant Surgeons Gibson, Price and Wood, and A. A. Surgeons Petteys, La Garde and Owsley.

Attached.

Lieutenant Colonel Richard I. Dodge, 23rd Infantry.

Major David S. Gordon, 2nd Cavalry.

Major Edwin F. Townsend, 9th Infantry.

Lieutenants Black, 2nd Cavalry, and McKinney, Miller and Tyler, 4th Cavalry.

Lieutenants Hofman and Delaney, 9th Infantry, and Lieutenant Heyl, 23rd Infantry.

2d Cavalry, Company K.

3d Cavalry, Companies H and K.

4th Cavalry, Headquarters and Companies B, D, E, F, I and M. (General R. S. McKenzie.)

5th Cavalry, Companies H and L.

4th Artillery, Batteries C, F, H and K.

9th Infantry, Companies A, B, D, F, I and K.

14th Infantry, Companies D and G.

23rd Infantry, Companies C, G and I.

DISTRICT OF THE YELLOWSTONE.
(Command of General N. A. Miles in July and August, 1879.)

The organization of General Miles' column, in the Campaign against the Sioux, during the summer of 1879 was as follows:

General Nelson A. Miles, Colonel 5th Infantry, Commanding.

Lieutenant Colonel Whistler, 5th Infantry, Commanding Battalion of Mounted Infantry, seven Companies.

Major E. M. Baker, Commanding 2nd Battalion, 2nd Cavalry, five Companies.

Major David S. Gordon, Commanding 8d Battalion, 2d Cavalry, three companies.

Major E. Rice, Commanding Three-gun Battery, including Hotchkiss Revolver. '

Staff —F. D. Baldwin, Captain and A. A. G., District of the Yellowstone.

H. K. Bailey, Lieutenant and A. D. C.

A. C. Girard, Surgeon and Chief Medical Officer.

E. D.Schue, Assistant Surgeon.

William Philo Clark, 1st Lieutenant 2d Cavalry, Chief of the Indian Scouts, 150 men.

W. E. Sabine, Acting Assistant Surgeon, Infantry Battalion.

O. F. Long, Engineer and Signal Officer.

F. F. Forbes, Depot of Supplies, Quartermaster.

W. H. C. Bowen, Field Quartermaster.

DEPARTMENT OF DAKOTA.
GENERAL TERRY'S COMMAND, AUGUST, 1876.

2d Cavalry, Troops, C, F, G, H, L and M, under Major James S. Brisbin.

7th Cavalry, Troops A, B, D, G, H, K, and M, (Troops C, E, F, I and L, died with Custer,) under Major Marcus A. Reno.

5th Infantry, under Gen. Nelson A. Miles.

7th Infantry, under Gen. John Gibbon.

17th Infantry (detachment), under Capt. F. D. Garretty.

22d Infantry (battalion), under Colonel Otis.

Light Artillery—one section.

The entire command, exclusive of scouts, numbered 83 officers and 1,536 enlisted men. Cavalry, 26 officers and 574 men. Infantry, 55 officers and 922 men. Artillery, 2 officers and 40 men.

www.ingramcontent.com/pod-product-compliance
Lightning Source LLC
LaVergne TN
LVHW051038080426
835508LV00019B/1590